NOT THE WORST OF TOM SHIELDS

NOT THE WORST OF
TOM SHIELDS

MAINSTREAM
PUBLISHING
EDINBURGH AND LONDON

First published in Great Britain in 1999 by
MAINSTREAM PUBLISHING COMPANY
(EDINBURGH) LTD
7 Albany Street
Edinburgh EH1 3UG

ISBN 1 84018 257 1

The material in this book was previously published in
Tom Shields' Diary and *Tom Shields Too*

A catalogue record for this book is available from the
British Library

Typeset in Garamond
Printed and bound in Great Britain by
Butler & Tanner Ltd

CONTENTS

APOCRYPHA

There is an old saying in the Diary business that certain stories are too good to check out. Unfortunately, this is not true. The libel laws prohibit such a luxury. But occasionally, once we have tried manfully to establish the truth of a story and failed, we still print it, with no names, on the grounds that it will do no one any harm.

A WOMAN is driving home from her work at Glasgow Airport. Some way along the M8, she spots a microwave oven lying on the verge. She stops and stows the oven in the boot of her car. She drives off but only gets a few hundred yards along the motorway when she is pulled into the side by a police car. The police tell her not to worry but could they have their speed-testing device back, please?

THIS story is supposed to have happened at the Brixton riots, but we cannot believe this of our boys in blue.

A young PC has lost his nerve and run away from the bricks and petrol bombs of the front line. He is taking shelter, head in hands, in a shop doorway. Next thing he sees is a pair of well-polished boots. A voice booms out that he should be ashamed of himself. He has let the force, and himself, down.

'I'm sorry, sergeant,' he says without looking up.

'What do you mean "sergeant"? I'm an inspector.'

To which the PC replied: 'I'm sorry, sir, I didn't think I'd retreated that far.'

THE average Scot's lack of foreign languages is highlighted in this little tale of a chap who went on a Mediterranean cruise. Being on his own, he was asked if he would mind sharing a dinner table with another passenger, a Frenchman, who was also travelling alone. The Frenchman spoke no English and the Scotsman, a Mr Bob Spiers, spoke no French.

At the first meal, the French chap said 'Bon appetit' to which the Scot replied 'Bob Spiers'. At the second and third meals the Frenchman said 'Bon appetit' to which the Scotsman replied 'Bob Spiers'.

The ship's purser asked Mr Spiers how he was getting on with his table companion. 'He's a friendly enough chap,' Spiers replied, 'but he keeps forgetting we've met and keeps introducing himself as Bon Appetit.'

The purser explained that this was French for 'enjoy your meal'.

Thus clued up, Mr Spiers greeted the Frenchman at the next meal with the words 'Bon appetit'. The Frenchman smiled and replied: 'Bob Spiers.'

AN apprentice joiner called in to fix a neighbour's pulley as a favour.

Having completed the work, he

went through to the parlour and said to the woman: 'That's your pulley fixed, Mrs Brown. Noo ye can get yer claes up.'

The lady, taken aback, said: 'Well, okay, but I was just going to give you a bottle of whisky.'

THE Diary credited this story to Sydney Devine but we subsequently heard it attributed to Andy Cameron and other radio presenters who deal with children's jokes, so it has to go under the heading of apocryphal.

A wee boy contacts the phone-in with the query: 'What vegetable brings tears to your eyes?'

No, the answer was not an onion. Nor was it any other potentially nippy veg which the presenter suggested. So, which vegetable brings tears to your eyes?

'A turnip,' said the wee boy.

A turnip?

'Aye, if you get hit in the ba's wi' a turnip, it brings tears to your eyes,' quoth the urchin.

SIGN in Ayrshire pub: 'Welcome – A Pint, a Pie, and a Kind Word.' A visitor duly followed the suggestion on the sign. The barmaid slammed his pint in front of him without a word. She was equally taciturn when she dumped an extremely greasy and aged pie on the bar.

'What about the kind word?' he asked.

'Don't eat the pie,' she retorted.

A GLASGOW housewife emptied her shopping on to the kitchen table. Returning minutes later she discovered that a pack of Penguin biscuits had been opened and two taken. 'Ye wee scoundrel' (or words to that effect), she said. 'Ah'll get the polis tae ye.'

Ten minutes later, as the urchin played outside, a police constable (in pursuit of other inquiries) approached the close-mouth. Anxious to get his version in first, the boy stopped the PC with the words: 'It wisnae me that stole the chocolate biscuits. And anyway that old bitch doesnae huv a TV licence.'

THIS is the story of an embarrassing encounter between an Ayrshire doctor and a young married woman patient.

The woman, whose husband had been away at sea for some time, was lying back on the doctor's couch for an intimate examination. Just as the GP was about to begin, the woman said: 'You'll have to do something about the cobwebs.'

The GP, slightly puzzled by the remark and assuming it was a reference to the long time her sailor husband had been away, replied: 'I'll leave that for your husband to deal with.'

The woman, having recovered from a severe fit of the giggles, explained that she was referring to the cobwebs on the ceiling of his surgery.

A GROUP of executives from a top Japanese car firm was in Gleneagles Hotel for a conference.

They had ordered full Highland dress and the six were making their way down the grand staircase for dinner when horror-struck staff noticed they were all wearing their kilts back to front. Sporrans, kilt pins, pleats – the lot – were facing backwards.

Experts in sorting out just about every situation, the loyal staff stepped in, erected a makeshift screen of towels and, right there in the foyer, turned the backside-foremost garments round with a resounding 'wheech'.

It is reliably reported that the Japanese delegation returned home with tales of the marvellous Scottish customs which are associated with the wearing of the kilt.

It is not known whether anything was worn under the kilt on this occasion or whether everything was in perfect working order.

THE City of Culture celebrations gave rein to Glasgow's talent for xenophobia. Hence the tale of the German visitor to the city who witnessed a Glasgow wummin skelping her wean in Central Station.

The German reproached the woman saying: 'In Germany we do not hit our children.'

'Is that right?' the woman replied. 'In Partick we don't gas Jews.'

THEN there was the following exchange:

Japanese Tourist: 'Excuse me, can you direct me to George Square?'

Glesca Keelie: 'You found Pearl Harbor easily enough. Find George Square your f****** self.'

AN Edinburgh couple had to move to Glasgow because of the husband's job. In the Glasgow way, the couple were quickly befriended by the wummin next door.

Now, it was this Edinburgh lady's custom of a morning to entertain a gentleman friend. One morning in the course of the entertainment, the chap suffered a heart attack and died.

Distraught, the lady consulted her neighbour for advice. After only a few moments of thought, the Glasgow woman said: 'Nae problem, hen, jist stick a shammy in his haun' and drap him oot the windae.'

THIS conversation, overheard at the Plaza Ballroom, is hopefully apocryphal.

Two young ladies exiting from toilets. One says: 'Senga, d'you know you've got a Tampax behind your ear?'

To which Senga replied: 'Oh, God, what huv ah done wi' ma fag?'

OF similar nature is the tale of a doctor whose colleague remarks: 'Do you know you've got a suppository behind your ear?'

'Is that right?' the doctor replies. 'In that case whit erse has goat ma pencil?'

THIS is supposed to have happened to a burgher of Hamilton. There he is, in his dungarees, under the car doing a spot of vehicular DIY. His wife pops off to the shops.

Here comes his wife back from the shops. She spots the legs sticking out from under the car. Being in a mischievous mood, she gives a tweak – a friendly but firm tweak – just where the legs of the dungarees meet.

Then she walks into the kitchen to find her husband making a cup of tea. And in walks a mechanic from the local garage with blood pouring from the wound suffered when his head suddenly and involuntarily hit the underside of the car.

OFFICE parties are a fertile source of apocryphal stories. This one involved a young lady, usually of impeccable behaviour, at a British Telecom staffie in Glasgow.

She had taken too much drink and was poured into a taxi. At her destination, she made her way unsteadily up the path. When her father opened the door, she began to apologise profusely, if slightly incoherently.

Her dad, a man of the world, told her not to worry, come in, have a cup of coffee. 'Anyway, you don't have to apologise to me,' he explained. 'You seem to have forgotten you don't live here anymore. You got married three months ago.'

THEN there was the tale of the man who woke up with a black eye the morning after the office party.

'I'm sorry, dear,' he told his darling wife, 'I don't know how I came home with this black eye.'

'That's all right, dear,' she replied. 'You got it after you came home.'

ANOTHER husband, returning in a terrible state at 4 a.m., so infuriated his wife that she threw the alarm clock at him. As his colleagues remarked the next day: 'It's amazing how time flies when you're enjoying yourself.'

WE heard of one Glasgow infant who appeared to enjoy his holidays in the South of France. His mother was making a belated attempt to wean the toddler off the breast. As we said, the wee lad had a great time. His mother didn't really. Spending, as she did, much time prising her hungry son off a number of very surprised women on the topless beach.

NOT only were souls saved during Billy Graham's last evangelistic mission to Scotland, but wee faith-healing miracles were also being done. Thus it was that two poor unfortunates, a woman on crutches and a man with a terrible stutter, went forward to be cured. They both went behind a screen on the stage while the great man led the prayers on their behalf. 'Senga, throw away your left crutch,' he cried. The left crutch came flying over the screen. 'Senga, throw away your right crutch,' he cried. The right crutch came flying over the screen. There was a loud thump. Billy shouted out: 'Senga, what has happened?'
'S-s-s-she's f-f-f-f-fell o-o-o-on he-h-h-h-her a-a-a-a-arse,' came the reply.

THE Diary pursued this story to the ends of the earth – well, Banffshire, actually, where it was supposed to have happened. It starts with an advertisement in the cars-for-sale column of a Banffshire local newspaper. The ad says 'BMW for sale. £10'. Everyone assumed it is a misprint. But one chap phones up to find out what the price should be. 'No. £10 is the correct price,' says the lady at the other end of the phone. 'But a BMW of that age and model is worth at least £7,000,' the chap replies. The lady, in a firm tone of voice, says the price is £10. The deal is duly done. The explanation is that the car belonged to the lady's husband. The same husband who had left for South Africa with the new woman in his life. 'What about the BMW?' his wife had asked as he left. 'Oh, just sell it and send me on the proceeds,' he said.

THIS story is set in one of the swish glass lifts of the terribly upmarket Princes Square shopping centre in Glasgow. Among the passengers are a woman and her wee boy, aged about seven. The wee boy is proudly sporting a new pair of those trainers that cost the best part of £100. Also in the lift is an attractive woman who, during the journey, turns round and slaps the man standing beside her. She says something to the effect that he is a filthy pervert and ought to be arrested. The argument continues after the lift arrives at the ground floor with the angry lady trying to find a security guard. The mother hustles her son away from the scene with words along the lines of, 'Is that not terrible?' Her son agrees and explains: 'She was standing on my new trainers, so I nipped her bum to get her to move.'

A YOUNG lady turns up for an operation at the gynaecology ward. Her hair is dyed green. Her pubic hair is also dyed green. In addition she has a tattoo on her stomach which reads: 'Keep off the grass.' When she comes out of the anaesthetic the nurse tells her: 'I'm sorry. We had to mow your lawn.'

THE Diary was inundated with versions of this apocryphal story. We heard variously of the lawyer from Dundee, the old lady from Dunfermline, and the Glasgow policeman who was in a lift in a New York hotel. Also in the lift were a well-heeled black chap and his minder. 'Hit the floor,' barked the well-heeled chap. The Scottish lawyer/old lady/policeman promptly dived to the floor, only to hear the laughter of the other two occupants as the minder pressed a button on the lift control panel. The story ends when the lawyer/old lady/policeman goes to pay the bill and finds it has already been taken care of by the rich chap in the lift – film star Eddie Murphy, who says he has not laughed so much since the last time he was at the bank.

ON a coach transporting holidaymakers from Glasgow to Paris, many of them on their way to sample Euro Disney, what does the courier person spot but a little old lady sitting with a TV set on her lap. 'Why are you taking a TV set to Paris?' is the obvious question. 'I don't want to miss *Coronation Street,*' is the reply. 'But French television doesn't have *Coronation Street.*' 'Exactly. That's why I'm taking my own set.'

FOR this tale we have to go back to a green, grassy slope adjacent to the River Boyne late in the evening of 12 July 1690. King Billy, for it is he, is wandering around the battlefield. He chances upon his father-in-law, the vanquished King James VI as was, sitting dejectedly on the afore-mentioned green, grassy slope.

'I can't believe it,' King James says to King Billy. 'I don't know how we managed to lose. We outnumbered you. We out-manoeuvred you. We outflanked you . . .'

'Don't worry about it,' King Billy reassures him. 'It's just another battle. In a fortnight's time who'll remember the Battle of the Boyne?'

A JAPANESE soldier emerges from the Malaysian jungle many years after the end of the Second World War. He is duly flown home to be reunited with his wife. After an emotional reunion, with much ritual bowing, the husband asks his wife: 'Honourable wife, have you been faithful to me?'

To which she replies: 'Honourable husband, I have indeed been faithful.'

The husband continues: 'Honourable wife, I think you lie. I have heard you've been living with a Gordon Highlander from Inverurie.'

'Fa tellt ye that?' she demands.

A GIRL was sobbing in the maternity ward and the doctor asked the sister

why. 'She can't breast feed,' answered sister. 'Then you know what to do,' he went on. 'It's hardening of the nipples. Get some olive oil and cotton-wool and make up some soaks and get her to put them on.' Upon his departure the sister consoled the girl: 'It's all right, dear, Doctor wants you to put on some olive-oil soaks.'

'Awright,' said the lassie. 'I'll put them oan if ye want – but will they no make a hell of a mess of ma feet?'

A TALE about confusion in Highland dancing circles. A teacher from deepest Argyll offered his assistance to the organiser of a Highland dancing competition in darkest Govan. He was allocated the job of checking off the names and numbers of the competitors. All went well until he was approached and addressed by a young lady. He scanned his list of competitors and had to admit: 'I'm sorry, I don't seem to have a Joanna Pye down here. Which section are you dancing in, dear?'

'Ah'm no' in any section,' she replied. 'Ah'm fae the kitchen. D'ye wanna pie?'

A NEWLY hired travelling salesman wrote his first sales report to the office. Its sheer illiteracy stunned the top brass: 'I have seen this lot what hasn't never bot nuthin fromm us, and I sole them a buncha goods for a thousand quid. I am now going to Manncester.'

Before he could be given the sack, or at least sent on a course for to learn English, there came this letter from Manchester: 'I cum hear an sole them half a millyun.'

The next morning the two letters were tacked to the staff bulletin board with this memo from the managing director: 'We bin spending two much time trying to spel instead of sel. You should all gett out an do wot he dun.'

THE scene is a Glasgow park on the day of the big Orange Walk. A chap heavily laden with a suitcase goes up to a polisman and asks if it would be in order for him to set up a small bookstall. The policeman can think of no objections but asks the chap what books he would be selling. It is a book on King William, the very hero of the Orange Order types who have taken over the park for the purpose of celebrating the Battle of the Boyne.

That will be of great interest to the lieges, the PC observes. 'Yes,' said the author and publisher. 'It's the true story of King William. Did you know that he didn't have a white horse and he was a homosexual . . .?' On police advice, the bookstall was not set up.

THE personnel section of a Govan firm organised a series of interviews for junior clerical posts. The personnel officer is none too hopeful, having spent two days wading through application forms which list hobbies such as 'walking my pit-bull' and 'playing darts'. These, incidentally, from the female applicants. 'Wheel the first one in,' ordains the personnel officer.

The hopeful young lady enters the room, keen to make a good impression and tries to be as outgoing and chatty as possible. Pulling at her blouse where sweat is sticking it to her body, she ventures the meteorological comment: 'Soafy clammy!'

'Come in, Miss Clammy. Take a seat,' says the personnel officer.

THIS tale concerns an Italian café owner in a small Scots town who never quite mastered the English language. This made him easy prey for local youths who delighted in taking the mickey. He would be asked at various times, to his confusion and frustration, for a 'packet o' bumbee's feathers' or a 'quarter o' roon squares'. In addition to the verbals, the callow youths were not averse to flinging their hot-pea specials at each other.

Then, one Christmas, overdosing on goodwill, the lads decided to stop giving the old man such a hard time.

They called him over to their table and informed him of their intention to reform. His delight was huge. 'Yerraverranicea boays,' he exclaimed. 'Nae maira roona squares an' bumbee feathers or scoota peas a' owera ma shoap. Itsa great! An' ah'll dae something forra you boays. Ah'll no spit in yer coaffee nae mair!'

MANY years ago, an Italian café in Perth had a windy-up gramophone which was a target for mischief by the local bad boys. So much so that the café proprietor used to reprimand them with the words: 'Hey, boays. No flicka da peas doon the hoarna the gramophone. You'll choke Harry Lauder.'

SENILITY is not funny. But life is. Thus we pass on to you the story of an old chap sitting crying on a park bench. A kindly young passer-by stops and asks what's the matter. In between heart-rending sobs, the old fellow explains that he recently got married to his next-door neighbour's 22-year-old Swedish au pair. She was a wonderful cook, ironed his shirts beautifully, and kept the house to perfection. She had also rekindled long-forgotten passions. 'So why are you crying?' the kindly passer-by enquired. To which the old chap replied: 'I can't remember where I live.'

SHIPYARD humour is not dead: we hear of a Norwegian manager at the Kvaerner yard in Govan who asked a

shipwright to walk more quickly to his job, as they do in Norway. Slightly miffed at such a direction, the Clydesider replied: 'Look pal, this is a boiler-suit ah'm wearin'! No an effin' track suit.'

A YOUNG student at Glasgow Dental School had been allocated to treat an elderly woman who was being fitted with a new pair of false teeth. On each visit, the woman expressed her gratitude for his care and attention by bringing him a gift of a bag of almonds. The student was always suitably grateful, thanking her very much and saying how much he liked almonds.

On her last visit, when the wallies had been well installed, the dentist-to-be said to her: 'Thanks for the bags of almonds you've been bringing me; you must have a great supply of them somewhere.' To which she replied: 'Well, son, I love thae sugared almonds, but it's just the sugar I like, not the almonds.'

A MIDWIFE is paying the last of a series of visits to a lady in Bridgeton who's just had another bairn, taking the tribe into double digits.

To mark the occasion, the mother persuades the midwife to stay for a cuppa and a wee scone. The midwife duly compliments the mother on her baking skills, remarking that the scones are delicious. 'Yes,' says the mother, 'I always think they're lighter and tastier when they are made with your own milk.'

TWO elderly women standing in the post-office queue in darkest Hardgate waiting to collect their pensions are showing great interest in a girl in front of them in the queue. She is wearing a pair of 70 denier tights, a form of very thick, very black, and very opaque leggings which are apparently fashionable these days.

As the girl leaves after being served, one old dear turns confidentially to the other and says: 'Mary, do you mind when we were young whit happened to girls who wore thae black woolly stockings?' 'Aye,' Mary replies. 'Nothing.'

A TALE from the Hebrides of a non-fisherman invited for a wee trip on a boat out to gather in the catch from some lobster creels. The guest is feeling queasy because of the slight swell, although a recent dalliance with the drink cannot be ruled out as a factor.

As he is watching the lobster fishermen at work, said chap is overcome and is sick over the side, losing his false teeth in the process. This causes much hilarity among the crew, who decided to prolong the fun.

They borrow the skipper's false teeth and place them in a creel as it is brought on deck. What a miracle, they explain. What a chance in a million for the sea to yield up the dentures which had been so cruelly lost. The victim of their hoax is quite amazed and puts in the said false teeth. But they remain in his mouth for only a few seconds. 'Ach, these aren't my teeth,' he says as he takes out the skipper's dentures and throws them into the sea.

THIS story about a mother and daughter demonstrates the vicissitudes of dealing with an elderly relative who is a few crumbs short of the full Madeira cake. The devoted daughter was out shopping one day when she came across a videotape of her mother's all-time favourite film – *The Bells of St Mary's*, starring Bing Crosby. She bought it as a wee treat.

The mother, not at her best that day, was having trouble understanding what a video is. The daughter took the easy way out and told mother simply that her favourite film was on the telly that night.

The pair duly settled down to watch the movie. Towards the end of

the film, the daughter realised there was something else on TV that she wanted to see but if they continued to watch *The Bells of St Mary's* she'd miss the start.

She considered but decided against trying to explain to mum that with the wonders of modern technology they could catch the end of the film later. Surreptitiously reaching for the remote control, she fast-forwarded the videotape.

As the film sped by, the old lady spotted something was wrong. 'Is that those people next door hoovering again?' she asked.

GRANNY is looking after her five-year-old grandson who has been sent home in disgrace from school for being cheeky to the jannie. The boy is warned by granny that 'Santa doesn't come to bad boys'.

The boy responds by sticking out his tongue. Time for stern measures. A cuff on the bonce is not politically correct so granny goes into an elaborate number, picks up the telephone, dials a few digits at random, and says: 'Right, Santa, don't bring any presents for . . .' and proceeds to give the wean's name and address. (Which we have withheld, since he may yet appear at the children's panel.)

Granny puts down the phone, quite pleased with her ploy. 'I'll just phone Santa back and tell him it's okay!' responds the uppity bairn. 'You don't know the number,' says granny. After only a few moments' thought, the wee man grabs the phone and presses the redial button.

AN elderly Scots exile lady, over from the States for a holiday, was relating to friends how proud she was of her grandsons. But she was also worried that they were overdoing their volunteer work for the church. She explained that since her arrival they seemed to spend nearly every evening down at the mission and often slept in the next day because of the late hours involved. No one had the heart to tell her that The Mission was the name of a local pub.

THE scene is a safari park which has been blessed by a school trip from the Possil area of Glasgow. A number of the little angels have escaped from their bus and are frolicking in the long grass. A concerned safari-park ranger drives up in his Daktari-style jeep shouting: 'Boys! The lions! The lions!' To which one of the lads ripostes: 'Don't worry, mister. We never touched your lions.'

A GLASGOW rugby fan is in Paris, in full Highland dress and somewhat the worse for wear, having encountered a team of bears from Bordeaux who have forced him to drink much whisky. He has to leave the pub early and retire to his hotel room before he falls down. When his room-mate returns, reasonably sober, he finds the kiltie lying totally naked on the bed apart from his ghillie brogues – those shoes with the criss-cross laces up the leg. Having covered his pal's embarrassment, the room-mate is untying the laces when the drunken kiltie comes to. 'Just put my shoes in the wardrobe beside my clothes,' he says.

'What wardrobe?' asks his pal (for

it was a very cheap Paris hotel). 'That wardrobe,' says the kiltie, pointing to the verandah door. 'Oh, this wardrobe,' says the room-mate, looking at the full Highland kit lying crumpled in the well of the building four floors below.

A TRUE story, we are told, from a funeral in Glasgow's East End. They are burying old Jimmy, who had been a bit of a drinker till the night he birled home from the pub and died. After his wee lie-in at home (no, it's not the joke about how well Jimmy was looking because he hadn't had a drink for three days) his sons are carrying the coffin out to the hearse. The path is icy and the sons hit a slidey bit. They are weaving left and right in an effort to keep their feet and a hold of the coffin.

The grieving widow, who had never been short of a comment, says: 'Look at that. He's going out the way he always came in.'

CRANHILL, Glasgow, is the scene of this tale of life as it is lived these days.

A local minister answers the knock at his manse door to be confronted by a child in the company of an irate parent. The child has a gory head wound, stitches and all. And, says the father, it is all the fault of the church. Kindly explain, says the minister.

Well, explains the father, it's that unbreakable glass in the church windows. His darling child had been engaged in the harmless practice of chucking a half brick at the windows when the brick bounced back and hit him on the head.

WE are not sure whether this comes under the heading of *Apocryphal Tales or Shaggy Dog Stories* but at least it is clean.

A customer in a corner grocer's shop is most impressed to see a dog enter the shop with a shopping bag, wait its turn in the queue, place the bag on the counter, dip inside, find a purse, and give it to the assistant. The grocer takes a shopping list from inside the purse, fills the bag with the requested items, extracts the money, puts the change back into the purse, places the purse inside the bag, and sends the dog off on its way.

The customer, intrigued by this canine talent, decides to follow the dog home. He watches as the dog goes up to the front door and barks three times. Nothing happens. The dog jumps up and rings the doorbell three times. Eventually the door opens, his owner comes out, takes the shopping bag, and slaps the dog around the ear.

Horrified, the onlooker berates the owner for his cruelty to an outstandingly intelligent dog. 'He's

clever all right,' says the owner. 'But that's the third time he's lost his front-door key.'

MORMONS chapping at your door can be a bore but it is not usual to bring in the polis to deal with them. We heard of a call to a Glasgow police office from a distraught woman claiming that she had been visited by a Mormon. She had slammed the door in his face but he wouldn't go away and was still knocking. When the polis arrived, they discovered that the man was indeed still there and was knocking incessantly. The lady of the house had trapped his coat in the door.

A GLASGOW community worker of English ethnic origin had not quite mastered the nuances of the local patois. At a meeting the community worker was desperately trying to get volunteers to form a committee. A wee lady in the front row had her hand half-raised, unsure whether or not to volunteer.

'Ah!' said the English community worker, pointing to the woman. 'What about you?'

'I'm swithering,' the still-undecided woman replies.

'Good,' says the community worker. 'That's Mrs Swithering. Now, anyone else?'

The same community worker announced that she was taking the afternoon off to have a look around the city. 'Are you just going for a wee donner?' asks a colleague of Glasgow ethnic origin. 'Certainly not. I'm a vegetarian,' was the indignant answer.

THIS is a wee tale from the Royal Liff state hospital, Dundee. A refurbishment was in progress and, as part of the material required, a lorry-load of sand was delivered. As the driver piloted his lorry through the entrance gates, he was flagged down by a well-dressed chap who enquired what his business was in the hospital.

Having heard the driver's mission, the chap told him to dump the sand at the entrance. Are you sure, the driver asked. Don't argue, do as you're told, the chap replied. The driver duly dumped his load of sand in the driveway, received a signature on his delivery docket and departed.

Yes, you've guessed. The patient duly walked away leaving the staff to deal with the problem of the pile of sand blocking the driveway.

THIS tale from Dumfries is said to have happened during a recent spell of good weather in the summer of 1993. You remember that bit of good weather. Just before we had the snow. The hero of our story was disporting

himself in warm-weather wear and did he not get a wee stone lodged in his sandal. He leaned against a handy metal structure and shook his leg violently in an effort to dislodge the stone. This performance attracted the attention of a passing roadsweeper. And what would you do if you saw a fellow man clutching a power-generator box and shaking violently, obviously suffering from an electric shock? You would do exactly what the Dumfries roadsweeper did. Remembering how dangerous electricity is, you would use your brush to whack the man free and save him from electrocution. Even though you might send the bewildered sandal-shaker to hospital in the process for treatment to a broken arm.

AS ITHERS SEE US

As part of a long-term quest 'Tae See Oorsels as Ithers See Us', the Diary monitored publications from England and many other foreign countries.

GLASGOW University football team, on tour in the USA, visited Wheaton College, near Chicago, the Bible-thumping alma mater of Billy Graham. The Glasgow chaps detected a certain reserve in the attitude of their American hosts. This, they discovered, was down to a circular letter which the college had distributed to their students, on the subject of the Glasgow Yooni team: 'Please keep in mind that these young men are not Christians. We have a great opportunity to share our lifestyle and Christian principles with them.

'All of them are drinkers! They have

been briefed on Wheaton's standards and the non-drinking procedures. Please be firm in reminding them of this, because they may try to bring their own drinks into your home.'

The Glasgow players, a bunch of red-blooded young men who liked the occasional lager, had to observe a strict 11 p.m. curfew. The two unlucky enough to be billeted with the college team coach had to get up at 5.30 a.m. for a cross-country run.

The Glaswegians did their best to cope with all this. But when a Wheatonite asked one of them: 'Do you really have no Christians in Scotland?' he replied: 'There were two or three, but we ate them.'

A JOURNALIST dispatched to Glasgow by the magazine *New Society* reported in February 1981: 'When I went to Glasgow last month I saw only two drunks.' The reason was not an outbreak of sobriety but the 'fact' that most Glaswegians could not afford the bus fares to visit the city centre.

The magazine also reported that Mr Fred Edwards, the city's 'restless and brilliant' social work director, had gathered round him 'a team of SAS social workers' which was making 'creative blitzkriegs on community problems'. The magazine did not indicate if the brilliant Mr Edwards had any plans to sort out the bus fares crisis.

IN the same month, very much pre-Year of Culture status, a book called *An Australian's Guide to Britain* (which carried the imprimatur of British Airways) said of the city: 'Glasgow is not well supplied with good accommodation and in any case is not worthy of an overnight stay. However, a visit of a few hours will probably be judged worth while.'

AN advertisement for Dewar's whisky in American magazines caused some wry amusement among the inhabitants of the picturesque village of Culross. Under a photograph of an old chap walking his collie dog through the cobbled streets of the village, ran the words: 'He was never elected. But every night "Mayor" Orlo McBain is the last man to walk the streets of Culross, Scotland. He checks a knob, closes a gate and goes his way. The good things in life stay that way.'

'Who is this Mayor Orlo McBain?' we asked the Culross police.

'Never heard of him,' the constable said. 'If anyone was wandering around late at night checking knobs and closing gates I'm sure we would have noticed. The only character we have ever had was a woman called Fanny Scotland who used to ring the town bell.'

The mystery was solved when Mr Ian McLeod, curator of the large number of National Trust for Scotland properties in Culross, revealed that he was the man in the picture. A team had arrived in the village from a Chicago advertising agency and asked him to pose with a borrowed collie dog.

Mr McLeod said of the Orlo McBain story: 'It is dreadful nonsense, but if it helps sells Scotch in the USA it might do some good.'

The National Trust received a $100 donation and the owner of the dog got $25. Presumably the writer of the advertisement copy also got to sample rather a lot of the product!

ANOTHER whisky company to go in for couthy Scots advertising around this time was Macallan. One of their ads told the tale of Alfred, a barman at the Caledonian Club in London who refused to allow a Texan visitor to put ginger ale into a measure of 15-year-old Macallan malt. Alfred was quoted as saying to the Texan: 'I'll no' be a party to defacing national monuments.' Of the Macallan, Alfred was reputed to have told the Texan: 'I doubt if ye'll find better.'

We tracked down Alfred the barman at the Caledonian Club. He said: 'It's all a bit embarrassing. I don't speak like that. In fact, no one does in Burton-on-Trent where I come from. It was fun at the time but the joke is now wearing thin, especially since I only got one bottle of the stuff for letting them use my name.'

AS part of a national campaign, Castlemilk Law Centre, the only such centre in Scotland, wrote to Lord

The BBC Language Course for Children
Only Seven Years Old*...
and She's Already Speaking French?

Give **Your** Child That Critical Early Advantage!

Great for Summertime Learning

Hailsham, the Lord Chancellor, even though they knew he was not associated with the legal system in Scotland. The letter produced this response: 'Lord Hailsham is Lord Chancellor of Great Britain, which does not, as you know, include Scotland.'

IT is not only Sassenachs and other foreigners who can come up with a picture of Glasgow that is slightly agley. The organisers of an event called Welcome Home 1983 showed a little less than encyclopaedic knowledge of their own city by producing a list of famous Glaswegians including: Lord Kelvin, inventor of Bovril; Saint Kentigan (*sic*), who was burnt at the stake in 1582; Peter Kerrigan, patron saint of Glasgow; Harry Lauder, a tobacco merchant; Thomas Lipton, a famous socialist; Tam Harvey, the Glasgow glutton; and Madeleine Smith, 'famous murderer of the Boys' Brigade'.

The organisers blamed the historic gaffes on an errant word processor, a piece of kit not, as far as we know, invented by a Glaswegian.

Elspeth King, then curator of the People's Palace, was angered that the above list was somewhat short of female representation. She immediately came up with 18 names of notable Glasgow women. It started off with St Thenew (or Enoch), mother of St Kentigern, patron saint of the city. In her inimitable style, Elspeth described St Thenew as 'Scotland's first fully documented battered woman, rape victim and unmarried mother'. Her list included a number of suffragettes, the Diary's favourite being one Elizabeth Dorothea Chalmers Smith, a well-known doctor whose suffragette principles led her to set fire to 6 Park Gardens on 24 July 1913.

No, Dr Smith was not ahead of her time in burning to the ground the HQ of the male chauvinist Scottish Football Association. The SFA did not move in until 1957. In 1913, the premises were occupied by the Lord Provost of Glasgow. Still, the thought was there.

MR Tony Benn, chairing a Labour Party meeting in London, on eco-

nomic strategy, declared that to make question time fair he would take questions alternately from men and women. The system worked well until there were no women left to put questions. With barely a pause, Mr Benn looked around the audience and asked: 'Is there anyone here from Scotland?' Presumably on the basis that in the absence of a woman, a man in a kilt will do.

RALEIGH (Glasgow) Ltd, a whisky producer, received the following telex from a Norwegian student:

Dear Mr Raleigh,

In the late July my companion, Mr H.G. Toreskaas and myself are going on an expedition of studies to Scotland. The purpose of the expedition is primarily to study the different brands of Scottish whisky and secondly to make a pre-project for my master degree in anthropology, which will be a comparative study of sheep shepherds' working methods in Scotland and Norway, stressed on the

threatening of wolves of lack of threatening? (How is the stock of wolves in Scotland?)

To carry through our expedition, we need a tandem bicycle (we have heard much about the extreme fog in England and due to that we must have a tandem so that we don't get lost for each other). We prefer to rent the tandem in Aberdeen. If that is unpossible we'll have to buy a tandem in Aberdeen. We would ask you to advice us a bicycle shop in Aberdeen where this is possible and return the address, telephone number and telex. Is it possible to get a price offer (a) for rent; (b) for sale?

We thank you very much for your co-operation in advance, and your name will be listed in the honouring list in the preface of our report.

A KISSOGRAM agency in London offers a Drunken Scots service. The act consists of a male employee (usually a genuine Scot) who turns up in kilt, a funny hat, bloomers, clutching a can of beer and proceeds to be a drunk Jock. For an extra payment, the Jockogram will show what is worn under his kilt. Presumably for no extra charge he will deliver a Glasgow kiss.

Other national stereotypes offered by the agency? A blond Swede or a witch doctor. If they had an Englisho-gram it would no doubt be someone who would bore the party to death with details of traffic conditions during his journey.

THE magazine *New Society* carried a report on down-and-outs in London. Naturally, one of the interviewees was a Scot: 'Jimmy has the cheerful, childlike face of "Oor Wullie" from the Scottish cartoon strip.'

Oor Jimmy goes on ('in a serious Dundee voice') to describe his drinking habits: 'I'm a very hard drinker. I'll drink anything. I had three bottles of aftershave and a bucket. I went out and got some hair lacquer. I put it all in the bucket and I drank it. I was staggering about bumping into walls. I was in the sick bay for three weeks.' No wonder Oor Wullie's hair stands on end if that's what Dundonians do with their buckets.

MUHAMMAD Mahfouz, correspondent of the *Saudi Gazette*, on a visit to Scotland, provided an insight into that rare breed, the Highlander. The Highlanders, he said, 'live in the mountains, which is a rather forbidding zone, and a collection of islands in the north-west'. According to Muhammad, Highlanders are still fighting, and losing, the wars of 1715 and 1745. The Highlanders 'have a lot of tolerance for hardships. They have scorn for ordinary work and technical skills and love to fight, to drink, and to sail.'

THE annual report of the Commissioner for Local Administration in Scotland is a weighty tome, but it is not without its lighter moments. It records a letter from an inquiring student which said: 'I would be extremely grateful if you could send me information on the geography, climate, countryside, costumes, music and national dancing of Scotland. If this isn't possible, could you please send me the address of the Scottish Embassy.' The student lives in England.

THE *Sunday Correspondent* newspaper of blessed memory contained a report about 'Glasgow's most frightening pub, the Saracen's Head, frequented by early-morning Barras workers. It is known as the Sarrie Heid (sore head) locally, because few people leave the establishment without one.'

The writer informed us further that it is 'easier to get a cappuccino in the city centre than it is to get a haggis supper (battered entrails and chips), such is the explosion of cafes and designer bars'.

AN ARTICLE in the Spanish newspaper *El Correo Español*, headed '*Glasgow, muerte y resurreccion*', focused on the city's football culture. Beside a photograph of Hampden strewn with beer bottles (as it was in the old days, they emphasise) the reporter tells of a visit to Ibrox where he found the fans singing '*un himno estremecedor*'. *Estremecedor* literally means shivering or shuddering.

The song, even translated into Spanish, should be familiar:

Hola, hola, somos los muchachos de
* Billy*
Hola, hola, nos conoceras por nuestro
* ruido*
Con sangre de catolicos hasta la rodilla
Rindete o moriras
Somos los muchachos de Billy.

We are sure no translation is necessary and we look forward to hearing it from the terraces if the Gers draw a Spanish club in the European Cup.

WE have become used to chronicling in the Diary the amazing ignorance (and we don't mean that in a bad way, by the way) of your average English person about Scotland and the Scottish way of life. We did not expect Labour's former deputy leader Roy Hattersley to add to the great ledger of English idiocy. But he has. Mr Hattersley was interviewed in *Citizens*, the magazine of Charter 88, the organisation which was campaigning for a written constitution

for the United Kingdom. The wide-ranging article touched on the question of devolution of power.

Mr H had this to say: 'I propose that we create regions which do have real powers. There could be, for example, a different educational system in Scotland. But these powers will be granted to them by Parliament. It can't possibly be a secession with Scotland announcing that they're taking all these powers. Westminster has to give those powers to Scotland.' And, perhaps, when Westminster is giving Scotland its own educational system, they could throw in a separate Scottish legal system. With London's permission we could even have our own national rugby and football teams. The possibilities are endless. But we suppose, Mr Hattersley, that a separate Scottish Labour Party is out of the question.

THE DONKEYS, a book which tells the story of the British Expeditionary Force in 1915, has been reissued in paperback. Some of the captions to the photographs will give pause to any veterans of the Battle of Loos in September of that year – or indeed to descendants of those who lost their lives. One caption refers to 'looking back at the English parapet'. The parapet in question had been manned by the 2nd Cameronians. Another photograph is described as an English outpost and yet another as 'the English line'. The positions in question were held entirely by Highland regiments. *The Donkeys* was written by the late Tory MP Alan Clark who was a Minister of State at the MoD.

WHEN nationalist fervour was rife before the 1992 election there was a short debate on what you would call an independent Scottish currency. One suggestion was the mickle, with 1,314 mickles making a muckle. The muckle would float or sink with the punt. A jibe at a well-known politician who transferred allegiances from Labour to SNP was that 'we'll need a 30 pieces o' sillar note' for the new currency. There was strong support for a national name as the French do with the franc. Ours could be the jock. A jock would consist of 100 weans. And ten jocks would be a tamson, made up of 1,000 of his weans.

A LETTER from the Next Directory to a resident of Benbecula, who wished to do some business with the mail-order firm, said: 'Unfortunately we are unable to send you a copy of the directory as we cannot send goods abroad and deal in foreign currencies.

The reason for this is firstly the high cost of postage, and secondly that we have no facilities for customs procedures for exporting.' Next suggested that if the Benbeculan still wanted goods from their directory, he ask a friend or relative with an address in the UK to act as an intermediary.

AWAY FROM IT ALL

Editing the Diary column is mainly a solitary pursuit – opening piles of mail, answering numerous telephone calls, reading endless newspapers and magazines to keep abreast of world affairs. Occasionally, the editor lets you out of the office on an assignment that has already been turned down by everyone else including the office boy. Here are some examples.

SATURDAY: I have been told Butlin's is a different world. It is in fact a different planet, as I discover when I stay at their Ayr centre. Otherwise, why are so many of the guests wearing headbands complete with ping-pong balls on the end of springs, headwear apparently known as antennae? When at Butlin's . . .

Wearing my antennae, I report for tea in the dining-room. Why is waitress pouring coffee into my soup plate? It is in fact brown soup. 'At least that's what it purports to be,' says waitress. Butlin's have some very literate waitresses. Survive soup and rest of meal, which is very reminiscent of school dinners. Children want to go to beach. Gate to beach padlocked each night at 6 p.m. Beginning to feel trapped.

Go to cinema (entrance free). Film is *Escape to Victory* about Second World War prison camp. Still feeling trapped, leave cinema.

Take refuge from rain in building called Beachcomber Bar. Tropical setting very pleasant until thunder, lightning and rain start *inside* building. Don't worry, only special effects, says waitress. Order campari and soda and find, for some reason, Butlin's

give large measure for price of single. Nice place, Butlin's.

SUNDAY: Raining. Head for church but diverted into adjacent showground, where all rides are free. Queue at dodgems. Queue at roundabout which tilts at great speed and brings tears to your eyes.

Arrive late for service. Minister giving sermon on 'The first shall be last and the last shall be first'. He should tell that to the man in charge of the dodgems queue. Soup at lunch is red but tastes the same as the brown. Lose in afternoon at table tennis to niece. Lose at pitch and putt, lose at bowls. Go back to showground and lose lunch on waltzers.

Children have joined Butlin's clubs (Beaver for age six to nine, 913 Club for older ones) and have a programme of activities that leaves them with approx. five minutes free time each day. Nice place, Butlin's.

MONDAY: Redcoat at breakfast urges us to clap for the sun. It rains. Lose to wife at table tennis. Lose lunchtime sweep at table on colour of soup. (I chose yellow but it is green.)

Catch brief glimpse of son at Paxo

Rooster Rock show. Paxo Rooster is redcoat wearing chicken's head. (Amazing what they have to do for their £43 a week.) About 3,000 children doing something called Birdie Dance. Camp compère, very amusing chap called Gerry Griffin from Forfar, has theory that some parents don't come themselves but throw children over fence. Retreat to Beachcomber Bar which has moat over which children must not pass.

TUESDAY: Lose to wife again at table tennis. Get revenge by saying she has fair chance of winning Miss Whitbread competition to find 'cheerful, charming, and chubby' lady. On reflection, wife would have no chance in competition – it's full of confirmed Butlinites obviously weaned on years of three school dinners a day. Go along to talent competition but again would have no chance against Butlin regulars who just happen to have brought along dancing costumes, sheet music, guitars, saxophones, etc.

See son momentarily as he passes on overhead railway. Determined to win something. Repair to Beachcomber for camparis as fuel for Knobbly Knees contest. Too many camparis, too late to enter. Just as well as Gerry Griffin has contestants stripped to waist, kissing each other, and doing Tarzan calls.

WEDNESDAY: Challenge eight-year-old at table tennis and lose. Little know that he is Beaver Club ace player. Sun shines for Donkey Derby. Put money on number eight which immediately starts to cough and retch. Comes last after throwing child jockey.

Compère Griffin, parodying Butlin's tradition of applauding everything in sight, asks for a big clap for Tote board. We all applaud. Think I'm finally getting into spirit of things.

Catch son at evening meal (soup brown, by the way). Ask if he would

like to play table tennis at which I know he is not good. Too busy, dad. Cinema, dodgems, pentathlon competition. Possibly spare some time Friday.

THURSDAY: No wigs . . . Lose at putting, lose soup sweepstake (it was red, not green). Spend most of day watching competitions. Glamorous Grandmothers ('No long dresses, trouser suits, wigs or hair pieces to be worn,' says brochure), all slim and obviously on self-catering. So many competitions, now getting confused. Is it Miss Lovely Hair or Miss Lovely Legs next? Or even Miss Lovely Hairy Legs? Anyway, lots of legs on display.

FRIDAY: Lose to son at table tennis but only by 22-20. Lose at snooker, putting. Despite school dinners, have lost half a stone in week. Celebrate with camparis in Beachcomber Bar. Wonder what volcano looks like close up. Prepare to wade through tropical lake (with plastic crocodiles) to find out but tall chap with green jacket and badge saying 'security' advises it is not good idea.

Join Paxo Rooster, 3,000 children doing Birdie Dance, and 43 Redcoats in upstairs ballroom for farewell party till 1 a.m.

SATURDAY: Time to leave. Re-united with children. Buy antennae as presents for friends. Drive out of camp wondering how ever readjust to planet earth. Stop at perimeter fence for last look. Throw children over and drive off fast.

WHILST on holiday bus tour of the French wine districts, far from Butlin's, the editor of the Diary was kind enough to send this postcard:

SUNDAY: Join bus at Gloucester Road bus station, London. Surely some mistake. Have booked (with four other ageing adolescent chums) for cosmopolitan, gourmet, connoisseur eight-day holiday of lifetime traversing France in luxury coach in company of other fun-seekers. Why sitting at back of boring ordinary bus? Why other passengers all grey haired? Fernando the courier not exactly understanding. What expect for £160? Driving to Dover in thunderstorm. Overtaken by super-duper German bus with video, inside toilet, plush seats, disco, swimming-pool, bar, restaurant and not a grey hair in sight. Lady in front of us is worrying about state of French toilets.

Reach France and Famous Five in back seat cheering up. Fernando makes announcement about 'bus rules'. Smokers must sit on right, non-smokers on left. Rota system for seats at front of bus. One of Famous Five (not me) now drinking litre of Martini by neck and decides to make own announcement. 'Will all people who are dead please sit on right-hand side,' he says. Arrive Reims: chicken and chips for dinner. Lady who has still not been to toilet asks for cup of tea from wine waiter.

MONDAY: Early visit to Moët champagne factory in Epernay. Things looking up as find free bar. Fernando approach and say: 'No, no. Visit cellars first, then free champagne.' Explain to Fernando only two

things need to know about champagne. Is it properly chilled? Who paying? Lady still hasn't been to toilet. French ambience induced by Moët visit evaporates as Fernando arranges stop for lunch at a supermarket. If this is Safeway it must be Monday.

Arrive Beaune. More like Bo'ness on a wet Sunday. One of the connoisseurs has a bottle of Coke with his *boeuf bourguignon.* Dessert is a choc ice still in wrapper. One of Famous Five has had enough. 'Is this a restaurant or a cinema?' he shouts in reference to choc ice for pudding.

Escape from English fellow travellers to a little *boîte* called the Club Americain. Find only other people in it are Maurice, a property developer from Berkshire, his son (Maurice minor) and an architect from Stewarton. They are here to open Pickwick English pub.

TUESDAY: Day off from bus. Visit Dijon which is pleasantly full of French people. Real French meal in real French restaurant. Unfortunately lose balance and come to grief in one of those real French toilets. Know now why lady in bus has thing about French toilets.

WEDNESDAY: Eight-hour bus journey to Bordeaux ahead of us. Three of Famous Five do very un-British thing. Cut and run. Abandon bus and get train to Paris. French railways amazing. Book seats on high-speed train by computer from station. Immaculate buffet car serves smoked salmon salad, steaks, chilled white wine. British Rail could learn something here. Arrive Paris. Book into the Hôtel Opéra-Comique which name sums up the holiday so far.

Dinner at Boffinger's at the Place de la Bastille. Surprised to get in since one of remaining Famous Five (not me) is wearing jeans and a black summit. Fixed menu at £10 starts with seafood platter size of a dustbin

lid and gets even better the further you go through the card.

After dinner Terrible Trio (as we are now called) find ourselves at loose end in place called Pigalle. Nice Frenchman stops us and says the Piano Bar up the street is just the spot for nightcap. Place must have been some sort of health club since full of women wearing swimsuits and other casual clothes. Small bottle of Heineken lager costs 30 francs. Try to tell owner that he could get case of 24 bottles for that price in supermarket and brewery must be overcharging him. Lady in swimsuit approaches and asks will I buy her drink. At these prices can't buy myself drink. Will I buy her packet of cigarettes? Say I am surprised to hear member of health club is smoker. About to offer her some chewing gum when she leaves to talk to party of Germans just brought in by same chap we met in street.

THURSDAY: Lunch at a brasserie near the Gare du Nord. *Choucroute* and beer. Feel just like Inspector Maigret. Try to book seats on express train to London. Fully booked. Have to buy tickets for ordinary train. Thing is packed like bloody cattle train. French could learn a thing or two from British Rail. Take refuge in buffet where lashings of chilled wine and Perrier restore faith in French rail system.

Daunted by prospect of overnight stop in London which, as you know, is full of English. Get off train at Calais and find it full of English people. Visit made worth while by superb meal in Vietnamese restaurant which whets appetite for one which is promised to open in Glasgow later this year. (But will they make spicy pancake rolls like Mr Chung in Calais?) Evening stroll along main street. Hear sound of breaking glass from café. English hooligans? No, *patron* and his wife have fallen out and are throwing crockery at each other. V. entertaining.

FRIDAY: Would like to rejoin bus but can't remember itinerary. Train from London to Glasgow. Wondering if all worth money and effort. Scots soldier sitting opposite tells me he has got compassionate leave from his unit in Germany. Is travelling to Hampden to see his team, Rangers, in cup final. Takes all sorts to make world, *n'est-ce pas?*

BARLINNIE

The Diary visits the Bar-L.

BARLINNIE is an open prison. The thousand or so inmates who are dubbed up in their peters as you read this may disagree, but what we are talking about is access from interested external parties to the great microcosm of prison life that is the Bar-L. From governor Peter Withers down, the staff proudly boasts that there is no hidden agenda at Barlinnie.

When a well-known Scottish tabloid newspaper asked the Bar-L authorities to comment on allegations of prisoner maltreatment, the reporter was invited to visit any part of the prison and ask any questions. The reporter did so and, as deputy governor Robbie Glenn says, 'gave us a clean bill of health'.

'So, what will you be writing about us, then?' Robbie Glenn asked the journalist. 'Nothing. There's no story here,' was the reply. The story of Barlinnie's new regime since the rooftop riots has been well documented. The visitor's trail is well worn. Just before my visit, photographers from the Cranhill Arts Project were in the prison at 7.30 a.m. one Sunday morning to capture the slopping-out parade for their archive of Glasgow life.

You would be as likely to meet a party from a woman's guild as a serious investigative reporter as the Bar-L pursues its open-door policy; open door for visitors that is.

My invitation to visit Barlinnie came after I wrote a wee story in the *Herald* Diary about a shop in Glasgow which was selling a novelty whisky called Barlinnie Bevvy, without permission from the authorities. I wrote that we hoped it appealed to the governor's sense of humour. Peter Withers was quickly on the phone with the question: 'What sense of humour?' He then said it was all in good fun and suggested that a bottle of the whisky be delivered to the prison, presumably for their archives.

Then deputy governor Robbie Glenn picked up on the Diary's reference to Barlinnie as 'Riddrie's best-known B&B'. 'We prefer to think of it as the Riddrie Hilton,' I heard him regale an audience during one of his famous after-dinner speeches. 'It is possibly Glasgow's most successful hotel. It has high room-occupancy rates. Unlike other hotels, our residents are carefully vetted and always arrive with a police escort. They are obviously happy with

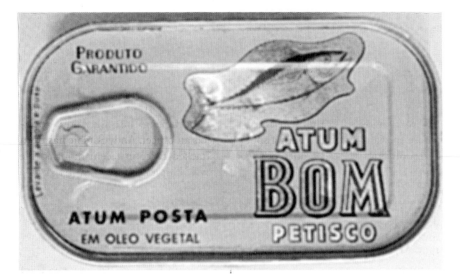

PRODUTO
GARANTIDO

ATUM POSTA
EM OLEO VEGETAL

ATUM
BOM
PETISCO

the service. They return with astonishing regularity, sometimes bringing friends and family with them.'

Robbie Glenn invited me to sample a taste of Barlinnie with the words: 'You'll find it very interesting and once you leave you won't want to come back as an uninvited guest.'

The Victorian bleakness of Barlinnie brings to mind prisoner Wilde's words written about his spell in Reading Gaol:

> *The vilest deeds like poison weeds,*
> *Bloom well in prison air;*
> *It is only what is good in Man*
> *That wastes and withers there:*
> *Pale Anguish keeps the heavy gate,*
> *And the warder is despair.*

In my case the warder was John McRoberts, who, I suspect, was given the job as my tour guide because he is a leading exponent of the Bar-L sense of humour. (He is not a warder by the way; they are officers, senior officers, principal officers, and governors.) He is a veteran of the riots at both Barlinnie and Shotts who sometimes daydreams about a post at an open prison in the countryside where the most pressing problem can be whose turn it is to milk the cows. But he knows he would get bored and miss the day-to-day challenge of man-management and crisis control. Or keeping the prisoners off the roof as it is also known.

John McRoberts is the Care Bear in E Hall. The official job description is caseworker and his task is to look after the prisoners' welfare and speed them as humanely and efficiently as possible through their prison careers. He is no soft touch, but has a genuine concern for his charges. A concern which he can express either in sociological language (for which he takes some stick from certain of his fellow officers) or in very straightforward terms.

'Most of the people I have to deal with in here are social inadequates with chronic alcohol-abuse problems which have placed them outside society,' he says. Or, to put it another way: 'Most of the people locked up in Barlinnie wouldn't hurt a fly. Then they go outside and get stuck into that singing ginger and get done for breach of the peace.

'Look at old Bob,' he says, referring to a long-term Barlinnie resident whose speciality is breach with a spot of shoplifting. 'He goes out vowing never to return. Then he has a few drinks, needs money for a few more, pops into Marks & Spencer, and thinks he's invisible. You're the worst shoplifter in Glasgow, aren't you, Bob?'

In his Care Bear's den in E Hall, John McRoberts keeps a big tank of tropical fish. When a prisoner comes in to discuss a problem, he is always sat in front of the fish tank. Often there is little John can do about the prisoner's problem. Usually they just want a bit of attention, a change of routine, and a therapeutic look at the fish.

'Did you phone the kennels, Mr McRoberts?' a prisoner asks. His alsatian is doing time in kennels while he is in the Bar-L. The Care Bear has to keep in touch with the kennels to give progress reports on the well-being of the dog. It is hardly I-Was-a-Prisoner-on-the-Chain-Gang stuff.

Another prisoner has a more unusual family problem. He is wondering how his father is getting on. His father has left the relative safety of darkest Ayrshire to be a mercenary in Croatia.

So what makes a good prison officer? A brains trust of officers with varying lengths of service consider this topic over a coffee in the office of C Hall, a melting pot where upwards of 250 untried prisoners of all persuasions are contained. You need to be a psychologist, a psychiatrist, a kindly social worker, a strict disciplinarian, a keen student of the criminal mind . . . 'And it helps if you're good at the boxing. Just ask Andy,' interjects an officer. Andy Ritchie has been attacked twice in recent months. He says: 'This job is full of surprises. One morning you open a cell door to a reasonably polite greeting, the next to a punch in the nose.' Andy Ritchie says he still has a 'reasonable relationship' with both the attackers.

He grew up in Blackhill, the tough housing estate near Barlinnie. While it is common for the career path of your average Blackhill youth to take him to the Bar-L, it is unusual for him to end up as a custodian. 'You could say it was not a great culture shock for me to come to work in Barlinnie,' Andy Ritchie says.

Like every other young officer, Andy Ritchie had to learn fast. 'You have your basic training but nothing can prepare you for the real thing.' From your first day, when some lag will look at the newcomer's uniform and opine: 'Your ma's turned ye oot nice,' the tyro officer is on a steep and interesting learning curve.

To the wall of the office in C Hall, there is affixed a notice bearing a piece of Bar-L cracker-barrel philosophy aimed at the younger members of staff: 'Old age and treachery will always overcome youth and skill.'

By necessity, Barlinnie humour is a black humour. All human life is there and most of the prejudices. There is a true story about the unfortunate who found himself inside for having sex

BRUCE SPRINGSTEIN, 35, has been a proofreader and inventory analyst, processed loan applications and even shagged fuzzy orange basketballs for a car promotion as a temp in Milwaukee, Wisconsin. He has no medical insurance and does not own a car or a house.

with a dog. For his first meal, a bone was thrown into the cell. He asked what was going on to be told that if it was good enough for his girlfriend, it was good enough for him. This was many years ago and would, of course, never happen in these more enlightened days.

Also from darker days there is the story of a huge African who found himself incarcerated in Barlinnie. The warders promised him a special meal as a change from the routine. At teatime they threw the smallest duty warder into his cell.

These days the humour is gentler but still with an edge. A mischievous officer asked for volunteers for a party to go and wash the windows at Cornton Vale. The prospect of a trip outside, not to mention the chance of some female company, meant that in no time at all the squad was assembled and ready to march off, buckets and cloths in hand. It was then they realised, amid gales of laughter from officers and fellow prisoners, how unlikely a mission they had volunteered for.

Then there was the prisoner from

England who had to come to Glasgow to give evidence at a trial. He left his open prison on his own, travelled by train to Glasgow, took a bus to Barlinnie, and knocked on the door to announce that he had arrived for his night's bed and breakfast. Rules is rules and he was taken in, handcuffed and locked in a holding cell until they could work out where to put him.

There is, of course, much scope for the practical joke. Like the one played on a senior officer who had a mania for cleanliness, an almost impossible pursuit in a prison more than 100 years old. 'What's that?' he would bark. 'Dust, sir!' or, 'Litter, sir!' would be the reply to an obvious question.

A piece of newspaper was covered in brown sauce and left out for inspection. 'What's that?' came the almost apoplectic inquiry. The prisoner in the cell stuck his finger in the mess, licked it, and replied casually, 'Shite, sir!'

Inmates like Coutsie are a rich source of grim humour. Even when he's outside the Bar-L, which isn't often, his life tends to get inextricably mixed with the prison. His problem in life is too much of the singing ginger. There he was standing at a corner in Duke Street, sipping at his can of strong lager, when he espied the Barlinnie bus taking its cargo back from the courts. The bus stopped at the traffic lights. Coutsie enquired of the driver, whom he knows well, if there was any chance of a pound for a drink. The driver declined. Coutsie lay down in front of the bus. The driver relented, got down from the bus and gave Coutsie his £1 blackmail money.

Coutsie's job at the prison includes helping the chaplains set up for services. Given his position of trust, he says, he would never think of assuaging his thirst by swigging the communion wine. 'Anyway, it's only one per cent,' he says.

It's easy to laugh at Coutsie's patter and forget the man behind the well-lived-in face, the sort of face you get in Tam Shepherd's, suggests an officer. Or from a lifetime of cheap drink.

Coutsie did his first spell in Barlinnie in 1961. The longest he has been out since is five weeks. He has 205 convictions, mostly for breach of the peace. During banter with John McRoberts and other officers, Coutsie proclaims that he taught them everything they know. But he is sadly lacking skills which will sustain him out of a prison environment. Apart from a skill in hijacking prison buses, he is adept at rooting out caches of booze hidden in the environs of Celtic Park by fans anxious to avoid the penalties of the Criminal Justice Scotland Act without losing their carry-out. It is hardly a training for life.

While the Bar-L undoubtedly has its share of tough men, the majority of its population are like Coutsie, the flotsam and jetsam of society. People who should be receiving treatment and rehabilitation. The sad fact is that it is cheaper for the authorities to keep these people in prison and this is increasingly the case as hospitals close their doors on the problem.

Another significant part of the prison population are those in for car theft, driving while banned, or some other motoring offence. A whole generation of young men appear to be locked up because of their obsession with motor cars. At one point, after meeting six of these motor villains in succession, I wondered if there were any real violent men in the Bar-L. Then I met the man who had stabbed his girlfriend. But, as his pal said in mitigation, if you met her, you'd stab her too.

There are, of course, some of the real thugs who can make life a misery for their fellow inmates. Drugs are the big currency in prisons these days. The more successful the police are in putting drug dealers and users away, the bigger a problem it becomes for the prison service. Thus a new inmate, even someone not remotely connected with the drugs culture, can find himself involved. Called to the visiting-room, he might find himself confronted by a strange woman who will give him a lingering kiss and pass a packet of drugs into his mouth. His task is to swallow it, bring it out (either up or down), and hand the contents over to the drugs barons. Or else.

Families might find there is a knock on the door and be handed a wee parcel which they have to smuggle in on their next visit. Or else. (To digress from the subject of drugs, older officers reminisce about the good old days when the lags would try to alleviate the boredom of Barlinnie life by making a batch of hooch with some raisins, sugar and yeast from the cookhouse. To avoid detection, the Barlinnie brew had to be drunk young, resulting in a laxative as well as an intoxicating effect. One cheeky bunch of hooch-makers kept the stuff in the fire bucket outside the senior officer's door.)

The new regime at Barlinnie, introduced after the roof riots, is aimed at controlling the hard men and making the individual prisoner less vulnerable. The dining-rooms system has been abandoned. With upwards of 200 men in one room, there were never enough officers on hand to prevent intimidation or react at a flashpoint. Prisoners now eat in their cells and are moved to work and recreation in smaller numbers. The officers feel more in control. The prisoners feel safer.

Robbie Glenn, with his enthusiasm for the place, claims there is probably more violence in your average Glasgow primary school playground than there is in Barlinnie. I thought I had stumbled across what the aforementioned tabloid journalist might have called a story. The windscreen of the yellow hired van used to transport food from the cookhouse to the halls was pitted with gunshot holes. A failed escape attempt? No, the van had been on hire recently to a well-known Scottish arts organisation for a tour of France. The driver had fallen foul of a French farmer who took a pot-shot at the windscreen.

If Barlinnie is a safer place these days for its uninvited guests, and the conditions are less crowded, the reality of incarceration is no less awful. The admission hall gives an immediate impression of abandon hope all ye who enter here. In a setting of Victorian squalor, the new inmate is divested of his worldly trappings, showered, issued with a set of clean but well-worn prison clothes, given a Barlinnie bowl (his first taste of prison food), then locked in a four-foot square holding cell while awaiting allocation to a prison hall. It is a soul-destroying experience, even for the most hardened criminals.

On one of my visits, the sound from one of the holding cells was a young man sobbing and calling out for his mother. The same young man who was pictured smiling as he left court with a life sentence for murder. But his future, such as it is, will not be at Barlinnie. Apart from the Special Unit with its infamous inhabitants, the Bar-L caters for prisoners serving sentences up to 18 months. Their main concern will be to do their time, avoid trouble, land a good job in the gnome-painting shed, and get access to as many creature comforts as possible.

Which brings us to the Barlinnie food. The cooks are proud of what they achieve on a budget of £6.38 for a whole week's food for each prisoner. One of the governors has to sample the menu each day and write his comments in the book. Robbie Glenn likes his prison food and puts in comments such as: 'The liver *au poivre* is an interesting addition to the menu.'

The old standard fare of porridge, mince and stews has been replaced by curries, sweet and sour dishes, and when there is a bargain to be had at the fish market, salmon or trout. Me? I had the Barlinnie bridie. Home-made, like everything at the Bar-L, delicious and containing more meat than us chaps on the outside are used to.

The pink custard was something else. I didn't taste it. Its very appearance, I'm sure, is against the Geneva Convention.

BOOZE

The section on alcoholic drink is necessarily short because ardent spirits and heavy ales have played little part in the years of the Herald *Diary.*

THE National Trust for Scotland had the honour of running the most up-market shebeen in Scotland. The shebeen (which, as you will all no doubt know, is an illegal drinking den) operated at the Trust's headquarters in Edinburgh's douce Charlotte Square.

The Trust's executive committee met there on a monthly basis and, before lunch, refreshments of an alcoholic nature were served.

The chaps on the executive, not wishing to spend the revenue donated by Trust members, were in the habit of organising a pay bar where the likes of your Marquess of Bute and the Earl of Wemyss and March would fork out for their gin and tonic, dry sherry, or can of Tennent's Super.

All very laudable, canny, and cost conscious – but totally illegal since the Trust did not have a licence to sell excisable liquor on their premises.

The illegality of it all did not go unnoticed by a disenchanted former member of staff who blew the gaff to Lothian Police licence division. The police were obliged to turn up at the lunch, interrupt the talk of heritage and history, and advise the Trust that their upper-class drinking den must close forthwith.

KICK like a mule . . . On a trip to Cyprus courtesy of the RAF, the Diary was introduced to a wine called Kokkinelli. It is a kind of Cypriot Lanliq, made of already strong local red wine fortified with brandy. Kokkinelli is consumed in great quantities by British airmen, especially since it is provided free with meals in many of the small tavernas near the bases.

The wine can have unusual side effects. One airman, under its influence, hijacked a donkey from the village to get back to base. When challenged by the guard at the gate, he spurred on the donkey and tried to persuade it to jump over the barrier. The donkey refused but the airman flew over the barrier beautifully, landing at the feet of the military policeman.

Another imbiber made it safely back to his quarters where he proceeded to hang his clothes over his bed before falling asleep in the wardrobe.

Kokkinelli is a precocious little wine, as they say in the Gallowgate.

A PRECOCIOUS nine-year-old enters a public house and shouts to the waitress to bring him a whisky.

The waitress looks at the height of him and asks: 'Do you want to get me into trouble?'

'Maybe later,' he says, 'but get me that drink first.'

A PLUMBER carrying out a job of work for a genteel Ayr lady was suffering from the effects of a ferocious hangover. He persevered with the work in hand and the lady, spotting that he was in need of some refreshment, asked: 'Would you like an apple?'

He considered the kind offer and, concluding that it did not quite meet the needs of his predicament, declined.

'Well, then, how about a half?' she asked.

'Oh, I'm sure I could manage that,' he responded brightly – at which point the lady produced a knife and cut the apple in two.

BURNS

One of the seasonal events of the Diary is the arrival of Burns Supper jokes. These are eagerly awaited. And some of them we haven't even heard before.

A CANNIBAL chief was guest of honour at a Burns Supper organised by the white administration in a British outpost of West Africa. The chief thoroughly enjoyed the ritual, the drink, but most of all the food, of which he partook mightily.

At one point the company were asked to be upstanding. 'What are we doing now?' the chief enquired.

'We're going to toast the lassies,' his host told him.

'No thanks, I couldn't eat another thing,' the chief replied.

SPEAKING at Burns Suppers can be a frightening proposition and speakers have been known to take refuge in strong drink. This can be dangerous.

Take the case of one chap, who shall remain nameless, who was to give the Toast to the Lassies. He had consumed so much whisky by the time it came for him to speak that all he could do was stagger to his feet, sway about a bit, blurt out 'Fair fa' your honest, sonsy face, chieftain o' the puddin' race', and collapse in his seat.

THEN there was the speaker who turned up to give the Immortal Memory at a Burns Supper but on the way to the club had suffered an accident to his dentures. He mumbled his apologies to the club secretary and explained why he would be unable to speak.

The quick-thinking secretary told him not to worry, made a quick phone call and said that help was on its way. Ten minutes later another club member arrived, with a box full of dentures. The speaker was able to find a suitable set and went ahead with his speech.

Afterwards, he approached the secretary and told him that the dentures he found in the box was actually a better fit than his own pair. 'Give my thanks to your dentist friend,' he added.

'I will,' the secretary replied, 'but he isn't a dentist. He's an undertaker.'

BURNS'S way with the lassies is recorded in the story of when he was out for a walk in the country. He encountered a beautiful milkmaid in a narrow lane. The milkmaid was carrying two pails on a yoke over her shoulders and there was no room for the two to pass. This gave Burns the

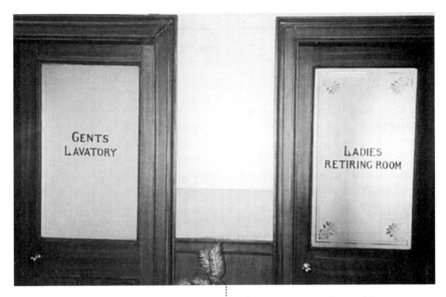

chance to indulge in a bit of chat. He asked her if she knew who he was.

'No,' she replied.

'I'm Rabbie Burns,' he told her.

'In that case, I suppose I'd better put these pails down right now,' she said.

AN American tourist visiting Ayrshire at the height of the Burns season was delighted to be invited to a supper. He said proudly that he already knew quite a bit about the Bard. He could even quote from Burns's poem about Ayr:

Ayr, there's no' a toon surpasses
For pullin' tails off horses' asses.

A REGULAR Burns speaker, who again shall remain nameless, appeared at a supper where the turnout was quite small. At the end of the evening, the secretary offered him a fee, which he declined as the club was obviously not affluent. The delighted secretary announced this to the members with the information that

the money saved would go into a special fund 'to allow us to afford some really good speakers next year'.

A CHAP from Cumbernauld gave us this recollection of the time he was invited to play the piano at a local Celtic supporters' club Burns Night.

'That the evening was not going to be one for the purists became evident when the first singer ('Ah'll jist start and you foallie') opened with the well-known Burns song 'Galway Bay'. 'The Wild Colonial Boy' was demanded as an encore.

The sangs and clatter continued, with Kevin Barry giving his young life, Sean South approaching barracks walls, and glorious St Patrick being hailed. The evening deteriorated further when a member of the audience threw a screwtop at the portrait of Rabbie Burns on the wall on the grounds that 'that Masonic bastard's been staring doon at us a' night'.

At the end of the night, the chairman, ignoring the pianist's request for anonymity, said: 'I'd like to thank the pianist, Mr William Waddell.'

The chairman managed to assuage the bears growling at the mention of William Waddell by saying: 'C'mon, he widnae know a' oor songs if he wisnae a Tim.'

HUGH McNamee recalls the occasion he was asked to play the piano at a Burns Night at the social club of a factory in Bridgeton.

'I noticed, after playing the first verse of the well-known songs, a poor response to the other verses. Some poems were spoken rather badly and it began to dawn on me that the gentlemen were not particularly knowledgeable about the Bard but were more intent on a good night out, an impression confirmed by the amount of whisky on the tables.'

When he played some of the lesser-known songs, there was even less response and after a time Mr McNamee was approached by one of the guests, who said: 'Hey, Jimmy. F*** Burns. Let's have "Singing the Blues".'

BUSINESS

The Diary is popular with business readers. Here it visits the cutting edge of the world of commerce.

LET it not be said that there is no sense of humour to be found in the Inland Revenue – well, a pretty bizarre imagination at least. The scene for this story is a large tax office in Kingston-upon-Thames. The Revenue was in the process of hiving off a number of jobs from Kingston to Nottingham.

In a brilliant piece of lateral thinking, it was decided to prepare for this exodus by pretending that the staff had already left for Nottingham. The Nottingham Division was separated from the rest of the office.

Doors were erected bearing the name 'Nottingham'. To make the point quite clear, an artist was brought in to paint murals of Sherwood Forest complete with Robin Hood and Maid Marian.

In best Civil Service tradition, a memo was issued to all staff setting out the rules: 'With effect from Monday, 2 March, and until further notice, Sections 4, 5 and 6 are to be regarded for all official purposes as being in Nottingham. No visits for official purposes may be made to those sections by anyone outside the Nottingham Division.

'There is, of course, no ban on unofficial or social visits, though please avoid discussing official matters in the process. Official contacts are to be made by telephone or by memo only . . . Should a visit be unavoidable, a note needs to be made of the reason and the time taken. Allowance should be made for the fact that a return visit from London to Nottingham (and vice versa) would take a day.'

With mind-boggling thoroughness, the Revenue had a system to simulate the 24-hour delay in sending documents from Kingston to Nottingham. 'Items coming into the Nottingham Division will be brought into Sections 4, 5 and 6 in a barrow and left for 24 hours.'

But where there is an emergency, a judicial review or a complaint by an MP 'it may be appropriate to consider a "fax"'. To simulate a fax, a Kingston tax officer would walk past the Nottingham section and hand the piece of paper over to a messenger who would then take it to 'Nottingham'.

At this point the rules suffered an unwelcome attack of common sense. 'Staff will be expected to use their discretion when exceptional circum-

stances arise . . . The excuse that the office was "pretending to be in Nottingham" would sound pretty thin if it caused an additional delay.'

ANYTHING is fair game these days for the ubiquitous newspaper advertising supplement. But perhaps the Aberdeen *Press and Journal* was pushing matters a bit by inviting advertisers to buy their way into a supplement to 'celebrate the 300th anniversary of the massacre of Glencoe'. One chap who certainly thought so was Mr Rob MacDonald Parker, director of the Clan Donald Centre on Skye, given that the MacDonalds of Glencoe, victims of the bloody murders, were his kith and kin. He received a letter inviting his tourist attraction to pay for advertising space in this celebratory supplement. He was not impressed. Particularly since the letter was signed

by a *Press and Journal* advertising executive by the name of Adrian Campbell.

ACCOUNTANCY isn't the most exciting way of life. For instance, when was the last time you heard of a youngster running away to join Ernst & Young? But a bold move by Colonel John Blashford-Snell, the man behind Operation Raleigh, could change all this. He issued this challenge to chartered accountants: 'Operation Raleigh, the organisation that gives young people a taste of adventure and leadership on ventures world-wide, is looking for short-term secondees from accounting profession to act as field accountants on its expeditions. Volunteers would be sent to expedition locations to carry out usual accounting and liaison with local banks, businesses, and sponsors as well as Raleigh headquarters, up to preparing final accounts. . . .'

The Diary managed to get hold of the chief accountant's report on a recent Operation Raleigh expedition to the North Pole:

- *Leith, 21 March:* The team set sail in good spirits. Managed to sell the ship to a Hong Kong company and negotiate a lease-back on very favourable terms. Have high hopes of reaching the Pole and making a profit.

- *Cape Farewell, Greenland, 20 April:* Disaster. Our insolvency expert was washed overboard this morning, leaving only myself, three trainee accountants, two secretaries, four bookkeepers, and a data-systems manager for the arduous task ahead.

- *Ellesmere Island, 3 May:* Our first base camp. Our IBM computers are working well despite the freezing cold. Would like to take the entire accounts department all the way to the Pole, but Colonel Blashford-Snell says there is no room on the sled. Will have to put the spread-sheets on to a lap-top and hope for the best.

- *Fifty miles from the Pole, 12 July:* Sixteen of the young explorers have died of frostbite. One of the team leaders blames it on my decision back in Leith to cut the clothing budget by 50 per cent. He doesn't seem to understand the need for tight cost control. Point out that the wastage rate in young explorers, in fact, compares favourably with previous expeditions.

- *Twenty-five miles from Pole, 3 August:* A bitter blow. My book-keeper plunged to her death down a ravine, taking the lap-top with her. Luckily I had the double-entry ledger in my rucksack at the time.

- *Five miles from the Pole, 10 August:* Farquhar, our last trainee accountant, is suffering from severe frost-bite after an all-night session working without gloves on a very tricky VAT problem. Says he is now just a hindrance to the accounts department and walks out into the blizzard saying he is off 'to make a final reconciliation and may be some time'. Have written to Edinburgh recommending him for the Institute of Chartered Accountants' highest award.

- *North Pole, 15 August:* Colonel Blashford-Snell raises a Union Jack at the Pole. Use my ice-axe to bury a copy of the interim accounts. Feel the expedition has been most interesting but long to be back at my desk in Glasgow implementing some exciting new Compliance Review Techniques into our standard audit procedures in response to the latest round of Companies Act legislation.

A TRUE story of a chartered accountant on holiday in France who took his family to visit a cathedral. 'Daddy,' said number-one son, who was obviously set to follow in the true (accounting) faith, 'what are all these plus signs doing everywhere?'

DEEPLY PHILOSOPHICAL QUESTIONS

The Diary has posed many questions to its readers through the years.

- Why do aircraft toilets have frosted windows?

- Did Paul ever get a reply from the Ephesians?

- How many more witnesses do they need before Jehovah's trial starts?

- How did the man who invented the bicycle know it was the bicycle?

- Did the guy who lost the lost chord have it insured?

- If a brick lands on your head can you claim a lump sum?

Allan Miller of Bishopton felt obliged to respond to our query as to whether anyone had ever seen a parson with a nose like a chicken's arse. 'The answer remains no,' says Mr Miller, 'but they must surely have hit the crossbar when they cast Karl Malden as the priest in *On the Waterfront*.'

- Whatever happened to the first nine *Malcolm* movies?

- Why is there no other word for 'synonym'?

- Why is there only one word for 'thesaurus'?

- Why is the alphabet in that order?

- Why can't you buy inessential oils?

- Why do people wear bum-bags at the front?

- Why does sour cream have a sell-by date?

- What was the greatest thing *before* sliced bread?

- Where do the sick people of Lourdes go?

- Why is 'abbreviation' such a long word?

- Why are water biscuits so dry?

- Why, if Glasgow is such a great place, are there travel agents on every corner?

- Why does the phrase 'Look, pal' in Glaswegian have nothing to do with friendship?

- Why do people in Dumfries and Galloway region refer to Langholm as the Malvinas?

- If a single bed is 3ft wide, how come a double bed is only 4ft 6in?

- How do they always get fish the right size to fit the batter?

- Why don8t typewriters have separate keys for apostrophes?

- Who taught Kirkpatrick McMillan to ride a bike?

- Whose bicycle pump did Dunlop borrow to blow up the first pneumatic tyre?

- Why do badgers have such rough arses? And who discovered the fact?

- What does acronym stand for?

- What happened to First and Second Lanark?

- Why do people only go to a health centre when they're ill?

- How do you grow seedless grapes?

- Why can't we shuffle the letters in anagram to make any other words?

- Why don't the United Nations declare Scotland a No Midge zone?

- Why isn't a 4x4 vehicle simply known as a 16 vehicle?

- Why do referees always use Partick Thistle colours when cautioning or sending off players?

- What if nothing happens at the end of the day?

- What will happen to the football pools if managers can't get a result?

- Should a blind man pay for stair-heid lighting?

- If bankers can count, why do their counters have six windows but only two tellers?

- Why is it that people who like a refreshment are always falling down?

- Why do alarms go off instead of on?

- Is acne an occupational hazard for football strikers, as in 'Duncan Ferguson picked his spot before tucking the ball awa'?

- Is the use of French phrases passé?

- How did they measure hailstones before golfballs were invented?

- Did Rabbie Burns ever attend a James Currie Supper?

- Has anyone ever actually eaten a Kellogg's pop tart for breakfast?

- Why do seagulls fly upside down over Saltcoats?

Please note, we don't actually expect answers to our deeply philosophical questions.

EDUCATION

The Diary's occasional forays into the world of education are invariably due to concerned individuals writing to give us an insight into school life. To be more exact, teachers tell us of the idiocies of their pupils, parents tell us of the teacher's latest fit of madness, and everybody gets in touch to tell the world about the headmaster's latest manifestation of believing he is God.

A LETTER arrived at a Strathclyde school, addressed to a Mrs Young. The staff worked out that it was intended for their Mrs Ewing. The letter was from a former pupil of the school. Mrs Ewing wondered why he had written to her since she had never actually had the pleasure of teaching him. The letter made it all clear: 'I am writing to you because your name is the only one I can spell.'

STRATHCLYDE Regional Council's further education subcommittee know how to be brief and to the point. Consider this minute from one of their meetings: 'With reference to the minutes of the Community Development Committee when that committee had considered a report commissioned by the Glasgow Divisional Deprivation Group relative to Community Development in Springburn and had agreed to continue consideration of the matter to allow the chairman and the vice-chairman of that committee to discuss the report with the appropriate members and officials in the first instance, the subcommittee, having considered the said report, agreed to continue consideration of the matter pending the outcome of the discussion referred to.' Got that?

A CIRCULAR on the role of head teachers in primary schools, issued by the Committee on Primary Education, contained this piece of double-think: 'In accordance with precedent, the head teacher is referred to as he and the class teachers as she. No discrimination is intended.'

THE department of artificial intelligence at Edinburgh University was working on computer programmes which would be able to translate speech instantaneously from one language to another. A difficult task, as you can imagine. One test proved just how difficult. When the phrase 'the spirit is willing but the flesh is weak' was translated into Russian and back into English, it came out as 'the vodka is strong but the meat is rotten'.

A MATHS teacher in a school on the south side of Glasgow decided to make the arithmetic exam more interesting for some of the underachievers in his class. He framed questions to which the class could relate. They had to estimate, for

AUTHORISED AGENTS FOR

IMPACT
SCHOOL OF
MOTORING
from £7·50

BOOK HERE
AUTOMATIC or MANUAL
D.O.T. APPROVED INSTRUCTORS

instance, the extra profit earned by a shopkeeper who sold cigarettes and matches singly compared to selling by the packet. Another question asked the pupils to work out a complex betting slip.

The class were unusually absorbed in their exam. The silence was only broken when one boy put up his hand to ask why the punter had not paid his tax on the betting slip.

GLASGOW students have their own rhyming slang name for a lower second honours degree, or two-two as it is known in academic circles. It is called a Desmond, after the well-known South African bishop.

THE owner of a Renfrewshire printing firm was interviewing candidates for an apprenticeship. The businessman was very hot on literacy and numeracy, attributes which he had found very useful in employees. He asked one young man how good his arithmetic was.

'No' bad,' was the reply.

He was then asked to divide 1,000 by four. After a long pause the candidate said: 'Actually, I'm more of a calculator man myself.'

INNUMERACY struck in Greenock, too, where a Diary reader asked an assistant in a bakery shop for a dozen rolls.

'What's a dozen?' he heard the young girl ask an older colleague.

The girl duly put 12 rolls in a bag. 'Could you make that a dozen and a half, please?' the customer asked.

At which point the assistant cut a roll in half and dropped it into the bag.

AN edict in Strathclyde schools forbade smoking, even by teachers, except in designated rooms. Thus the staff rooms at Eastbank Academy become no-go areas for dominies addicted to the weed. These poor, lost souls had to find alternative accommodation for the burning of the weed and inhalation of nicotine.

Appropriately enough, they took refuge in a disused girls' toilet.

STRATHCLYDE education officials are rigorous in rooting out racist attitudes in their schools. This instance involved a routine visit to a school dining-hall.

One of the dinner ladies was explaining the breakdown of lunching habits among pupils: 'We have the homies, the dinnies, and the packies,' she explained.

After a sharp intake of breath from the visiting heid yin, the lady was informed that the last word mentioned was not acceptable language.

Luckily she was able to explain that it was not a reference to the children's ethnic origins, merely to the fact that they brought packed lunches to school.

THESE were among the answers given by pupils in a general knowledge quiz held in a school in darkest Lanarkshire. The school will remain unnamed to protect the innocent. (We are talking about the teachers, of course.)

Asked to name the five continents, a darling child replied: 'A, E, I, O, U.' Another ventured that the author of *Treasure Island* was Anneka Rice.

The prize for lateral thinking went to the child who was asked how a blind person would know if he or she had arrived at a pedestrian crossing. The answer, of course, is that there are bumps at the edge of the pavement. Nothing so prosaic for this lad, who said the blind person would know 'when the dug stoaps'.

MORE school quiz gems, this time from the rehearsals for the Glasgow Libraries' Primary School Quiz:

- What is the Kremlin? 'A wee furry hing fae that Steven Spielberg fillum.'

- Where are the Crown Jewels kept? 'Oan the Queen's heid.'

- What did Noah send out of the ark first to see if the flood had stopped? 'His wife.'

PAISLEY polis were involved in a project with local schools, the aim being to teach children how to react to a variety of dangerous situations. One of the exhibits was an ordinary room full of potential nasties such as an iron lying face down on an ironing board and a chip pan brimful of fat.

'Now why mustn't we touch any of these things?' a polisman inquired of a primary seven class from a local school.

'Because we'll leave our fingerprints on them,' was the response from one cherubic wee lassie.

THE Use of Language and That: A new teacher at Annan Academy (a young lady from south of the border) was appalled to see a fourth-year boy running full pelt along the main corridor at 4 p.m. She stopped him and asked why he was running. 'I'm trying to catch the 'Fechan bus,' he replied. She promptly doled out a one-hour detention for his use of foul language. Which is why the lad was so late getting home to Ecclefechan.

FROM examination papers from a school in deepest Ayrshire we can pass on to youse such information as:

- The capital of Scotland is S.

- The highest mountain in Scotland is Ben Everest.

- Wanlockhead is similar to Leadhills . . . and they both have minefields around them.

- The Sahara is a hot dessert.

FROM the news book of a Govan primary-school pupil: 'Emperor Hirohito had a very big funeral. It took 50 men to carry the beer.'

TWO fresh-faced five-year-olds found themselves involved in a play-ground fight in their first week at school. The boy on top finally tired of administering a right doing and enquired of his opponent: 'Have you had enough?'

'I don't know,' replied the other. 'This is my first fight.'

ONE of the more delicate problems teachers have to deal with is when a pupil is deficient in the Lifebuoy department. One teacher was com-pelled to take wee Jimmy aside and impart some advice on personal hygiene. The next day Jimmy's irate mother confronted the teacher with the statement: 'Ma son's in school tae be telt, no' smelt.' She added a scrap of information which did not come as news to the teachers; 'He's no' an effan' geranium.'

GREAT School Absence Notes of Our Time: A teacher at a well-known penal institution (aka school) in the deep south-west of Glasgow swears genuinely to have received the follow-ing parental missive: 'Dear Sir, Please excuse John for being absent as he spewed up the whole of Peat Road.'

The text of another absence note was not all that unusual. The missive from wee Jimmy's mum was of a standard variety, stating that he had been awfy no' well and had been kept off the school. What struck the teacher was that the note was well crumpled and looked as if the mother had picked up any old scrap of paper she could find. Indeed she had. When the teacher turned the scrap of paper over she found another message reading: 'Your dinner's in the oven. If you want sex later, just wake me up.'

The letter from a mother explain-ing her wee boy's non-attendance was graphic and to the point: 'Dear Miss, Sorry Peter isn't at school. I gave him syrup of figs last night. He hasn't been yet, but when he goes, he'll come.'

FROM the Mouths of Babes: The cast of the nativity play at St Joseph's playgroup, Clarkston, were busy rehearsing their lines. Imagine the scene. The three wise men have followed the star and have reached the stable. 'I bring gold,' says the first wise bairn. 'I bring myrrh,' says the second. The concept of frankincense is proving difficult for the third wee wise man as he offers hopefully: 'I'll just bring the sandwiches.'

THIS from an anonymous school-teacher in a primary school of

Catholic origins in the South Side of Glasgow which goes to great pains to encourage non-diocesan children to attend. The weans are looking forward to the advent of Christmas. The principal is helping set up the stable scene with Mary, Jesus and Joseph, the three kings, some lowing cattle *et al.* While thus engaged he is approached by a child of a non-Catholic denomination. 'Sir,' the child asks, looking at the plethora of straw in the manger, 'does the school keep hamsters?'

A PUPIL at a Lanarkshire school returned home after a sex education lesson so well versed in the subject that he was able to tell his parents that 'boys have got a penis and girls have got a fat china'.

THE swan-like transformation of sundry polytechnics into universities was the subject of some ribaldry in the Diary. A particular target was the Glasgow Caledonian University which, even in its days as Glasgow College of Technology, was referred to as the University of Coocaddens. This was because the upstart education establishment had delusions of grandeur and kept changing its name in attempts to go upmarket.

Now life has overtaken fiction and Glasgow Polytechnic, as the college was known for a few years, has the status of university. But the search for a suitable name was not without tribulation. The first choice was City University, but Mr Norman Thompson, a founding but now former member of the staff of the illustrious educational establishment, wrote: 'I would seriously counsel against the adoption of the title City University . . . In a city which abhors pomposity and responds to it actively, the title "city" would be all too easily mispronounced.' There were some serious suggestions such as Buchanan University, after the former train-station site on which the college is built, but these were quickly ignored.

We discovered that entry qualifications to Glasgow's third yoonie were stricter than we thought and not merely having to quote your mother's Co-op number. Two sets of books must be completed – one fully coloured in (without going over the lines) and the other with all the dots joined up. The poly also demands mathematical proficiency to the standard of undertaking long division together with proven ability to 'carry one' in hard sums.

The poly's aspiration to be called Queen's University, Glasgow, was kicked into touch and they then went for Glasgow Merchants University. This was soon amended on campus to the Patter Merchants University, the Bevvy Merchants University, and the Scrap Merchants University. Another alternative suggestion is that the new yoonie be called the Gardner Merchant University after the esteemed catering company which has the contract to feed the staff. The concept of the Merchants University was quickly dropped.

A study of the 1828 David Smith map of the Cowcaddens showed that there had once been a lunatic asylum on the site of Glasgow's third yoonie. This institution was the Magdalene Asylum, giving a precedent for the elegant Magdalene College, Glasgow. Or the inelegant Looney Yoonie. Another idea was that the proximity of the campus to the old Normal School led naturally to the Normal University. There was a school of thought that this was an ideal opportunity to commemorate that great thinker Duns Scotus. So how about Dun Larnin University or even Dunstudian Yoonie?

Another serious suggestion was University of Caledonia, prompted by the fact that the stockyards of the railway of that name once occupied the site. And this obviously struck a chord, with Glasgow Caledonian University the actual name chosen by a ballot paper of staff and students. The successful title was thus described in a news release: 'Glasgow Caledonian University. The title is pronounceable and distinctive both in its full form and in its acronym. This title abbreviates easily, e.g. Cally, Cal-U (as in the American form).' This led to speculation of such snippets of overheard conversation as 'I'm at the Cally Yoonie' or 'Yes, Farquhar's doing awfy well. He's majoring in bulk solids handling at Cal-U. No, not Los Angeles, the wan in the Coocaddens.'

The blurb continued: 'The images associated with Caledonian are used in marketing worldwide to evoke trust, integrity, and a quality of life worth seeking.'

But the ribaldry was not over for poor Glasgow Caledonian University. Instead of abbreviating to Cal-U, it was generally felt more likely that it would be shortened to CU. Which has an altogether different meaning, Jimmy. And it was not long before people were suggesting it should have been called Caledonian MacBrain University.

ESCAPE TO SIBERIA

Siberia, once the one-way ticket destination for Soviet deportees, is now desperate to attract visitors of a different kind as talk switches from hard labour to hard currency. Tom Shields visited there – and returned to tell this tale.

THE Russians sent me to Siberia. In a break with tradition they let me back out after a fortnight so that I could tell you lot what a splendid holiday spot it is. It is, I can tell you, a splendid holiday spot. That is, if you can call a place that is bigger than the US a spot. Anyway, Intourist is hotter than ever in pursuit of tourist hard currency. But Moscow and Leningrad, the traditional Russian visitor venues, are full to bursting.

Siberia, the land of pioneers, prisoners and political exiles, still has plenty of space. Intourist is selling Siberia as the great outdoors adventure, which is why I found myself in the company of experts on hiking, rambling, fishing, birdwatching, cycling, and sundry other healthy activities.

There was also an Irishman whose speciality was finding the local pub, investigating the level of crack in Siberia, and nosing around the shops. This seemed like a more interesting adventure. I decided to follow the Irish itinerary.

So here we are in Abakan which, as I'm sure you know, is capital of the ancient land of Khakassia. Sunny Khakassia, as it is rightfully called, for the annual average is 300 days of sunshine. This land is famous for its fertile soil and rich mineral resources, full-flowing rivers and healthful lakes and for its taiga, abundant in mushrooms, berries and nuts.

Okay, I admit all that last bit is straight from the Intourist brochure. The reality is that the town looks a bit like Drumchapel. There is nothing in the shops unless you want a pair of plastic sandals. There are no postcards of Abakan but there are views of Leningrad and Samantha Fox's chest.

The souvenir shop in the hotel is empty, but in the lift I am offered a soldier's hat for £5, which seems like a bargain. I decline the offer to buy the medals from the Afghanistan war.

The hotel offers little for those of us on the hedonist adventure trip. It has none of the facilities you would expect in a Western hotel, although it does have a cement mixer in the foyer.

It has a bar which is open only four hours a day in this neo-prohibitionist land. Inspection of the rest of down-

DONNACHIE'S BAR, Cobh

Due to the sad death of Paddy, the Bar, to all intents and purposes, will remain closed during our grief; but so as not to inconvenience our esteemed customers, the door will remain ajar. 'Tis what Paddy wanted.
Thank you, **DONNACHIE FAMILY**

town Abakan reveals that the hotel is actually the liveliest spot around. In a leafy square some of the locals are passing round a big glass container of brown liquid. It is apple juice, and this is what the Abakan lads mean by going out for a jar.

When the bar opens later we discover it is selling apple juice, ice cream, and vodka if you ask nicely. At closing time a local is spectacularly sick over the bar counter. Was it too much apple juice or simply a bad ice cream?

Abakan, it has to be said, is not great for the crack, but the other special interests are thriving. The birdwatcher has been down at the riverbank and has seen a white-throated needletail, a sparrowhawk and a pippet. Someone else has been horse-riding at a farm run by the Soviet union of miners. The cyclist has teamed up with a local wheelers' club whose membership seems to consist entirely of blonde nymphets in Lycra trousers. He is now enviously referred to as the pedalophile.

Us less active tourists have been taking in Shushenskoye, the village where Lenin spent his years of Siberian exile. Compared with the living conditions of the present-day Abakanites, whom he freed from Tsarist slavery, Lenin spent his Siberian exile in some comfort in a substantial wooden house with a sauna. Shushenskoye looks for all the world like an olde-worlde timeshare development.

There is some great shopping to be done at the Shushenskoye souvenir stall. Badges and busts of Lenin galore. Samantha Fox's bust is also available in key ring or postcard form.

On, farther east, to Irkutsk, the capital of the Buryat region and the oldest city in Siberia. From here the first Russian caravans of merchants set off to China and Mongolia. The look of Irkutsk reflects its 300-year-old history. It boasts many ancient stone buildings of original architecture and time-blackened wooden mansions. (Yes, that's the Intourist brochure speaking again.) In Scottish terms, I would place Irkutsk as a lively but faded Paisley. In Russian terms, it's a shopper's paradise.

Bookshops with marvellous posters costing pennies. Record shops with Paul McCartney and Elton John LPs or the boxed sets of Bolshoi operas for under £2. Brilliant jewellery made from local semi-precious stones.

The local Harrods has a magnificent moose's head on sale for 490 roubles (about £49). I want to buy but can hardly lift it, never mind carry it home. The people in the shop are very sympathetic but no, they do not deliver to Glasgow.

There is a busy marketplace where you can have your photo taken with a

real live tiger. A small, chained-up, real live tiger. But still it looks a risky business.

A kiosk is selling photographs of the Tsar, poor photocopies of a sex manual, and full colour posters of our Samantha.

In winter, when the temperature descends to minus 40 degrees centigrade, the Irkutsk market sells milk in blocks. I pine for the opportunity to ask people if they would like one lump or two in their tea. But the autumn weather is hot. The trouble with Siberia is that in the winter it is all ice and in the summer there is no ice.

The Irkutsk market has more fresh fruit and veg than I had seen in the rest of Russia put together. The giant watermelons are an essential purchase. The chances are in Siberia if you're on the hedonist adventure holiday, you will have been sitting up half the night drinking vodka with Mongolians, Russians, Ukrainians, Moldavians or, if you're stuck, Americans.

This leaves you in the morning with a thirst. In most places a soft drink is out of the question. So is mineral water, which Siberian hotels appear not to sell until lunchtime.

The tap water is not recommended. Any milk on the breakfast table will be of the soor milk cairt variety. There is usually a jug of juice which will vary in colour from purple to green, yellow to brown, depending on the berries from which it is squeezed. This juice is not the berries and will not quench your morning thirst. But the watermelons will. It is your Siberian Irn Bru.

The hotel is comfortable and caught in a fascinating time-warp. *Yellow Submarine* is playing on the video in the foyer. In the tourist hard-currency bar, a Californian rock band called Alien Blackness, all long hair and cowboy boots, is enjoying its three-month Siberian tour, paid for out of the Soviet Government's arts budget.

But what are the outdoors people up to? They are at Lake Baikal, the world's largest freshwater lake, which is just up the road. Baikal is a unique creation of nature, striking with its primordial beauty. (Yes, we're back into the Intourist brochure.) Its water is crystal clear and transparent – apart from the bit that's polluted by the pulp mill, but that will be closed by 1992.

Some of the outdoor activists are away fishing. In typical Russian style, it involves more than getting in a boat and dangling a line in the water. They sail away for half a day and spend the night in a hut in a small settlement where the locals make them buckets of borsch for their tea. At 2 a.m. they are wakened and taken out to a raft where they fish by floodlight.

It is a great adventure and it

doesn't really matter that they don't catch a single fish. This is surprising since Lake Baikal has 2,500 species of fish. With all these varieties, it is puzzling that every day the hotel serves the same kind of fish. Thankfully it is tasty, a kind of salmon or trout called omul.

The activists have a choice of hiking, climbing, sub-aqua, wind-surfing and sailing. The less-activists can lie on the sandy beach or sample a Russian steam bath.

The pedalophile wishes it was winter when the lake freezes over and you can cycle on it. The birdwatcher is ecstatic: he has just seen a caper-caillie and a Siberian tit.

There is no sign, however, of Samantha in the souvenir shop. But I have found, through the free economy market, a splendid set of antlers for only £30. All I have to do is get them back to Glasgow via Ulan-Ude, Yakutsk, Moscow, Leningrad and London.

Say what you like about Aeroflot. The uncertain in-flight food (well, why not a Penguin biscuit for your dessert?); the certainty that your in-flight refreshment will be a cup of some coloured juice; and the flies buzzing around the cabins (there must be some extremely far-travelled Russian flies).

But Aeroflot's relaxed policy on hand luggage is brilliant. A set of antlers? No problem.

We're off, antlers and all, to Ulan-Ude, the southernmost stop on my Siberian adventure. This capital of the Buryat region, bordering Mongolia, is the original outpost of the Cossacks and today retains much of its frontier atmosphere. (Yes, more brochure-speak.) Architecturally, much of Ulan-Ude is like Castlemilk. Except Castlemilk does not have a Buddhist monastery or a 30-foot-high bronze head of Lenin. Ulan-Ude also has the most strikingly beautiful women in all the Russias. The Irishman says so and in thse matters I bow to his considerable expertise.

The Buddhists, I have to say, are a bunch of nippy sweeties. I got a row for having my hands in my pockets inside the temple. And I thought I was conducting an intelligent inter-view with the chief lama, asking how he spent a typical day. (He prays a lot, talks to his flock, and watches TV at night; favourite programme the *Nine O'Clock News*.)

All very nice and ethnographic, I thought, until one of the Russians tells me that during the interview the lama asked the interpreter: 'Why is this man asking me so many stupid questions?' To think I could have been away spotting eagles with the birdman.

There was nothing but friendliness, however, at Yakutsk, the last and most northerly stop on the Siberian tour. Yakutsk is near the Arctic Circle, a town built on concrete pillars in the permafrost zone.

In Scottish terms, it is Stornoway on ice. A wild, isolated place which for eight months of the year is cut off from the rest of the world.

Because of its isolation, the hotel facilities are of a basic nature. An English member of our party decides that his bathroom constitutes too much of an adventure, even for Siberia. 'You can't ask me to sit on this!' he shouts, brandishing a rather pitted and scratched toilet seat at the receptionist. Then he throws the toilet seat across the foyer and storms back to his room.

The Irishman is able to put the matter into perspective. 'Would you have that sanded down and delivered to my room? I don't have a toilet seat at all.'

Yakutsk is the least promising of the Siberian venues but it provides the best food I tasted in two weeks in Russia. The occasion was a boat trip on the River Lena to a picnic site. In Siberian fashion, the round trip by hydrofoil is 300 miles. The landscape is straight out of a Yukon adventure movie.

There is a sign which says do not drop litter and do not chase the bears. I promise not to do either.

While the activists scale the Lena Pillars, the hedonists sit at the camp fire and watch Alosha, the 17-year-old YTS chef, and his wee sister Lana who has skived school to help him, make a magnificent fish soup and some wonderful Siberian stovies. There's champagne and brandy to wash it down. You could get to like the great outdoors.

The Irishman, who is allergic to the great outdoors, has been exploring Yakutsk and has found a Moldavian rock band on tour. He learns that Yakutsk can be a wild place at night with the odd drug addict and mugger lying in wait for miners who come into town with their pockets stuffed with roubles.

One of the Moldavians says that if you are going out late, do what he does and carry a big stick.

After a noisy and hectic gold-rush-style night in the hotel dining-room (complete with Wild West fight) I decide to retire early to wrap up my antlers.

The Irishman does not want to waste the last night in Siberia. He ventures into the night clutching a bottle of vodka and a big stick to go to a party he's heard about.

It's an adventurous life in Siberia.

FILMS

As more and more Gaelic programmes hogged prime viewing time on Scotland's TV stations, the Diary put forward the suggestion that the annual £10 million budget of the Comataidh Telebhisein Gaidhlig *might be better spent on a truly blockbuster movie. Various suggestions as to possible titles soon came flooding in:*

Home Ochone: Lost in Uist
Jurassic Park Bar
Wee Free Men and a Baby
An American in Harris
The Rocky Morar Picture Show
The Great Tain Robbery
Kisimul Kate
For a Few Shielings More
Plaid Again Sam
Out of Affric
Seven Sheep for Seven Brothers
Ceilidh's Heroes
Calum X
Full Tweed Jacket
High Dunoon
Every Which Way But Lewis
Born Wee Free
Wee Free Amigos
Sabbath, Bloody Sabbath

Two Muileachs for Sister Sara
The Crinan Game
Nuns on the Rhum
Blade Rona
The Tain Commandments
Lorna Dounreay
The Scarba Pimpernel
Brora! Brora! Brora!
Vaternish Down
From Here to Ettrick Bay
Flash Invergordon
Peggy's Ewe Got Married
Shinty Shinty Bang Bang
Cyrano de Berneray
The Great Golspie
Sleeping Beauly
Conan the Barra Bairn
Apokeachips Now

Worthy of a world première on a rainy night in Oban were:

It's a Mod, Mod, Mod, Mod World
Children of a Lesser Mod
Obanator and the follow-up *Obanator Dhu*
A Streetcar Named Kintyre
Plaid Runner
Desperately Seeking Objective One Status
Crofter Kane
Rebel Without a Croft
Where Seagulls Dare
Single White Cheviot
The Sword and the Scone
The Cuillin Fields
The Spey Who Came in from the Cold
The Bodach Snatchers
Invasion of the Bothy Thatchers
Ossians Eleven
When Barra Met Islay
Honey I Shrunk the Kilts
Padraig Post Always Rings Twice

The *Murdo* movies were very popular:

Murdo Most Foul
Murdo She Wrote
Murdo and His Amazing Technicolor Tweed Jacket
Murdo on the Orient Express

Edinburgh did not feature by name but was obviously the setting for *Guess Who Will Have Had Their Dinner?*. Some devious entrants tried to curry favour with our sponsors (a famous whisky company) by suggesting such titles as *Glengoyne with the Wind* and *Glengoyne Glen Ross*.

Elvis Presley was an inspiration for such Scottish remakes as *Love Me*

Senga, Follow That Dram, and *Viva Lasswade*. Not to mention *Loving Ewe*. *In Bed with Ma Donald* saw a more recent pop icon Gaelicised.

Non-Gaelic-speaking areas soon demanded their own movies, the Northern Isles inspiring:

Conan the Orcadian
Yell Freedom
Hoy Noon
The Unsters
No Orcadians for Miss Blandish
Hoy Anxiety

And *Fair Isle Attraction* – you know the movie where Glenn Close rips off Michael Douglas's cardigan in a steamy sex session.

Speakers of the Doric tongue made a strong case for £10 million a year to make their own movies, including a remake of that wonderful musical *Three Quines in a Fountain* and these:

The Loon's A Balloon
Grampian the Wonder Horse
Laurencekirk of Arabia
Bothy Nichts Fever
It's a Maud, Maud, Maud, Maud World
Turra! Turra! Turra!
Fit Like Doc?

FOOD

For a change it is the turn of the consumed to have their say. I have talked to head waiters and chefs from some of our better restaurants about the occasions when the customer was not right. To protect the innocent and the livelihoods of certain head waiters, my informants must remain anonymous.

THERE is an old and oft-repeated joke about a young man in a Glasgow restaurant who is asked by the waiter if he would like ginger with his melon. He replies that he will stick to the red wine, the same as the rest of the company. There is no recorded instance of this happening but the spirit of the untutored diner lives on with the person who ordered steak tartare and then complained that it was raw. Or the customer who asked for his steak tartare to be well done.

Not to mention the lady who complained to the manager of an Italian restaurant about their practice of providing powdered milk which had made her coffee taste disgusting. Not surprising, he replied, since she had just put two spoonfuls of parmesan cheese into her cup.

Or the customer in a wine bar who ordered soup followed by a main course with a side salad. The waitress placed his cutlery and a bowl containing French dressing on his table and went to the kitchen to fetch his soup. She returned to find the customer eating the bowl of French dressing. She left him to finish this rather unusual soup course and was not surprised when he took refuge in the toilet and was unable to tackle the rest of his meal. Compared to this, the quite common practice of drinking the water from fingerbowls pales into insignificance.

There was another obvious connoisseur who told a waiter that there was a leaf floating in the French dressing. It must have blown in through the open window, she added. Unbayleafable, the waiter might have said, if he were into elaborate puns.

MOST head waiters will tell you that they do not mind dealing with diners who, faced with a menu bulging with gastronomic goodies, admit that they just want something simple. A well-known Glasgow lawyer is famous for by-passing the glories of haute, nouvelle and sundry other cuisines in favour of a regular lunchtime order of plain omelette and mashed potatoes, albeit washed down by a bottle of fine wine costing about £20.

Another customer on whom the niceties of *à la carte, table d'hôte* and surprise menus are obviously lost, plumped for smoked salmon from the list of starters. Asked what else he would like he ordered and received on a side plate a portion of chips and peas.

IT is the customer who thinks he or she knows it all about good food and fine wines that causes the most heartache to the chef and head waiter. The owner of an establishment which prides itself on value for money quality wines still remembers with sorrow the Chambertin 1959 which he was offering at the apparently knock-down price of £19.95 a bottle. A customer consulting his wine diary discovered that it was an exceptional year. He ordered a bottle only to return it without drinking on the grounds that the wine was a brown colour and not red. Instead of trying to explain about the changes in colour as a wine ages, the chef took the bottle back and shared it with a wine-loving customer who was also in the restaurant. The wine waiter, unable to resist a comment to the offending diner, asked him if he had managed to retain the nice pink colour he had been born with.

The same chef has had his wild strawberries, brought in triumph from the market, rejected by a diner, who said they were too small.

THERE is a school of thought among head waiters that there is a growing band of professional complainers: people who are convinced they can get a free meal, a reduced bill, or even a free drink just by being difficult.

One person complained that the pheasant was of a poor standard. He took his complaint as far as the consumer problem page of a Sunday newspaper before admitting that it was in fact the first time he had ever tried pheasant and had no idea how it should taste.

Another difficult customer demanded a 50 per cent reduction on his bill. The food had been excellent, he said, but the waiter should have informed him of the various other menus he could have had. Where other diners produce a credit card to pay he placed his lawyer's card on the table. The waiter stood firm, phoned the police, received full payment and is still awaiting the writ.

THE problem of menu items not being available for the customer has been around for a long time. There was a famous waitress employed at a west coast hotel during the 1950s, heyday of bus and steamer trips from Glasgow. One day, by chance a Friday, due to a typist's error haddock and chips was missing from the lunch menu. The waitress, whose speed and dexterity could have won any Trencherman award for service, but who unfortunately sounded like Francie and Josie's first cousin, was told to inform the customers of the omission, as briefly as possible.

This she did, by standing at the

door of the restaurant and calling out: 'Hauns up a' youse yins that are Cathlics.'

OTHER forms of skulduggery which are by no means uncommon in restaurants including leaving by mistake with the wrong coat or umbrella. The Marks and Spencer raincoat swapped for the Burberry is a good trick.

One restaurant in Glasgow is still trying to remedy the situation where a regular and valued customer is using a new umbrella he inadvertently picked up instead of his own battered specimen some months ago.

THERE is anti-social behaviour which is not deliberate but which is usually alcohol-induced. A waiter who worked in the old 101 Restaurant in Glasgow recalls an upmarket but rather well-oiled lady diner who plunged down a flight of steps. Only slightly hurt but in a state of considerable shock she was asked by a member of staff who was comforting her as she lay on the floor if she would like a medicinal brandy.

'Make it a whisky and soda,' was the reply.

Also from the 101 days comes the story of a beautifully turned-out woman who had also enjoyed too much wine. She went to the ladies and walked back through the restaurant with the back of her skirt tucked inside her knickers. It fell to the poor head waiter to inform her of the situation.

But when it comes to bad behaviour in restaurants the Americans lead the field . . .

A Texan complete with boots and stetson was not prepared to wait his turn in the cocktail bar along with other customers who had not booked a table in a busy hotel restaurant. When a table became vacant he jumped the queue and sat down. The waiters, in a scene reminiscent of a *Scotch and Wry* sketch, ignored his constant shouts to be given a menu. Eventually the head waiter simply walked up and took away the table leaving the Texan sitting in a chair in the middle of the restaurant. He got the message and returned to the bar.

Another American customer resident in one of Scotland's better hotels was getting firmly on the waiters' nerves with his regular demand: 'Hey, boy, get me a pitcher of water.' One morning he made this request in his usual loud voice to a waiter who was not feeling at his best. The waiter walked over to an oil painting of a river scene which adorned the restaurant wall. He took it down and handed it to the American with the words: 'Here is your picture of water, sir.' The American didn't get the joke. The waiter was suspended for a week.

FOOTBALL

The game of football featured as prominently in the Diary as it does in the Scottish male psyche. The stories were mainly unclassifiable and those repeated below are in no particular order.

SOCCER in the USA is a whole different ball game. We have become used to cheerleaders, Wurlitzers, and five action replays of each goal. But will we ever accept the term used by Tampa Bay Rowdies to describe their supporters? Down Tampa way the bears on the terracing are called fannies.

INSIGHT into the essentially warm-hearted nature of the Old Firm rivalry.

On the retirement of Willie Waddell, after a successful career as a player, manager and director of Rangers, Jock Wallace, Rangers' manager, said: 'I have no comment to make.'

Desmond White, chairman of Celtic, said: 'This is Rangers' business

and has nothing to do with Celtic, so I have no comment to make . . .'

JAMIE Fairley, a talented midfielder on the books of Hamilton Accies in 1980, was expected soon to move on to bigger things. His answers to an interview in the club programme gave an inkling of where his heart lay:

Favourite colour? Green.
Favourite team as a boy? Celtic.
Highlight of career so far? Playing against Celtic in a friendly match.
Person you would most like to meet? His Holiness Pope John Paul II.

Footnote: Jamie Fairley was subsequently transferred, not to Celtic, but to Motherwell FC.

OTHER allegiances were to be discovered in the programme produced by Stenhousemuir FC for their 1986 Skol Cup match against Rangers. It contained profiles of two Stenhousemuir players, Harry Erwin and Jim Sinnet, in which both fairly nailed their colours (blue) to the mast.

Asked to choose their favourite other teams, both named Rangers. Favourite away ground of both was Ibrox. Both named the best goal they had ever seen as one by Davie Cooper for Rangers against Celtic. Favourite players, past and present, were John Greig, Derek Johnstone and Davie Cooper, with Maradona the only non-Ranger to get a mention.

Fair enough, you might think, until you reach the next question: 'Who would you like to throw a bucket of water at?' Mr Erwin replied: 'The Celtic team.' Mr Sinnet said: 'Celtic and T. Burns.'

Mr Sinnet's other entries included; 'Hobbies – going to watch Rangers. Favourite reading material – *Rangers News*.' He also informed us that his favourite listening was 'flute band music'. Mr Erwin won the bad taste award for his entry: 'Favourite funny man – The Pope.'

Footnote: Stenhousemuir later apologised to Celtic.

GEORGE Best graced the Scottish football scene briefly in 1980 with Hibernian FC. Despite his drinking problems, George really did his best for the Hi-Bees. On his departure this was duly acknowledged by the Hibernian Supporters Association. A warm little tale, spoiled only slightly by the association's choice of a whisky decanter and glasses as his going-away present.

THE construction of the new Ibrox stadium was one of the wonders of the '80s. Two Rangers fans were looking at the stand which had just been completed at the traditional Celtic end of the ground. 'Look at that. Is that no' brilliant?' one opined.

'Aye,' his pal replied. Then after a pause he added: 'Too good fur thae animals.'

BOHEMIANS Football club of Dublin were in Glasgow to play Rangers in European competition. At a press conference, a reporter, referring to the possibility of sectarian rivalry spoiling the match, asked the manager of the Dublin team: 'Do you have any reservations about coming to Glasgow to play Rangers?'

'Sure,' he replied, 'we're staying at the Albany.'

ONE of the industries associated with the game of football is that conducted by the urchins who frequent the environs of football stadia and greet arriving motorists with the 'offer' to 'look after your motor, mister'. One visitor to Celtic Park declined the offer and pointed to the Alsatian in the back seat which, he was sure, was security enough. He returned to find all four tyres flat and a note on the windscreen saying: 'Get your Alsatian to blow them up for you.'

THE gentle wit of the Scottish football fan was apparent yet again at the World Cup in Mexico. After the Scots lost 1–0 to Denmark, both sets of fans were hurling friendly chants at each other. Thanks to barriers of accent, if not language, the Danes kept smiling through a little ditty which went: 'You can stick your streaky bacon up your arse.'

LEGEND has it that a bunch of Celtic fans in Bellshill, Lanarkshire, renamed their supporters club the John F. Kennedy, in memory of the assassinated American president. Legend also has it that their Rangers counterparts changed their name to the Lee Harvey Oswald Loyal.

THE Rangers fans were quick to welcome Israeli internationalist Avi Cohen. He came on to the Ibrox turf to the strains of that old song: 'Shalom, shalom, we are the Billy Boys . . .'

FORMER Rangers manager Graeme Souness's unfortunate experiences of being sent off halfway through football matches led to a cocktail being named after him. You simply ask the barman for a Souness.

'What's a Souness?' he will say.

'Just one half then I'm off,' is the reply.

WHEN the buying and rapid reselling of players by former Rangers manager Graeme Souness reached its peak in 1988, the club announced that in future team members would have sell-by dates instead of numbers on their jerseys.

THREE international footballers, one Irish, one English and one Scottish, have the same names as birds. Name them. Answer: Bertie Peacock, Frank Swift and Matt Busby.

IN the autumn of 1988, a run of poor performances by Celtic FC led to a large mailbag which subsequently became known as the Parkhead Jokelist:

• Have you seen the new Celtic strip? It has green and white hoops with a red neck.

• What's the connection between Celtic's season and the Glasgow Garden Festival? They were both finished by September.

• Two men on a desert island. One says: 'That's Celtic beaten again.' 'How do you know?' asks his pal. 'Well, it's Saturday, isn't it?'

• Celtic's new signing is Chinese. He is called Win Wan Soon.

• The club's new sponsor is Tampax, to help them through this difficult period.

• Manager Billy McNeill dug up the pitch at Parkhead in mid-season and planted potatoes. Why? So Celtic would have something to lift at the end of the season.

Goalkeeper Ian Andrews had a short and unfortunate career at Celtic.

• What's the difference between Ian Andrews and Eamonn Andrews, they asked? Eamonn was good on the box.

- What's the difference between Ian Andrews and Cinderella? Cinderella got to the ball.

- What do Ian Andrews and Michael Jackson have in common? They both wear gloves for no apparent reason.

- Why is Ian Andrews known as Ena Sharples? Because he spends so much time with his head in a net.

There was a disaster at the diamond mine where the Seven Dwarfs worked. The wee men were all missing, feared dead. After many hours digging through to the shaft where the dwarfs were trapped, the rescuers heard a voice singing: 'Sure, it's a grand old team to play for . . .'

'At least Dopey's safe,' they were able to report to a worried Snow White.

- How did Ken Dodd solve his income tax problems? He sold off his Diddy-men to Celtic.

- What's the difference between Celtic and the Star of David? The Star of David has six points.

- Celtic have signed Steve Davis because they are so many points behind in the Premier League they require snookers.

HEART of Midlothian FC have also been the subject of ribald humour. It was rumoured in 1988 that their goalkeeper Henry Smith was to quit football to work as a salesman in Wallace Mercer's property company. Did he have any experience in this line? Yes, he had recently sold two semis.

Researchers in Edinburgh made a significant breakthrough in AIDS prevention. Wear a pair of Henry Smith's gloves. They never catch anything.

ALBION Rovers had a half-back line in the 1970s called Currie, Sage and Rice.

PELE, who visited Scotland in the summer of 1989 for the junior World Cup, is held in awe by Scottish football fans. Thus when the Great Man, waiting in a crowded departure lounge at Glasgow Airport, got up to give a woman his seat, her husband intervened: 'Don't you know who he is? Give Pele back his seat.'

FATHER Neil McGarrity was one of the young priests ordained by Archbishop Winning in Glasgow in summer 1989. As is usual, he received a gift from friends and parishioners at St Stephen's, Dalmuir. In his case the gift was somewhat unusual: a complete Rangers strip, McEwan's lager logo and all, with the name 'Father Neil' emblazoned on the back.

THE reactions to the separate, but quite similar, problems facing Salman Rushdie and Mo Johnston were the subject of much comment by Diary readers. For example:
Question: What is 6ft 1in, blond, blue-eyed and lives in Reykjavik?
Answer: Salman Rushdie.

THEN there was the tale of the Glasgow taxi driver who was called to pick up a hire at a mosque on the south side of Glasgow. He had waited for ten minutes and still had no passenger. He asked for a message to be passed on, but after a further ten minutes still had not picked up. Exasperated, he finally entered the foyer of the mosque and shouted: 'Taxi for Rushdie!'

WITHIN half an hour of the news that Mo Johnston had signed for Rangers, a Diary reader was on to say that he knew where Mo would be living when he came to Scotland from Nantes in France: 'He's sharing a flat with Salman Rushdie.'
    Another fan was on to say: 'At least Salman Rushdie only has the Muslims after him.'
    Immediately after the signing, a number of traditional Old Firm songs were being rewritten, such as:

The Soldier's Sash
The Cry Was Mo Surrender
Hello, Hello, We Were the Billy Boys
Rangers fans were to be heard singing:
    Hello, hello, Mo is a Billy boy!
    Hello, hello, we're glad it's not Big Roy!

WE had news of a Rangers fan whose wife had given birth to quadruplets. He decided to call them Eeny, Meeny, Miny and Billy.

IT was said that one of the first things Mo Johnston did after spurning Celtic in favour of Rangers was to go to confession. He told the priest: 'Bless me, father, for I have signed . . .'

CELTIC fans were claiming that Mo would be sending his children to Judas Iscariot primary school.

A DIARY football peace-keeping award went to Ally McCoist of Rangers.
    A player from an opposing team had just been grounded by a robust tackle from Terry Hurlock. 'I'll get you, you English bastard,' the recumbent player shouted.
    'Take it easy,' said McCoist as he helped him to his feet. 'Anyway, which one did you mean? There are seven English bastards in the team.'

SCOTTISH goalkeeper Jim Leighton was quoted in *Match Weekly* magazine as saying: 'One of the worst crimes of which a goalkeeper can be found guilty is being caught flat-footed by a long-range, surprise shot that hits the back of the net.'
    The next week the luckless goalie

suffered the indignity at Hampden Park of seeing a long-range, surprise shot from Norway's Johnsen hit the back of the Scottish net.

THE 1990–91 season was not one of St Mirren's best. They ended bottom of the Premier League. The Diary's man at Love Street had a theory that the choice of pre-match music may have had something to do with it.

It was bad enough at one home match when the sparsely populated terraces 30 minutes before kick-off echoed to the sound of the Beatles singing 'Look at all the lonely people . . .' Worse still was the choice of the last record before the match started – Ray Charles's soulful rendering of 'It's Crying Time Again'.

WITH a World Cup match against Norway in the offing, the Diary was sent a useful little publication called *What You Want to Say and How to Say It in Norwegian.*

First we had the familiar chant *Folg, folg* (Follow, follow).

After queuing for a half-time pie, the Norwegian fan would no doubt say: *Mange task for deres gjaestfrihed* (Many thanks for your hospitality).

In the likely absence of any taxis being available outside Hampden, a more traditional Norwegian form of transport might come in handy: *Vi onsker at leie et rensdyr* (We wish to hire a reindeer).

Scottish fans wishing to make the Norwegians feel welcome should say: *Kan jeg byde dem noget?* (Can I offer you some refreshments?) On shaking hands with our Norwegian friends, we say: *Set het der* (Put it there).

The phrasebook section, titled 'About Town', had such handy phrases as: *Er der nogen god variete her?* (Is there a good music hall?) Even handier is: *Hvis vi faar en morsom aften, vu vi betale dem got* (If you give us a good time we will pay you well), not to mention: *Vis os alt* (Show us everything).

There are a few phrases for which, we feared, we would not find a use: *Krol mmine mustacher* (Put the irons on my moustache); *Jeg onsker en friktion* (Put some tonic on my head); and *Server mine eg i et eggeglas* (Serve my eggs in a glass).

It had one phrase which, we hoped, the Norwegians would use after the match: *Jeg er syg* (I am sick).

THE Gulf War and football came together with this conundrum: What is the difference between Saddam Hussein and Graeme Souness?

One is a fanatical fundamentalist tyrant who is prepared to sacrifice his people to achieve his aims. The other is president of Iraq.

AN intriguing concept arose out of the bid by the Scottish Professional Footballers' Association to negotiate a share of broadcast fees earned by TV companies.

Ruling on the matter, Trade and Industry Minister Lord Hesketh said that footballers do not enjoy any protection of their 'intellectual property' in the form of playing skills, under the Copyright, Designs and Patents Act 1988.

The very idea of your average footballer having intellectual any-thing, never mind intellectual property, appealed to the Diary.

Until you start to think about:

- Wee Jimmy Johnstone's jink;

- Jim Baxter's keepie-uppie skill;

- Denis Law's levitation and heading ability;

- Johnny Hubbard's penalty kicks;

- Peter Lorimer's thunderbolt free kicks; *and*

- Franz Beckenbauer's leadership qualities.

There were some less serious intellectual properties on which certain footballers could claim copyright:

- Gazza's greetin';

- Willie Johnston's Speed;

- Willie Miller's refereeing ability;

- Bobby Moore's light touch;

- Mo Johnston's crossing ability;

- Charlie Tully's cheek;

- Davie Wilson's diving ability;

- Frank Haffey's singing voice;

- Maradona's handling of the game;

- Derek Johnstone's gravitas;

- Terry Butcher's open door policy;

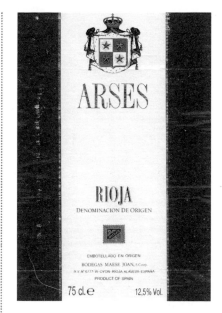

- Roy Aitken's perseverance in the face of overwhelming public opinion;

- Tony Higgins's brainpower (unfortunately, all of it in his head);

- Davie Cooper's sinistrality;

- Andy Ritchie's fan dancing;

- George Best's stamina (not solely related to the football pitch);

- Jim McLean's *bonhomie*;

- Bill Bremner's *sangfroid*;

- Emlyn Hughes's reticence;

- Lou Macari's mental arithmetic (handy in the bookie's);

- Stewart Kennedy's anglophilia;

- Jimmy Greaves's liquidity;

- Bobby Charlton's hair-raising shooting ability;

- Alex Miller's *joie de vivre.*

SOCIAL work departments across the land were ordered by the Government during the Gulf War to set up bereavement counselling teams in readiness for bad news and casualties.

A Strathclyde social worker, asked to fill in a form giving details of his expertise on disaster and traumas counselling, simply entered: 'Celtic supporter.'

To the Editor,
Glasgow Herald

Dear Sir,

Thank you for the three-day pass away from writing about the General Election. I used the time to visit London with some friends from the Park Bar in Glasgow who were going down to see Scotland playing England at Wembley.

In case Mr Ted Croker, secretary of the English Football Association, should read this, it must be empha-

sised that these chaps, although called Macleod, MacDonald, Campbell and McKinnon and speaking Gaelic a lot, are really of English descent and have not obtained their Wembley tickets by deceit.

They were driven north to find work during the Home Counties Clearances of which Mr Croker has no doubt heard.

Anyway these Park Bar chaps have their own bus which they use to travel to events of social and cultural interest. The trips so far have been to Spain for the World Cup and to Switzerland for the European Championship game involving Scotland.

The bus is a 29-seater Bedford which first saw the light of day in 1961, the year England beat Scotland 9–3. How's that for an omen.

It has been converted, with bunk beds, toilet and kitchen sink to take 12 passengers to Scotland's football matches in barely discernible discomfort.

The venture is nearly wrecked at the outset when 12 £11 tickets sent recorded delivery by Cousin Murdo from the Croft in Milton Keynes a week ago fail to arrive. (Does Mr Croker have a part-time job as postman, too?)

Fortunately Wembley tickets in Glasgow on Tuesday night are about as scarce as a flute band in Bridgeton on 12 July and replacements are easily obtained.

The journey began outside the Park Bar just after 11 p.m. (a strange time to start a journey one might think but presumably the Park Bar bus veterans know best).

It is 3 a.m. and we are having

breakfast at Trust House Forte's charming motorway bistro at Charnock Richard. They must have Ted Croker as a consultant.

It is 4.30 a.m. and we are just short of Derby. The bus has had to stop for some work on the defective fuel line. Bonny Prince Charlie had much the same trouble, remarks Callum, one of the Park Bar bus's veterans.

It is 11 a.m. The Park Bar bus is in pole position in the Wembley Stadium carpark. Our next-door neighbour is a small grey van of uncertain vintage.

It is driven by a young chap wearing a kilt of even more uncertain vintage and a three-foot-wide tartan sombrero.

He is singing 'Spot the Looney'. In an otherwise deserted carpark it is not difficult to do so.

It is 3 p.m. at Trafalgar Square and the Scots fans are having what can best be described as a garden party. It is very busy and some of the chaps have climbed up on to the fountains obviously to get a better view of the proceedings.

There are a great number of Scottish fans here for the match despite Mr Croker's efforts to keep them away.

A straw poll reveals that 55 per cent of them are here like me to avoid the election, 10 per cent are here on business, 10 per cent are job-hunting, and 25 per cent don't know.

A substantial number just happen to be wearing tartan and have had Wembley tickets thrust upon them, probably by Cousin Murdo from the Croft in Milton Keynes.

There is a handful of arrests of Scots fans. The endlessly diplomatic London bobbies say the arrests are simply to protect the fans and the general public.

Callum suspects they are lifting Scots with tickets intended for English fans and that Mr Croker has a part-time job as a police informer.

It is 5 p.m. on the Tube to Wembley and every carriage, whether they like it or not, has its own Scottish choir.

'No swearing, boys,' says the choir leader in our carriage and then leads off into a repertoire which includes:

'I wish I was a kettle,
I'd be steaming every day.'

It is 6 p.m. and denizens of the Park Bar bus are receiving Cousin Murdo from the Croft in Milton Keynes with numerous other relatives and friends for a pre-match cocktail.

In fact, the whole carpark resembles a giant tartan cocktail party. The fellow in the uncertain kilt and the tartan sombrero is back again singing 'Spot the Looney'.

In the crowded car park it is more difficult to do so but not impossible.

It is 7.10 p.m. and the English FA have just announced that tickets can still be bought at the stadium. You don't even have to be English to buy them. Mr Croker's racist attitude to Scots fans obviously has not stopped him from extracting the maximum financial advantage for the English FA from the fixture. The attendance is 84,000 and receipts are £654,000.

It is 7.45 p.m. and the game begins. For further details please consult Jim Reynolds, of our sports pages or possibly the obituary column.

It is 10 p.m. and the Park Bar bus piper, I think his name is Callum, is playing a lament in the Wembley car park. Another bus veteran, obviously inured to disappointment, has cheered up and is asking a fetching WPC to dance.

It is midnight. The 12 Callums and I have gone out to enjoy a drink and a bit of crack, as the Highlanders put it. We should also celebrate Jock Stein's and Graeme Souness's last game in charge of Scotland, at least according to Callum.

The trouble is London is closed, at least to Scottish fans.

We find ourselves outside a club in Kensington High Street. The bouncer explains that it is a gay club.

'No problem,' says Callum grasping hold of my hand and adding: 'It's terrible what you have to do here to get a late drink in London. I've had more fun in Benbecula on a Monday night.'

It is 3 a.m. We take a taxi back to the bus at Wembley Stadium. The chap in the tartan sombrero has stretched out in a tartan sleeping-bag beside his van. There is only time for a quick chorus of 'Spot the Looney' before retiring to the relative comfort of the bus.

It is 10 a.m. on Friday morning and the bus is heading north. Looking on the bright side, we discuss Scotland's chances in the Under-21 World Cup in Mexico.

By coincidence one of the Callums has a sister who lives just outside Mexico City who, he is sure, would put us up.

By a narrow margin the vote is to head north and not for Mexico City.

But before this business in Mexico is over I would not count on the Park Bar bus contingent having a presence in Central America.

Meanwhile, for some, it is back to the election.

ONE of the tribulations of the summer of 1991 for Scottish football fans was having to put up with the 25th anniversary of that match at Wembley when those brave West German lads were cheated of the World Cup. Like the party of Scots from East Kilbride who had to cope with some of those typically loveable Cockney types in a Spanish holiday resort. 'Oi, Jock,' said one of the Cockneys, brandishing an English tabloid newspaper, ''Ere's a competition wot you lot should go for. The prize is a day wiv the men who won the World Cup for England.' 'Nae fear,' a Scot replied. 'Who wants to spend a day wi' a Russian referee and linesman?'

THE honeymoon period was short for Tony Cascarino, the £1.1m Celtic forward who suffered a long drought before scoring in a competitive match for the club. The Jokeline was soon buzzing:

● What is the difference between Tony Cascarino and Boris Becker? Boris Becker hits the net sometimes.

● What was the first question Terry Waite asked after his release in Beirut? Has Cascarino scored for Celtic yet?

- *Follow, Follow*, the Rangers fanzine, described Tony Cascarino as 'the biggest waste of money since Madonna's dad bought her a pair of pyjamas'.

FROM Liverpool we had a variation on the 'Watch your car for you, mister?' urchin school of marketing. In this case the driver, reluctant to fork out the £1, pointed to the Rottweiler in the back of the car. 'Look,' said the urchin to his accomplice, 'this guy's got a Rottweiler that can put out fires.'

YOU have to admire the dedication of your average football mandarin. Take David Will, chairman of Brechin City and a vice-president of FIFA, the sport's ruling body. There he was with Mrs Will at the World Cup draw in New York in 1991, doggedly making his way round a succession of dinners and official receptions. And him just back from a FIFA trip to China. It's amazing how the Angus lawyer manages to fit all this in as well as guiding Brechin City to their dominating position in the lower half of the Scottish second division. One thing he doesn't have to worry about in his FIFA travels is choosing what to wear. He was spotted in the Big Apple sporting a very smart grey suit with a small and stylish FIFA logo. Likewise his shirt and tie. We cannot say if FIFA also provide underpants.

A NEWLY wed Aberdeen fan's dear wife was wont to throw tantrums and insist he miss the game and accompany her on Saturday afternoon

shopping expeditions. His chums advised him to take a firm stand. The next time she tried to prevent his attendance at Pittodrie he was to put her over his knee and give her a good skelping. Thus there was the scene where this new household was rent with cries of discord. Enraged at her intransigence, the husband chased the wife into the bedroom, put her over his knee and spanked her. It was at this point that the thought occurred to him that the Dons weren't playing all that well at the time.

WHEN Motherwell FC won the Tennent's Scottish Cup final, an immediate reaction was 'This means they'll be in Europe – just like their local councillors'.

AS a young Rangers player, Alex Ferguson, now manager of Manchester United, was unhappy at being left out of the first team. He stormed into the office of the legendary manager Scott Symon. 'Why have I been in the second team for three weeks?' he asked. The magisterial Mr Symon replied: 'Because we don't have a third team.'

BOBBY Lennox, who played with Celtic during the good old Jock Stein, nine-in-a-row years, still plays the odd game in a team which consists of former players and media personalities. During a post-match, fluid-replacement and winding-down session, Mr Lennox lost a wager and as a forfeit had to sing 'The Sash'. He got as far as 'It is old and it is beautiful/And its colours they are fine . . .' Then he stopped. Asked to sing the rest, Mr Lennox confessed that he did not know any more of the words. He explained: 'When I was playing for Celtic, the Rangers fans would start singing "The Sash", but by the time they got to the second line we had usually scored and shut them up.'

NINTENDO have come up with Goals – an entertainment which for a mere £40 allows you 'to participate in an actual simulation of the World Cup'. The computer game was obviously created with the American market in mind. The blurb enthuses with considerable Corinthian spirit: 'Win amateur soccer's most glorious prize: the World Cup.' It goes on to explain how you can guide one of 16

national teams to a 'one-game' final. The final includes Japan but not Scotland. The Nintendo chaps obviously knew more than Andy Roxburgh about Scotland's chances.

Under hints and tactics, the instruction manual defines tackling as 'hooksliding' and adds: 'A safe strategy is shooting the ball as far up field as possible . . . it's a more effective strategy than trying slowly to move the ball up field by dribbling and passing.' Which is, of course, Nintendospeak for 'Get the ba' up the park!'.

ABERDEEN FC's young footballers were chosen as guinea pigs for a Scottish Professional Footballers' Association coaching course on how to deal with the media. 'Young players often have to face the media and many are not properly equipped to portray the proper image of themselves and the club,' said the course organiser. 'Our aim is to teach them what to do and what not to do to present the public with a good image.' Unfortunately the course clashed with a decision by the then Aberdeen manager Alex Smith, who was upset by speculation that his jaiket was on a shaky nail, to issue an edict banning individual players from talking to the media.

IF you have ever wondered what football physios have in those huge bags which they lug on to the park to treat injured players, goalkeeper Gordon Marshall provided a wee insight. When he was with Falkirk, manager Jim Duffy, doubling as physiotherapist, came on to the park and discovered he had nothing in his bag but a sponge and some hair gel. Ever the quick thinker, Jim simply ran some gel through the player's hair and told him: 'You look great. Now get up and play!'

WE know the English broadcasters occasionally have trouble with the names of Scottish football teams. But we fear the chap on BBC Radio Lancashire went too far when he announced as a score draw an encounter between Alloa and Stenhousemanure.

CONTRARY to some opinion, Ernie Walker, the former secretary of the Scottish Football Association, did not spend all his time travelling the world on SFA and FIFA business. Mr Walker apparently makes a regular point of taking in a football match from the fan's point of view. Thus, he was to be found in Annan to attend a Scottish Cup match between the local Athletic and Queen's Park. 'How much is it?' Ernie asked the man at the turnstile. 'Two pounds,' was the reply and, as Mr Walker reached for his wallet, 'but it won't be two pounds to you.' Just as Ernie was about to insist that, even though he was SFA secretary, he would pay to get in, the turnstile man added: 'It's only a pound for pensioners.'

SCOTTISH football fans overheard in a bar-restaurant in Cyprus: 'I'm getting worried about the Big Man up there dancing wi' that bloke,' said one of his friends. 'It's okay,' another said, 'it's common for men to dance with each other over here.' 'I know,' the first replied. 'But that's six dances he's had wi' him and two of them were slow numbers.'

Also: 'Do you know why Cypriots are so bad at football? Every time they get a corner they open a fruit shop.'

LEGEND has it that Lou Macari did not become manager of Celtic in 1991 because of his frankness at the interview. What would he do if he were manager, the board members asked. 'I'd sell Paul McStay for £3 million and John Collins for £2 million,' said Macari. The board, rather cheered at the thought of this substantial cash injection for the Biscuit Tin, asked: 'And then what would you do?' 'Simple,' replied Macari, 'put the lot on Rangers to win the Premier League.'

IT may be hard to believe now but when Mark Hateley first joined Rangers he was the subject of some booing and jeering because he had taken Ally McCoist's place. There was a swift change of heart, perhaps to do with him scoring loads of goals. The jeers were replaced with the refrain: 'Have told you, Hateley, that we love you . . .'

WHEN Graeme Souness was still an Ibrox hero, the fans regularly chanted 'Sou-ness, Sou-ness'. At one match a press photographer's messenger, who could best be described as being on the chunky side, walked along the trackside to collect some film. As he did so, a section of the fans changed their chant to 'Sumo, sumo . . .'.

IN the days when Stirling Albion played on an Astroturf surface, a

Kilmarnock player sustained a bad cut. As he lay receiving attention on the Annfield artificial pitch, a Stirling Terracing Tam shouted out: 'Hey, ref. Get him aff. He's bleeding on our carpet.'

THE scene is a campsite in Asti, Italy, during World Cup 1990. Two Scottish fans by the names of Joe and Sugsy, complete with ankle-length kilts, are impressing fellow campers of all nationalities with their culinary skills. They have decided to dine on bacon and beans. They return from the supermarket complaining loudly about the price of streaky bacon in Italy – about £12 a half-pound. Not only is it expensive but ye jist cannae fry it right, opines Sugsy before throwing the lot away. A terrible waste of good Parma ham, say campers who are a touch better informed about Italian nosh.

When the time comes to leave the Italian campsite, Franco the host gives a farewell party to the fans and makes pizzas to order. When Joe is asked what pizza topping he wants, it transpires his taste buds do not extend to tomato, cheese, or any of the other fancy Italian bits. 'Just butter,' he says.

SPOTTED perambulating the streets of sunny Norrkoping during the European Championships in 1992 was none other than Ernie Walker, a former secretary of the Scottish Football Association. Ernie was recognised by a passing Scots fan and asked: 'How's aboot a photie?' Ernie agreed and the fan engaged the services of a passing Dutch fan. The Dutchman duly took the snap and said: 'Now it is my turn.' As Ernie prepared to have his picture taken again, he was handed the camera by the Dutchman who put his arm around the Scots fan.

THE Scottish football fans won the hearts and minds of the Swedish during the championships by taking a wee drink but causing no trouble, while the English continued to disgrace the good name of Britain. One of the Tartan army in Gothenburg reported seeing a Scot, the worse for drink, being looked after by a Swede: 'It's the first time I've ever seen a drunk being carried into a bar by a bouncer.'

BUT the visits to Wembley to play the Auld Enemy used to bring out the worst in Scottish fans. Like the detachment who were billeted in a hotel just outside London. The bears were preparing themselves for the night out ahead by relaxing at their windows and balconies. Among the strollers below were a group of Scots carrying rucksacks. After an exchange of pleasantries between the balcony hangers and the street people, one of the latter, not relishing another night under the stars and loth to waste good drinking money on a hotel, asked: 'Hiv ye a spare bed up there? Ah've naewhere tae sleep.' 'Hang on and I'll see,' was the reply. A couple of minutes later the voice floated down from above: 'Nae bother, pal. Here you go.' Closely followed by a nice wee single bed with sheets and matching pillow.

THIS story is from a Glasgow fan who wishes to remain anonymous in case his wheelchair pass for future international matches is withdrawn. The SFA had been most helpful in arranging special disabled tickets for the Italia '90 World Cup. A kind lady at Park Gardens sent him a letter which he had to produce at Genoa tourist office to collect the tickets. Unfortunately, he had to cancel at the very last minute. He tried to let the SFA know but the officials had already left for Italy. It being a shame to waste the valuable tickets, the letter was passed on to another Scots fan. Thus a fan turned up, in a wheelchair hired from a local hospital, to collect the tickets. He was somewhat taken aback to find the mayor of Genoa there in person to present him with VIP tickets for the match. As our informant said: 'It was, perhaps, just as well that Scotland's performance against Costa Rica did not induce such a state of euphoria as to inspire the seated fan to leap to his feet.'

EVEN lady Scottish football fans have been known to stray. The scene is Barcelona in 1972 where Rangers' European Cup-Winners' Cup glory is being somewhat marred by a post-match riot. It is 5 a.m. and a group of Rangers fans are returning to Calella, swapping horror stories about the fate suffered by Rangers fans. One occupant says that he is worried about his wife. 'The last time I saw her she was wrestling with a Guardia Civil in the centre circle. If she's in the pokey, I'm in stook because the travellers' cheques are in her name.'

WE'RE not saying Airdrieonians are strangers to European competition but when they qualified in 1992, the staff at UEFA in Geneva could be heard referring to a team called Airdrie-Onions.

ST Mirren fans have always had a way with words. One denizen of Love Street, concerned that his team were not taking the direct route to goal, was heard to observe: 'They're jist goin' roon' and' roon' in squares.'

AN exhibition at the People's Palace in Glasgow dealing with 500 years of the Roman Catholic Church in the West of Scotland mentioned, of course, the contribution to the community of Celtic FC. It told how in 1888 Brother Walfrid and sundry other Catholic men of good standing formed a football club with the object of raising cash to feed the hungry and clothe the poor of the mainly Irish immigrant population of the East End of Glasgow. The exhibition featured a photograph of an early Celtic team. Except that subsequent research showed the photograph had been wrongly captioned in the museum files. It wasn't Celtic but another Glasgow football team. The

Tickets to : Turkey
Patmos Pireaus Ephessus
Car Hire - Air Tickets
Hotel Reservations

captain's badge, a lion rampant, might have given a clue. Yes, it was none other than Rangers.

AFTER a lengthy goal famine had struck Scotland, it was rumoured that on one foreign trip, striker Gordon Durie couldn't find his way into the team hotel. Someone had painted goalposts over the door.

STUART SLATER, Celtic's talented, goal-shy £1.5 million purchase from West Ham, became known to fans as Jigsaw. Why? Because he falls apart when he gets into the box.

CELTIC'S failure to attract a sponsor led to some ribaldry. For a team who had not won a trophy for four years, Winalot seemed an obvious choice. Then it was said that Oxo were interested. They planned to launch a special Celtic cube, in green, white and gold foil, to be known as the Laughing Stock.

It was reported that Celtic had at last found a sponsor for their new £50 million stadium at Cambuslang. The Tooth Fairy.

ITALIAN football just oozes style. Even down to the objects thrown by the crowd. Colin Davidson, a producer with *Scotsport Extra Time*, who found himself with a film crew behind the goals at an AC Milan home game, narrowly missed being crowned by a flying bottle of salad cream.

AT least someone has a sense of humour at Celtic Park. After the most barren and unsuccessful spell in the club's recent history, Celtic Pools ran a competition for supporters to say in no more than 12 words 'why Celtic are the best team in Europe'. Despite repeated requests, the Diary was never able to find out from Celtic what was the winning answer.

THERE appears to be no bounds to the allergy your average Celtic fan has to anything remotely concerned with Rangers. We hear of one Tim on a construction site who hated using the platform lift because it had been made by a company called Alimac. This meant it was an Alimac hoist.

WHEN Celtic introduced their own brand of peanuts, there was a promotional offer of a free packet for every fan who spent £1.50 or more at the Parkhead refreshment stalls. Thus we heard from a member of the Celtic Park faithful who, having purchased his two pies, two Bovrils, crisps and Mars bar, walked away to these words from the girl behind the counter: 'Haw, are ye no' wantin' yer nuts?'

WHILE most Celtic fans were swallowing the bitter pill and uttering phrases of congratulation as Rangers came close to winning a European Cup final place, it was not given to every Tim to be so sporting. Like the chap who was heard to say: 'If that happens, the best we can hope for is a plane crash.'

TERRY Cassidy achieved some notoriety in his brief but abrasive period as Celtic's chief executive. He even achieved the accolade of sharing a joke with Saddam Hussein. Saddam visits the mosque and asks Allah: 'Tell me, Allah, am I the baddest, worstest

man on earth or what?' Allah refers him to the magic mirror, of which he asks: 'Mirror, mirror, on the wall, who is the baddest of them all?' He gets his answer but is somewhat puzzled. Back he goes to Allah with the supplementary question: 'Who is this guy Terry Cassidy?'

ONE of Terry Cassidy's innovations at Parkhead was to hire a team of crack marketing men. One of these chaps was given the task of creating a new Celtic FC tie. Various designs were put forward to Mr Cassidy, followed by the question: 'What colour did you have in mind?' The boss, in a burst of uncharacteristic diplomacy, replied: 'I think we'll stick with green.'

IT was rumoured that the reason for Mr Cassidy's eventual sacking was that, when asked by the Celtic board how to save money on the new stadium, he replied: 'Don't build a trophy room.'

SHORTLY after the change of management at Ibrox in 1991, Ally McCoist revealed that he would have to undergo an operation before he could resume full duties for club and country. It was nothing to do with ankles or hamstrings. The Greatest Living Ranger said he was to be hospitalised for an operation 'to remove this smile I've had on my face ever since Souness left'.

THIS tale of a footballing odyssey to Marseille concerns a Lanarkshire lawyer who had been persuaded by his pals that nothing would do but

they would all take themselves off on the day-return flight to take in the Rangers European Cup match. He agreed to go but decided to keep it a secret from she who must be obeyed. Mainly because she wouldn't have let him go.

Thus he left the matrimonial home dressed as if he was off to the office. Yes, he was the guy on the Marseille charter wearing the pinstripe suit. He proceeded to have a jolly time until, as ill luck would have it, he was separated from his chums and found himself at the game in the midst of the dreaded Marseille fans. Worse still, he found himself being jostled and, fearing that he was the victim of a gang of Marseille cut-purses, he did what any Lanarkshire man would do, he resorted to physical force. Unfortunately they were not French felons but ordinary fans that he was assaulting and our man ended up in custody.

When he was eventually released at 11.30 p.m., his plane to Glasgow was long gone. You can imagine the trepidation with which he made the phone call: 'Hello, dear, I'm in Marseille . . .' Our man was last seen carrying home an Easter egg as big as himself.

FRECOSSAIS

IT came as a pleasant surprise while doing our bit for European unity in the single market in Normandy to discover that one of the cheeses which was receiving laldy is actually named after the Glasgow dormitory town of Bishopbriggs. For the benefit of those without a smattering of French, we are, of course, referring to Pont L'Eveque. This happy coincidence, or perhaps it was the Calvados chasers, led us to ponder on French versions of other Scottish place names, for instance, the three large residential *quartiers* of Glasgow known as Chateau du Lait, Paques-Maison, and Tambour-Chapelle. Other chic addresses in the Glasgow area would include: Colline-Tete, Taniere-des-Ours and Moulin-Individu. Heading out into Lanarkshire we find such places as Colline-des-Cloches and Les-Deux-Sont-Bien.

The Gallic Gazetteer was soon full of readers' suggestions:

Janvier-Decembre (Callender)
Un-Peu-d'Amour-Physique (Bonkle)
Je-Possede-Un (Iona)
L'Argent-J'ai (Moniaive)
Chien-Colline (Muthill)
Odeur-Tu-Lai (Mingulay)

La Ville d'Imposteur (Maxwelltown)
Terre-Derriere (Hyndland)
Petit-Verre-de-Kelvinside (Drem)
Claque-Mon-Pain-Indien (Slamannan)
Deteste Jean (Lothian)
Pleure-Dans-Un-Vert (Gretna Green)
L'Etoile-Propre (Anstruther)
Sans-Vache (Kyleakin)
Parbleu-en-Agiter (Auchenshuggle)
Eglise-Vache-Fromage (Kirkcudbright)
Peau-de-Derriere (Erskine)
Abeille-Parlez (Beattock)
Il y a Tant (Thurso)
J'ai Couru (Arran)
Mere-Grosse (Moffat)
Quel-Ruisseau (Whitburn)
Fini-Pechant (Dunsinnan)
Eglise-Tout-Le-Jour (Kirkcaldy)
Dormant (Kippen)
Partant (Leven)
Regrettez (Rhu)
Occupé (Tain)
Ma-Jambe (Mallaig)
Allez-Camionette (Govan)
Cuisine-Indienne (Currie)

A stretch of the imagination is required for the likes of:

Un-Ours-Mourant (Aberdeen)

Port-des-Dents-des-Hommes (Port of Menteith)

Even the map of the Verre-Allez Metro (Glesca Subway) came in for translation with such stops as Credit-au-Pair (Partick), Palais de Lally (Buchanan Street-Concert Hall), and Stade Edouard-Ours (Ibrox).

Being awfy linguistic, the teachers from Kyle Academy knew that *zizi* is French for 'willy'. Thus there is that nice wee toon on Arran called Beau-Zizi (Brodick). And you will have noticed how often the snow blocks the road between Pont de Zizi and Chaten-Outil.

Meanwhile back to the list:

Tuez-Mon-Peigne (Kilmacolm)
Venez-Frappez (Cumnock)
Voleur-Ville (Crookston, Glasgow)
La Ville de L'Oreille (Lugton)
Jambon-Fourbe (Cunninghame)
Tuez-Le-Fils-de-Monsieur-Nesbitt (Kilbirnie)
Colline de L'Art Nouveau (Newarthill)
En-Haut-Loi-Lande (Uplawmoor)
Muet-Fritures (Dumfries)
Huit (Echt)
Deux-Centimetres-en-Blanc (White-inch. There are actually 2.53 centimetres in an inch but we won't quibble.)

A follower of a well-known West End of Glasgow football club, Le Chardon (Thistle), spoke of his many happy hours spent at Le Mont des Sapins. On the subject of football, numerous folk suggested Parc-Tete as the obvious translation of Parkhead. We felt it might be more accurate in those

Un-Ours-Serieux (Aberdour)
C'est-Dechire-Loin (Stornoway)
Benediction-un-Foin-Camionette (Bunnahabhainn or Boon a Hay Van)

Eventually *notre tête* was nipping with having to do so much translation of:

Verre-Allez (Glasgow)
Matin-Cote (Morningside)
Manteaux-Salées (Saltcoats)
Tuez-L'Archevêque (Kilwinning)
Salle-de-L'Alouette (Larkhall)
Château-sans-Chien (Castle Douglas)
Bateau-Beau-Thé (Broughty Ferry)
Port-Maison-de-Rapide (Gatehouse of Fleet)
Nouvelle-Tonne-Ragout-Art (Newton Stewart)
La-Ville-de-Qui (Houston)
Tuez-Le-Petit-Jacques (Killiecrankie)
Camionette-Egarée (Strathaven)
Lance-Le (Hurlet)
Ils-Sont-D'Accord (Thurso)

difficult days to call it A La Recherche de Temps Perdu.

We now know that Kelso comes from the French Quel-Sot, meaning 'What an idiot!'. Dundee is renamed Jute-Alors and Aberdeen, in tribute to the renowned generosity of the denizens of Furryboots City, has been renamed Les Misérables. L'Ile-De-Quel-Klaxon is, of course, Isle of Whithorn. Poseur-Colline is, as you probably knew, the Camphill area of Glasgow. Ville-Des-Amoureux you will recognise as Winchburgh. But, enough of the Gallic Gazetteering. Fini. Or Je-Sortirai as Alloway is now known.

THE use of this Gallic-Scottish, or Frecossais as some came to call it, was not just limited to place names. We heard of an instance in Lanarkshire when a *bon viveur* in an *estaminet* in Mere-Bien one night ordered a round in French. '*Cinq demis de cloches, Jacques,*' he cried. A young lady sit-ting near the bar asked her boyfriend what had just been said. He replied gravely: 'He said it's half-past five.'

A PARTY of Glasgow councillors made the pilgrimage to see Rangers playing Marseille in the European Cup. On the return journey they were shopping in the duty-free section at Paris Charles de Gaulle airport. One of the cooncillors decided that an Easter egg would be a splendid present for the wife. He approached the mademoiselle behind the counter with the words: 'Any Easter eggs?' Predictably, the young lady did not understand. The cooncillor returned to his chums for some advice on matters linguistic and duly returned to the jeune fille with the amended question: 'Any Easter *oeufs?*'

A similar conversation involving a Scottish customer in French shop: '*Oeufs,*' he says. Assistant: '*Douze?*' Customer: 'Naw. Hen's . . .'

FUNERAL FUN

Death has no sting for the Herald *Diary. Many was the time we turned to the subject of funerals for the odd cheery wee story.*

WE were told about the chap whose task it was to arrange the transport at a family funeral. He contacted Strathclyde Buses to provide a coach to take mourners from the church to the crematorium.

Strathclyde Buses carried out the contract with the utmost professionalism. The only, tiny criticism was that some of the passengers felt that a Wee Happy Bus, complete with cheery face painted on the front, might not have been the ideal choice of vehicle for such an occasion.

FROM a Glasgow minister we heard this story of the generosity of a showground family. He was called upon to officiate at the funeral of a member of the family. After the ceremony, the drivers and other employees of the undertaker involved each received a thank-you envelope. They were surprised but none too delighted to discover on opening them later that the envelopes contained a complimentary ticket for a ride on the ghost train.

OUR report on the moving and uplifting service for Norman Buchan, the Labour MP, prompted a number of readers to tell us how they wanted to go, when they had to go. Music was, of course, important:

Alan Ward, a Cambuslang minister, recalled a parishioner at a previous kirk who left instructions for two good old Scots songs to be played at his funeral service. The coffin was to be brought in to the strains of 'Will Ye No' Come Back Again?'. His choice of music as the coffin was removed from the church was 'I'm No' Awa' Tae Bide Awa'.

An organist at an unnamed west coast crematorium passed on some recent requests. They included 'Old Shep' (for a dog lover), David Bowie's 'Starman', and 'Stranger in Paradise'. The organist was also asked to play the evangelical hymn 'Colours of Day' which includes the line 'Light up the fire and let the flames burn . . .' Entirely appropriate for a cremation.

Richard Easson of Tain told us that his father's grave request was 'Raindrops Keep Falling On My Head'. 'Unfortunately, we wouldn't get the Sacha Distel version,' he said.

'Smoke Gets In Your Eyes' received more than one nomination as the tune to end the cremation service, as did 'Keep the Home Fire Burning'. John Lennon's 'Imagine' appeared to be the anthem for the '60s generation. Another '60s person, Robert Callandar of Glasgow, had an unusual choice for his musical crème de la crematorium. Mr C let it be known that, despite the fact he is a big lad, he has every confidence in the ability of his male siblings to cart his coffin down the aisle. He has chosen the Hollies' 'He Ain't Heavy, He's My Brother' as the accompanying music.

Other gravest hits included Gracie Fields's 'Wish Me Luck As You Wave Me Goodbye', Eddie Cochran's 'Three Steps to Heaven' for the deceased who has led a blameless life, and Chuck Berry's 'No Particular Place To Go' for the person who does not believe in life after death.

And for a farewell to your friendly income tax or VAT inspector, how's about 'The Deil's Awa' wi' the Exciseman'.

An anonymous football fan wished to be dispatched to the strains of 'Cheerio, Cheerio, Cheerio'. But not everyone wanted to make their funeral a modern, upbeat one.

An artist of the Diary's acquaintance has decreed that when his time comes he wishes to be laid to rest on a faraway hillside. Inaccessible by road. The mourners will have to take turns carrying the coffin. In the pouring rain. Then they will sing all of Psalm 119, which runs to 176 verses. 'If I'm not having any fun, they're not having any fun,' is his logic.

And, by the way, there will be no women at the graveside. They will be back home preparing the boiled ham and the rest of the purvey.

GAZETTEER

The Diary's net spreads wide across Scotland, from the sundry delights of Kilwinning to Clootie City . . .

THEY behave in strange ways in Motherwell if the evidence in the following court case is any guide: a barman was cleared of starting a fire at his uncle's pub. We quote this snippet of evidence from the *Motherwell Times*'s coverage of the trial: 'He [the accused] blamed one of the pub customers with whom he had indulged in a drunken bout of sumo wrestling in the pub a few hours before the fire was discovered. The court heard that a police officer called to the fire found the accused with a tartan rug over his head hiding behind a Christmas tree in a close near the pub.'

ALSO from Motherwell is the tale of an industrial tribunal where a chap claimed unfair dismissal. His firm pointed out that he had thrown a cup of tea over a female colleague who was his former girlfriend. He claimed provocation because she had been nagging him in sign language. The tribunal found him two-thirds to blame.

IT was inevitable that a joke should emerge linking the Bank of Credit and Commerce International and the globetrotting Motherwell District Council. Apparently, initial fears that the Motherwell council might have lost some funds lodged with BCCI proved groundless since the Motherwell council keeps all its cash in travellers' cheques.

FROM Cunninghame District Council we heard the story of a councillor who had been deputed to go to London to accept an award from the British Tourist Authority. The gong was to be handed out by a royal personage at a lavish ceremony in a hotel in the Strand. The tribune of the people was duly given his air tickets, hotel voucher, and invitation. Reading the words '7pm for 7.15pm' on this last document, the councillor asked a council official: 'Are you sure we should be going to this? It seems an awful expense just for 15 minutes.'

DUMFRIES and Galloway Regional Council Public Library Byelaws ensure that users obey a strict code of conduct:

● No person shall spit in the library.

● No person shall sleep in the library

after having been requested to refrain from doing so by the librarian.

- Any person who in the opinion of the librarian is intoxicated or disorderly or so unclean in his person as would be likely to cause offence to other users of the library, shall not enter or use the library.

- No person shall lie on the furniture or fittings of the library or on the floor thereof except with the consent of the librarian.

- No person who is suffering from a contagious or infectious disease shall enter or use the library.

GORDON MURRAY, a former provost of Cumbernauld, lodged a housing application that could best be described as unusual. In a letter to Cumbernauld and Kilsyth District Council's chief executive, Mr Murray listed a number of circumstances which, he says, made a priority of the application by him and his wife, fellow councillor Margaret Murray. He said that the 'medical conditions which prompt this request' included:

- 'I have only one eye and my eyesight in the remaining eye is failing.'

- 'I have numerous gunshot wounds.'

- 'Most Labour councillors and some officials of the district council are convinced I have been suffering from Alzheimer's disease for some time. (Unfortunately my numerous medical consultants have not been able to confirm this to date, otherwise I might have escaped liability for poll tax.)'

- 'My once active sex life has become a distant memory.'

- 'My fair skin makes me liable to a number of skin diseases ranging from skin cancer to chronic dandruff (a dandruff so severe it will not react to Head & Shoulders or any of the modern miracle cures!).'

- 'My various medical conditions are aggravated by the fact that I am a compulsive eater and suffer from gross obesity.'

The other medical points ranged from arthritis of the spine, a disease of the blood vessels, and a heart attack.

While this was a touching letter,

council officials were puzzled as to why it had been written, since the councillors Murray already had a perfectly good house in Cumbernauld. It appeared that the letter was an attempt at satire, commenting on the fact that a Labour councillor had recently been granted a house on health grounds.

IT is no easy task to foil the talented thieves of the Glasgow garden suburb of Drumchapel. One anecdote concerned the construction of a garage to house a local school minibus. On the assumption that what ain't fastened down will be lifted, the authorities, on delivering the bricks with which to build the garage, thoughtfully provided also a watchman, a watchman's hut, and an Alsatian dog. One evening the watchman sloped off for a quick pint. On his return, he discovered that the bricks had indeed remained secure. However, both the watchman's hut and the Alsatian had been stolen.

ON a rare foray to the Borders we were asked: 'What label does a Hawick girl have on her knickers?' To which we replied: 'We don't know. What label does a Hawick girl wear on her knickers?' Answer: 'Next.'

A TALE from Ayrshire which sounds too silly to be true but we are assured is not apocryphal. It happened in Dalry, which might explain a lot. The scene is the Roche chemical plant in the douce Ayrshire toon. A Swiss engineer was on secondment from the parent company. His English was no' richt guid, to let you understaun'. One of the locals decided that what the Swiss chap needed was a book to help him with his English. The Swiss chap was delighted with this kind offer and duly read the book with the efficiency and thoroughness for which his nation is famous. He came in the next day with a few supplementary questions for the Dalry man. 'What means "Michty me!" and "Whit's wrang wi' the Bairn?".' Yes, he had been given a Broons book to study.

GLASGOW has changed in the last decade or so with the advent of Mayfest, the *annus mirabilis* of the European Year of Culture, and the general growth of the city's arts industry. Glasgow's lifestyle has changed too. Here is a list of the ways a typical Glasgow working chap was then and the way he is now.

THEN

Job description: Welder in Govan shipyard and part-time comedian.

House: One-room tenement flat in Partick, shared with wife and four children.

Breakfast: Two rashers of bacon, fried egg, black pudding and a potato scone, all in a City Bakeries roll.

Lunch: Spam sandwiches (Mondays and Wednesdays) and corned-beef sandwiches (Tuesdays and Thursdays); Fridays, a pie and four pints of heavy in pub.

Dinner: Actually, it was called your tea in those days and was corned-beef fritters (Mondays and Wednesdays) and spam fritters (Tuesdays and Thursdays); Fridays, another pie and eight pints of heavy in the pub.

Method of transport: Glasgow Corporation bus; no motor car.

Girlfriend: Senga, waitress in the works canteen.

Problem with girlfriend: His wife has just found out.

Favourite team: Celtic.

Last time he was in a fight: When some idiot stole his bottle of Lanliq at a party in Partick.

Idea of a good night out: Spend a tenner on a meal in an Italian restaurant and then on to a country and western music club.

Ambition: To get out of the shipyards.

NOW

Job description: Area liaison inward investment executive (business and the arts division) with Govan Enterprise and part-time comedian.

House: Bachelor studio flat in Partick; wife and four children living in the bungalow in Bearsden.

Breakfast: Two slices of prosciutto, eggs Benedict, *un morceau de boudin noir* and a potato scone, all in a City Bakeries croissant.

Lunch: Glass of Highland Spring, Ryvita and cottage cheese (Mondays to Thursdays); Fridays, spam roll and a Spritzer in pub.

Dinner: Now called dinner and consists, Mondays to Thursdays, of any low-fat, low-salt Marks and Spencer meal for one, washed down with Earl Grey tea. Fridays, pie and eight pints of Spritzer in the pub.

Method of transport: Strathclyde Bus; politically correct way to travel.

Girlfriend: Miranda, drama student who works part time as a waitress with outside catering company which provides executive buffets at Govan Enterprise.

Problem with girlfriend: His daughter, who's in Miranda's class at drama school, has just found out.

Favourite team: Boston Celtics.

Last time he was in a fight: When some idiot stole his bottle of Marques de Caceres gran reserva Rioja at a dinner party in Partick and replaced it with a bottle of Lanliq.

Idea of a good night out: Take in a concert by an Italian tenor and then for supper to a Tex-Mex cantina.

Ambition: To attract the shipbuilding industry back to Govan.

BINGO players will be familiar with such cries as '88, two fat ladies' and 'key of the door, 21'. In Dundee the bingo callers were wont to cry, to the consternation of women present, '76. Seven and six. Was she worth it?'

THERE was a famous Clootie City costermonger who was regularly heard to cry: 'Onions! Genuine Spanish onions! Nane o' yer foreign muck here!'

DUNDEE'S Labour clubs collapsed amidst a financial debacle with all sorts of allegations of criminal activity. One of the people involved received a communication containing two bullets and note with a Mafia-style warning: to whit, the single word 'Omertá'. The word, in typical Clootie City literary tradition, was in fact misspelt. It appeared on the note as 'O'Merta'. No doubt it was from the Irish Mafia.

A WORKERS' meeting was called by the management at Dundee's Michelin factory in an attempt to persuade the workforce to adopt a new shift system in which they would lose the right to have Saturday and Sunday off each week. You would still have a 'weekend' off, a management negotiator explained, except that it would not be Saturday and Sunday every week. One worker, a well-known sage, was asked by the management chap to explain why he was shaking his head. 'Am I to understand,' said the sage, 'that a Tuesday could be like a Saturday, and a Wednesday like a Sunday?' 'Exactly,' said the management man, pleased to have made the big breakthrough in understanding. 'Can you tell me how I'm going to get a *Sunday Post* on a Wednesday?' the worker replied. The proposal was rejected.

NO less a person than Ken Sykora, doyen broadcaster and presenter of Radio Scotland's *Eater's Digest*, told us that the chip was invented in Dundee. Not the microchip, the fried chip. Mr Sykora unearthed this fascinating fact in an interview with Kinross hotelier Terry Doyle. Mr Doyle insisted that the chip was created in Dundee by his great grandfather, Frenchman Edouard Dejernier. Monsieur Dejernier moved to Dundee in the 1870s, where he started up a chain of fish restaurants. He introduced the fritter and the 'finger' which later became known simply as the chip. His tattie innovation was carried abroad by visiting sailors. The delicacy was known as Frenchie's Fries, now better known as French fries.

ONE of Dundee's most famous sons is Lieutenant Montgomery Scott. He is better known as Scottie, as in 'Beam me up, Scottie'. Yes, the cantankerous engineer in *Star Trek* hails from the city of the Tay. This information can be verified in an episode in which Scottie fantasises about being a Highland laird. He reminisces: 'Och, I wish I was back in my native Dundee . . .'

A CLUE to the psyche of Dundee may be found in how Clootie City celebrated the anniversary of VE Day. The great and the good in Dundee

decided in their infinite wisdom that the returning soldiery, after six years of war, could not be trusted to conduct themselves in a manner fitting to this great occasion, so all the pubs were ordered to stay shut that night. There were no riots following this momentous decision, but there were a great many dumbfounded, depressed and drouthy demobbed Dundonians dandering dejectedly around the streets of dry Dundee.

JIM McLEAN, former manager, chairman and god of Dundee United, in a way epitomises the city. Mr McLean has a reputation for having an uncompromising nature. This was enhanced by a tale about his reaction to a letter from a young fan. The young Arab (as United fans are called) put pen to paper, as is every paying punter's right, to inform Mr McLean that he thought some of his team selections were wrong. The letter duly went into Mr McLean's in-tray. After Ayatollah McLean had dealt with the day's business (torturing apprentices, rebuilding the stadium, checking the Tannadice bank balance) he set off home, stopping on his way at the address from which the letter had come. He knocked on the door and asked the lady of the house if the boy was in. The boy duly appeared to be told by Mr McLean: 'Look, I pick the team.'

HOW do you recognise a Dundee police car? Simple. It's got a roof rack. This is a reference to one of the less glorious chapters in the history of Dundee's finest. Folklore has it that the Dundee force is the only one in the country that had to call out the day shift to the night shift. The incident occurred in the early 1970s when some of the night-shift boys in blue succumbed to temptation while investigating a burglary at a local pub, the Rowan Tree. Local urchins had much fun in the ensuing months by singing 'Rowan tree, Oh, rowan tree' to passing bobbies.

THE *Sun* newspaper reported under the heading 'Randy Ravers Flock To Cammy's Pit Of Passion', the opening of a Dundee club where sex was the motif. On entering the premises, clubbers were confronted by a giant phallic symbol; statues with Madonna-

NOW
IS YOUR
CHANCE
KNICKERS
DOWN
2 for £1

esque pointed boobs; a bar held up by bare-bottomed, knickerless, stockinged ladies' legs; and if that wasn't enough to move the earth, a specially woven sperm-patterned carpet. The steamy décor of the passion pit was lost on one Dundonian lass, who told the *Sun*: 'I didn't realise sex was the theme until someone pointed it out to me.'

IN Dundeespeak the number two is pronounced *twaa*. An example of this comes from the Dundee soldier who returned from war service in France. Asked how he liked that country, he replied: 'It's great. Every time you ask for twaa eggs, ye get three.'

THIS tale concerns a job which Dundee Council put out to tender. Three firms put in bids. An Aberdeen company offered to do the job for £3,000 on the basis of £1,000 for materials, £1,000 for labour, and £1,000 profit margin. An Edinburgh firm put in a bid of £6,000 – with £2,000 each earmarked for materials, labour and profit. A Dundee firm put

in a tender of £9,000 and was duly invited to meet a senior council official to give a breakdown of its estimate. 'Simple,' said the Dundee businessman. '£3,000 to you, £3,000 to me and £3,000 for the Aberdeen boys to do the work.'

DUNDEE cops were conducting inquiries in the Hawkhill area and one of the interviewees was a Dundee District Council cleansing department employee whose beat took in the locus of the crime. He was approached by one of Tayside's finest who surmised that the street sweeper might have seen something of value to their investigation. 'What is your name?' he asked. The cleansing operative told him. 'Address?' This information was duly given. 'Occupation?' the polisman asked. The road-sweeper looked at his dustcart, looked at his cleansing department uniform and said to the policeman: 'Actually, I'm a brain surgeon at the Dundee Royal Infirmary.' The police were not amused and took the unfortunate scaffie down to the nick where he was kept in custody for an hour for obstructing police inquiries. He was released with a warning 'not to be stupid in future'. Unrepentant, he replied: 'Well, you started it.'

JAMES McDONALD, a famous son of Dundee, died in Los Angeles. Both Dundee Labour MPs, Ernie Ross and John McAllion, put down an early-day motion at the House of Commons to ensure he did not go unmourned. The motion read: 'This House regrets the passing of Mr James McDonald, born in Dundee 84 years ago, who brought pleasure to millions for more than 40 years as the voice of Mickey Mouse and who provided the yodelling, whistling and sneezing for Walt Disney's classic 1937 cartoon film *Snow White and the Seven Dwarfs*, and expresses its sincere sympathy for his widow, Roberta.' It matters little that Mr McDonald's parents emigrated from Dundee when he was only a month old. The city by the Tay needs all the famous sons it can get.

ONE of Dundee's most famous politicians was Mr Edward 'Neddy' Scrymgeour, the Prohibition candidate who unseated Winston Churchill from his Dundee seat. As you will gather from his ticket, Neddy was a fierce critic of the drink. He had to suffer continual barracking from sundry drunks at his election meetings. Undeterred, he would warn these imbibers that, come prohibition, all the ales and ardent spirits in Dundee would be emptied into the River Tay. Equally undeterred, a gang of the said imbibers at one meeting reacted to this news by singing the hymn: 'Yes, we'll gather at the river . . .'

THERE was a local man who complained to his MP that his name wasn't on Kilwinning's war memorial. This was unfair he felt, since he had fought longer in the war than his brother whose name was on the memorial. This led certain local cynics to ask him: 'Settle an argument. Was it you or your brother that was killed in the war?'

A KILWINNING man decided to

take the train to Glasgow for the day. Asked how he had enjoyed his first visit to the big city, he replied: 'It's brilliant – and ah didnae know it was a' under gless.'

ANOTHER KILWINNING man was having his parentage discussed. 'Naw, she's no' his mither. She's his auntie. She hid him tae a sojer during the war.'

TWO chaps were having a drink in their local Kilwinning tavern. They ordered up another round of one pint of heavy and one of lager. The barmaid put the pints in front of them, but the wrong way round. The two broke off their conversation, stared in a puzzled fashion at the two pints and then changed seats.

A KILWINNING chap won the pools. Asked in the pub what he would do with his winnings, he said he would buy his mother a house, his sister a car, and (being a Catholic, unusual we know in Kilwinning) he

'would like tae pit in a windae at the chapel'. A fellow Kilwinningite (not of the same persuasion) said that for £20 he would 'pit in a' the windaes at the chapel'.

THE following tale of Kilwinning Protestant intransigence was sworn to be true by a Glasgow University student who says he was there at the time. He was invited by a fellow student to a party in Ayrshire's Burgh of Culture. Having arrived within the burgh limits, the students stopped their car and asked a local for directions.

The Kilwinningite peered into the car and asked: 'Ony papes in this caur?'

'Certainly not,' was the reply although there was at least one.

'Are you sure?' came the rejoinder.

'Mind you, it's hard to tell the difference. They look mair and mair like us.'

TWO Kilwinning men, serving with Monty in his desert campaign against the Germans, were in a foxhole doing their best to shelter from the relentless sun. 'Here, d'ye ken whit day it is the day?' asks one.

'Naw. Whit day is it the day?' his pal replied.

The first chap explains that it is Marymass Day, the big gala day in the area.

'They've got a grand day for it,' the second man says, peering up at the cloudless skies.

Another Kilwinningite claimed to have been at the annual Marymass festival 'hunners o' times'.

TWO Kilwinningites on a night out to Kilmarnock missed the last bus home. Being lawless types, they decided that instead of walking home they would break into the Western SMT garage and steal a bus. One climbed over the wall while the other kept watch. After 15 minutes had elapsed with no sign of his pal the man keeping watch shouted over the wall: 'Whit's keepin' ye?'

'Ah canny find a bus that says Kilwinning oan it,' he explained.

'Ya idiot,' says his pal, 'Take wan that says Irvine oan it and we'll walk the rest.'

A GREYHOUND in transit in a British Rail guard's van escaped on arrival at Kilwinning station. A Kilwinning BR employee chased the beast up the platform uttering the immortal words: 'Stoap that dug! It's a parcel!'

THE licensee of a Kilwinning hostelry noted for its unswerving support for things red, white and blue, had prepared for the next day's Orange Walk by painting a large slogan on the outside of her premises. It read: 'One queen, one crown, no Pope in our town.' To which a nocturnal graffitologist had added: 'Lucky old Pope.'

A CHAP enters a barber's shop in Kilwinning and joins the queue of men sitting. Observing that it might be some time before he is done, he seeks to pass the time by reading. 'Excuse me,' he says to the chap beside him, 'are you reading that paper you're sitting on?'

POSSIBLY the cruellest jibe about the fine burghers of Kilwinning is that when there is an escape from the state mental hospital at Carstairs, the police immediately throw a cordon around Kilwinning. 'If they get into Kilwinning, we'll never find them,' an official is reputed to have said.

KILWINNINGITES have their own peculiar way of putting things. Half-day closing is referred to as 'hauf-shut day'. A bank holiday has been heard described as 'hauf-shut day a' day the day'.

A DIARY reader shared with us his tale of a Kilwinning colleague in the RAF. When the chaps in the barracks room were being more than usually boisterous, the Kilwinningite would chide them with the words: 'D'ye think it's ootside yer in?'

DR GAGE was a well-known medical man in Kilwinning in the latter half of the last century and played a part in the introduction of a new, healthier water supply. The new water was welcomed by everyone apart from one lady, who told him: 'Doactor, the new watter willnae dae.' Asked to elaborate she explained: 'It's got neither taste nor smell.'

Dr Gage's duties also took him to the local poorhouse, where one old lady complained about the quality of the soup: 'It's no' biled right. Try this,' she said, producing a pea from her pocket. The doctor duly popped it into his mouth and agreed it was rock hard. 'Weel, doactor, that's exactly how it came through me this morning,' the lady informed him.

A KILWINNING lad announced his intention to marry a local girl known to be free with her favours. 'You're no' mairryin' that yin?' one of his pals said. 'Hauf the men in Stevenston huv been wi' her.'

After a moment's thought, the bridegroom, obviously something of a philosopher, replied: 'Och, it's no' a' that big a place, Stevenston.'

THE most famous hostelry in Kilwinning was the Winton Arms, a redoubt of Loyalism and Orangeism. Lily McCaffer, who presided over the Winton for many years, told the Diary there were so many stories

about her and her hotel that she never bothered to deny them.

The story about the time she sent home a regular who was wearing a green jumper with the words that he 'should know better' for example. Or the tale of the honeymoon couple who booked in, left their suitcases in their room, and went for a walk: on their way out of the hotel, they asked what time Mass was the next morning; on their way back after their walk they found their suitcases on the pavement. Then there was the priest in plain clothes whose identity was discovered, his pint confiscated and his money returned.

Lily said such things might have happened under an earlier management. But she admitted she never wore green 'because it's unlucky'.

OVERHEARD in a Kilwinning post office: 'Two stamps please. One quick and one slow.'

A KILWINNING social club installed a satellite TV system. The committee became worried that the dish, situated on a low roof, might be too easily nicked. As a result, they resolved to have a local tradesman construct a secure box over the dish. On a subsequent agenda was the problem of poor reception on the satellite TV system.

THIS tale of a Kilwinningite came from Mr W.B. Thomson of Kirkintilloch, who recalled the occasion of one of the last shows at the Glasgow Apollo. Jerry Lee Lewis was scheduled to headline the concert but had been unable to appear.

The box office was busy issuing refunds, so Mr Thomson retired to a nearby pub where he found sundry disconsolate Teddy boys. Most disconsolate of all was a figure in a yellow drape suit, seated forlornly at the end of the bar.

W.B. related: 'I eventually spoke to him and it turned out that he had come straight from his work in Kilwinning, oblivious of the cancellation. I suggested, as a consolation, that he may yet see his hero at another venue,. But he indicated that this wasn't a solution. "This is my effan problem . . . Look!" the Kilwinningite said, rolling up the left sleeve of his jacket to reveal the legend, freshly tattooed on his arm – Friday, 17 February 1987. Jerry Lee Lewis . . . His last show at Glasgow Apollo . . . The King Lives.'

Mr Thomson suggested the addition of a tasteful 'Cancelled', but the Kilwinningite was not impressed.

A KILWINNINGITE was telling his cronies in the pub about his weekend's activities: 'Ah ta'en the wife oot fur a meal,' he said.

'Whit did ye hiv?' a pal asked.

'Stertit wi' a prawn cocktail.'

'Away, that's a wummin's drink!' was the reply.

WE hear of a young Kilwinningite who got a job as a barman. Remarkably, the young man was not versed in the ways of public houses, as he displayed when he said to the manager: 'The man there wants a pint and a half of lager but for the life of me I can't find a glass big enough.'

A KILWINNINGITE, telling of an embarrassing situation in which a fellow burgher had found himself, averred: 'Ah tell ye. His face was as red as an orange.'

WE were also told of a Kilwinning Rangers supporter's imprecation to a defender as a visiting attacker threatened the home team's goal: 'Kill him! Knock him doon stane deid like a lump o' iron!'

THEN there is the tale of the stranger who asked for directions. A Kilwinningite said he couldn't go wrong: 'Take the first on the left and then doon the street, below the railway bridge that's no' there noo.'

SOME place Port Glasgow, as can be seen from this extract from a court report which appeared in the *Greenock Telegraph* under the heading 'SAUCE BOTTLE ATTACK VICTIM NEEDED 34 STITCHES':

'Mrs Myra Rancier (36) told the court there had been an argument and Brownie had punched Mrs Findlay, knocking her over a chair.

'But she admitted she had not seen everything that had happened as she was blind in one eye, was drinking super lager and had been reading Bunty comics at the time.'

STEAK pie features in assault. The accused entered a chip shop in Gourock holding a steak pie. He 'stood in front of customers and demanded four pickled onions . . . He turned towards the person standing behind him in the queue and asked, "What are you smiling at?" and struck the

man with his right hand which was holding the steak pie.' The man was found guilty of breach of the peace and fined £75.

THE Diary discovered a fellow student of Greenock life in Mr Iain Talman of Cardross. Mr Talman, a Gourockian by birth, has been collecting Greenock lore for many years.

He has amassed a rich collection of wee stories from the local courts, some of which suggest that Greenockians are not expert at escaping from the scene of the crime:

- The passer-by who was assaulted by a man who had emerged from a coin-operated photo kiosk. The assailant left his victim with wounds requiring four stitches to his scalp. He also left four photographs of himself which were discovered after he had made his escape. The accused, thus, was the first person in history to leave behind a perfect photofit for the police. He was caught and fined £30.

- The burglar who found his haul too heavy to carry and went to the neighbour of his victim to phone for a taxi.

ALIBIS and pleas in mitigation can also leave a little to be desired, like:

- The accused on a drunk and disorderly charge who explained that he had been celebrating his birthday. This did not impress the bailie who checked the date of birth on the charge sheet which showed the man had been celebrating a month too early.

- The bramble-pickers – two men found on a railway line with a bag containing a large quantity of copper wire claimed they found it while picking brambles. The depute fiscal somewhat spoiled their story by pointing out that the incident occurred in July, a time when there were no brambles.

- The man convicted of assault with a bottle who explained that he had consumed 17 bottles of wine that day.

- The accused on a breach of the peace charge who claimed he was being chased along the street by animals who were 20 feet high, seven feet wide and were breathing steam. His agent added that he was further upset because he had discovered his divorced wife in bed with an Englishman. 'I'm not sure whether it was because she was in bed with another man or because he was an Englishman.'

A young Greenockian succumbed to temptation, as he stood in a chemist shop by the charity Christmas stocking bulging with cash. He grabbed it and made his getaway. Police were waiting for him when he returned home with his booty. He really should not have been so surprised. They got his name and address from the prescription which he had taken to the chemist.

OTHER forms of behaviour which have led Greenockians into court are merely inexplicable, including:

- The shoplifter who stole a tin of dog food but had no dog.

- The woman who appeared in court to represent her husband on a wife-beating charge.

- A youth who was fined £20 for punching and kicking a litter bin and shouting 'Come on and fight'. The fiscal commented: 'He was presumably doing this because he knew that it couldn't retaliate.'

- The man who was arrested in a shop hitting his head against the walls and floor. He also assaulted a shop assistant with a packet of biscuits and therefore qualified for the Greenock hall of fame for attackers who used everyday objects (see previous references to sauce bottles, meat pies, etc).

Other examples include:

- The grandfather who assaulted his granddaughter in a supermarket with a shopping basket.

- The man who assaulted his wife and daughter with a TV set.

- The husband who stuffed an electricity bill into his wife's mouth. The accused told the police: 'I just cracked up when I saw the bill and rammed it down her scrawny little

A 70-year-old man was found guilty of stabbing his son with a bread knife, causing a six-inch-deep wound. The father explained that he was trying to establish from his son the whereabouts of his wife. He said he went to the kitchen to get the knife 'just like a father taking a strap to his child' to frighten him into telling the truth.

A man who lit fires in a close and two litter bins was caught walking along the street with two matches in his hand and another two in his mouth. When cautioned he said, 'there was no malice to hurt people . . . they were just wee bonfires like Guy Fawkes did – wee beacons to warn people like they did with the Spanish Armada.'

In the midst of all this surrealism in Greenock Sheriff Court, there is the wise and witty figure of Sheriff J. Irvine Smith. Sheriff Smith recently had to take the case of a well-known persistent offender who seems to prefer prison to life in Greenock.

Sheriff Smith looked up to see the accused, who exhibits definite camp characteristics, in the dock and said: 'Oh, no. Not you again.'

'Well, who were you expecting? Joan Crawford?' came the reply.

MEANWHILE, the *Greenock Telegraph* embarked upon the traditional circulation drive which involved a member of staff walking the boulevards and promenades of the Tail o' the Bank looking for people carrying copies of the newspaper. His happy task was to ask the reader a simple question and

throat.' (Greenockians have always had a way with words.) The defence lawyer said in mitigation that his client had been out for a drink and came home to find the electricity bill on the mantelpiece. 'It amounted to £130 for a period of six weeks . . . He feels his wife was the cause to a great extent of the amount of the electricity bill.' Sentence was deferred for six months.

THE Tail o' the Bank has a long tradition of unusual behaviour. Mr Talman's files include a story about a man who smashed a Port Glasgow shop window, stole a cloth cap, and was going to walk across the Clyde to Cardross. That was in 1885. *Plus ça change.*

Other famous Tail o' the Bank cases soon came to light:

then hand over a fiver. The young man charged with the task had an unfortunate start when he spotted a comely young lady carrying a copy of the paper. 'How would you like to earn a fiver?' he asked her. Before he had the chance to pose the simple question, she rewarded him with a hefty slap in the face.

BUT in the end the Diary discovered in its researches that Greenock is not without gentility and class.

Two well-to-do ladies of the select West End part of town were not impressed when they saw in their local paper that they had been the victims of chip pan fires.

One of the irate ladies telephoned the paper and informed reporting staff that she had not been using a chip pan. It was, as she told them in no uncertain terms, 'a deep fat fryer'.

The other good lady felt she had even greater ground for complaint, for, as she told them, she had been making *coq-au-vin* at the time.

GRACE

The subject of the humble Grace Before Meals produced a small but rich correspondence in the Diary.

WE have all heard of the Selkirk Grace but one which could rival it is the Langholm Grace brought to our attention by a local minister who has been introducing the victuals in these terms:

All creatures that on earth do well,
Wrax oot your haun' and help yoursel'.

A number of other Graces subsequently arrived in the Diary's mailbag including:

Holy, holy, roon' the table
Eat as much as you are able
Eat muckle, pooch nane
Holy, holy. Amen.

And the variation:

Roly, poly round the table
Eat as much as you are able
If you can, eat the table
Roly, poly. Amen.

Then there was the extremely couthy:

Ye'r at yer auntie's sae don't be blate,
There's halesome fairin' on ilka plate.
Meat fit for provost, laird or loon.
When ye'r fu' as a puggy, lick the spoon.

Or the more direct blessing:

Doon wi' yer heid
Up wi' yer paws
Thank the guid Lord
For the use o' yer jaws.

The humble potato came in for special treatment:

O Lord wha blest the loaves and fishes
Look upon these twa wee dishes,
An' tho' the tatties be but sma'
Lord mak them plenty for us a';
But if oor stomachs they do fill,
'Twill be another miracle.

Then there is the special grace for anglers:

Guid Lord, wha gars the bonnie
    specklin' troot.
Loup tae oor flees in loch an' river,
Grant us Thy grace, oor humble wish,
Tae Thee be praise an' glory ever.

THE Rangers football club has its own preprandial prayer:

Lord, heap blessings on the soup,
Heap blessings on the stovies.
Heap blessings on the Papes and Jews
The Moslems and Jehovies.
Heap blessings on all gathered here,
On absent friends and strangers,
And, if you've blessings left,
Please, heap them on the Rangers.

THE Scottish Medical Students Grace is admirably short:

For God's sake, fa' tae.

WE finish with the Aberdeenshire Grace:

God be wi' ye a' yer days
Plenty mate and plenty claes,
A timmer cup and a hoarn spoon
An ae tither tattie when tither's done.

HEALTH

The diary looks on with a healthy scepticism.

WITH staff cutbacks and inadequate resources, life is difficult for the nurses in Glasgow's hospital casualty units. It is not surprising, therefore, that some nurses take a hard line with the various down-and-outs who feign illness to obtain a bed for the night. One such sister in a hospital which shall remain nameless has perfected a technique whereby she approaches a patient suspected of pretending to be unconscious and grabs him firmly by the family jewels. She was called upon to use her skills recently by a young doctor who was unsure about the genuineness of a patient. Hearing the resulting screams, the doctor returned to the scene with the words: 'No, sister, not him. The man in the next cubicle.'

A GENTLEMAN from Bishopbriggs was in Stobhill Hospital for a vasectomy. He was awaiting this routine operation in a room with a number of other chaps, all of whom became slightly alarmed when a young nursing auxiliary came in clutching a cardboard box and asked the sister: 'What do you want done with these balls?' The box contained, of course, Christmas decorations.

AN apocryphal tale concerns Mr John Cockburn, an eminent surgeon at Aberdeen Royal Infirmary cardiac unit. He was guest speaker at a function run by a pharmaceutical company in Edinburgh and during the meal the company's young English representative kept referring to him as Cock-burn. 'It's Co'burn, as in the film actor,' John told him. The rep, by this time very nervous, kept repeating to himself as the time drew near to introduce the surgeon's speech, 'It's Co'burn, Co'burn', then promptly stood up to introduce John Heartburn, the respected cock surgeon.

A YOUNG man was proudly relating to his mother how he was on the nicotine patches and had given up smoking. His mum inspected the patch and recommended: 'What you should do is put on all the patches and get that nicotine out of your system in the one go.'

THE concept behind the nicotine patches quickly caught on. There were reports of a chap going around with a teabag taped to his arm who said he was trying to give up tea. Not

to mention the man with a pie on his arm to see if he could lose weight.

THE Body Shop factory in Easterhouse, Glasgow, where they make the designer soap, is one of the more desirable workplaces in the area. As you would expect from the principles established by founder Anita Roddick, everything involved is of the best. Workers are encouraged to pursue a healthy lifestyle by having access to quantities of the Body Shop lotions and ungents. The factory itself is of the modern times variety with designer overalls. An industrial paradise you would think and you would be right. Apart from one issue raised at a management staff meeting. 'Everything's fine,' said one chap, 'but could we not have white rolls instead of those brown ones in the canteen?'

INSULTS

A reference in the Diary to somebody in the Sarry Heid pub having a face like a melted wellie led a reader to speculate that the West of Scotland is richer in such descriptive facial phrases than any other region. The Diary was immediately submerged with many examples . . .

- A face like a hauf-chewed caramel.

- A face like a torn melodeon with the tune hinging oot.

- A face like a City Bakeries Hallowe'en cake.

- A face like a well-skelped erse.

- A face like a bag of spanners.

- A face like a burst couch.

- A face like a can of angry worms.

- A face like the hin' end o' a bus.

- A face you could chop sticks with.

- A face like a blind cobbler's thumb.

- A face like someone had set it on fire and put oot the flames wi' a shovel.

- A face like a ragman's trumpet.

- A face like a battered fart.

- A face like a robber's dog.

- A face like a horse in a huff.

- A face like a pudding supper wi' the jaundice.

- A face like a fish supper looking for a vinegar bottle.

- A face that has worn out three bodies.

- A face only a mother could love.

- A rerr face for hauntin' hooses.

- A face you'd never get tired of kicking.

- A face like a rivet-catcher's glove.

- A face like a torn kit-bag.

- A heid like a clootie dumpling.

- A splendid face for playing hide and seek.

- A face you couldnae mark wi' a pit boot.

- A face that wid turn milk soor.

- A face like the north end of a south-bound cow.

- A face that would turn a funeral up a side street.

- A face like the wrang end o' a Belfast ham.

- A face like a German bank – full of marks.

- A face like a sand-blasted meringue.

- A face like a chippit chantie.

- A face that would frighten the French.

- A face like a camel eating sherbet.

- A face that would get a piece at any door.

- A face like a relief map of the Himalayas.

- A face as long as Leith Walk.

- A face like a pun' o' knitted mince.

A WELL-KNOWN Hallowe'en game is often used to describe facial characteristics, as in: 'He looked as if he'd been dookin' for apples in a hot chip pan.' Or, of someone with a ruddy complexion: 'He looks like he's been dookin' for beetroot.'

AILEEN Fisher of Stranraer told how a ward maid at the Victoria Infirmary in Glasgow used to abuse nurses (including Ms Fisher) with the words: 'Your face would make a rerr Sunday arse for me.' Telling comments from others included:

- 'If I had a face like yours, I'd paint ma arse and walk on ma hauns.'

- 'He was so ugly that when he was born the doctor skelped his mother.'

- 'The last time I saw a heid like that it wis hinging oot a poacher's pocket.'

- 'If I'd a face like yours, I'd teach my bum to speak.'

- 'What are you going to do for a face when Quasimodo wants his arse back?'

- 'The last time I saw faces like that they were staring at me from a pirate ship.'

- 'The last time I saw an arse like that Sabu was hitting it with a stick.'

- 'He always reminds me o' a rat lookin' oot a jeely jar.'

- 'Is she ugly? If pigs could fly, she'd be a squadron leader.'

- 'If I had a face like that, I wouldn't bring it out on a clear night.'

- 'Tell me, is that your face or is your arse up for a breather?'

- 'You know – the wumman wi' the upside-doon legs.'

THE Diary gave an honourable

BOATS HAULED *and*
LAUNCHED 2.50 per. ft.
BOTTOMS WASHED
1.50 per. ft.

mention and wee prize to one Phil McGhee for his suggestion of 'a face like a scorpion's arse'. It was not exactly rib-tickling class, but the Diary had never had a competition entry before from an untried prisoner in D Hall of Barlinnie.

THE editor of the Diary himself was not immune to physiological insult. Some ******* suggested: 'A face like that man who writes the *Herald* Diary.' Another wit suggested that the picture which adorned the column looked 'like a werewolf peering over a dyke'.

YOU may also have heard of the Glasgow man who was so ugly as a child that strange men used to give him sweets to get out of their car.

LANGUAGE AND THAT

The Diary, as any reader would tell you, is dead into language. Thus, we are happy to offer a whole section on Gaelic, Lallans, English, Frécossais and that.

THE braid Scots dialect is usually to be found in the SNP's newspaper, the *Scots Independent*, or in letters to *The Scotsman*. But, in 1984, the magazine *Gay Scotland* brought the sonsy old words out of the closet by running a piece of fiction in the dialect. The tale concerned two chaps, Rab and Eck, who went 'fur a dauner intae the wuds'. The story contained numerous references to something called 'a moudie-wart'. The Scottish National Dictionary tells us that 'a moudie-wart' is a 'mole'. Obviously Rab and Eck were on some sort of nature trail. But then Rab related: 'We wis wuntlin a making a dirdum fit tae gar ilka mappie i the wud skeir stramulyert.'

A scene, we fear, we must leave to your imagination.

MUCH of the writing in braid Scots published by the *Scots Independent* was written by SNP activist Peter D. Wright. A typical article said: 'At the hinmaist National Cooncil convene in Larbert, Athole Cameron richtlie myndit the Scottish National Pairty o the neid tae saufgaird and forder the culture, tradeetion and heritage o oor beloued kintra o Scotland. Agin the creepin Anglicisation, deed ay Ameri-canisation alsweill, thare is muckle tae be dune tae mak siccar that a distinctive Scottish identitie is maintained.'

At least one fellow Nationalist disagreed. In a letter to the paper, he said: 'Peter's dialect is not authentic. No one in Scotland uses words like "fremmit" (foreign), "athel" (prince) or "wittinsblad" (which presumably means newspaper). This is just *Oor Wullie* language and an insult to the reader.'

Oor Wullie was not available fur tae comment.

A FARMER'S daughter, newly returned from university with a

degree in English, was finding some of her father's ways a trifle coarse. After her father announced that he was 'awa' to scatter a wheen o' dung' she asked her mother: 'Can we not persuade him to say manure instead of dung?'

'Wheesht, lassie,' the mother replied. 'It's taken me 20 years to get him to say dung.'

THE Diary was indebted to Donald John MacSween, a speaker at the Labour Party's Scottish conference in March 1984, for his help in compiling a glossary of trade union terms in Gaelic. This was in response to a statement by NUPE that the union intended to take more interest in the promotion of the language.

A toirt air bord, as you probably already knew, means: to take on board.

A toirt fa' comhair: to take cognisance.

Aig an deairbh am a tha seo: at this moment in time.

Neart an aonachd againn: this great movement of ours.

And, last but not least:

Dochason an luchd obrachd: the aspirations of the workforce.

A QUESTION in the entrance exam to Napier College's journalism course asked potential journos to explain what *An Communn Gaidhealach* was. One candidate answered: 'The president of Tanzania.'

ON a visit to the Outer Hebrides to take in the *Feis Barraigh* (the Barra Festival), the Diary increased its Gaelic word power simply by reading the programme:

Piobbaireachd le dram: licensed piping display.

Dannsa feillteach, einneir agus dram: carnival dinner dance with licence.

Bairbecuidh agus dram: licensed barbecue.

DOTAMAN, the BBC Gaelic programme for children, consistently gained a higher viewership than much of the rest of BBC Scotland's output. In particular, *Dotaman* regularly attracted more viewers than the channel's flagship politics and current affairs programme, *Right, Left and Centre.* The difference in the ratings had little to do with viewers' enthusiasm for the Gaelic language. The major factor was that *Dotaman* was presented by leggy Gaelette Cathy MacDonald who appeared in uniforms including a tight-fitting, whip-cracking ringmistress's outfit.

SCOTTISH Television hired MORI to conduct an opinion poll to find out what the Scottish public felt about Gaelic broadcasting. The sample of nearly 1,000 people were asked if they spoke Gaelic; 92 per cent said no, 4 per cent said yes, and 4 per cent didn't know.

AN English couple who had recently moved to Argyll applied to the local council to build a house. They intended to call the house *Tigh na Botan*. The Gaelic-speaking official pointed out that this was not a good idea, since the name translated as 'House of the Penis'. Perhaps they could try *Tigh na Batan* or 'Boat House', as they actually meant to call it.

A PRINCE Charles Gooder English Award went to whoever penned an advertisement in which Dundee District Council sought to recruit a press and information officer. It began: 'Due to the waygoing of the present post-holder, a vacancy has arisen for a press and information officer, which post was created to meet the changing needs in respect of the provision of information to the press and general public . . .'

No, experience with a quill pen was not required.

IN these days of sensitivity in matters of race, the colour nigger brown is no more. A Diary correspondent reported that this shade has been replaced on colour charts by something called African Flesh. Doesn't have the same ring to it somehow. Can you imagine your granny popping into Trerons for a pair of African Flesh gloves?

A TALE from Furryboots City. (Aberdeen, of course. 'Furryboots are ye fae, yersel'?)

A visitor to those north-eastern parts told how he attended a social evening in which part of the entertainment was an Elvis Presley look-and-soundalike competition.

One of the contestants appeared initially to be in with a great chance. The rhinestone-studded white suit, the snake-hipped movement, and that mean, bad-boy sneer.

It's a shame that he had to spoil it with his rendition of 'Blue Suede Shoes', which began: 'Yin for the money, twae for the show . . .'

SUCH was the volume of purchases by a lady at a supermarket that, while she was struggling to arrange them into tidy mountains of comestibles at the checkout, a box of cornflakes landed at her feet. On picking it up, and not knowing from which end of the conveyor belt it had escaped, she asked the girl at the till: 'Was this through?' To which the girl replied, in hurt and offended tones: 'Naw, it jist fell!'

AS part of the new freedom enjoyed by Russians, the Avis Press has been allowed to publish the *International Dictionary of Obscenities – A Guide to Dirty Words and Indecent Expressions.* Here are some of the less obscene examples:

Bzd'et: To fart silently.

Loshka gavna v bochki m'oda: A fly in the ointment. This translates literally as 'a spoonful of shit in a barrel of honey'.

Davalka: Nympho.

Bros' dumat' zhopay: quit thinking with your ass.

Kakat: To poop.

Irdun: A person who farts frequently.

OVERHEARD on a North Sea ferry. A Scottish granny is admonishing her half-German grandwean: 'Gretchen! If ye dinnae stoap that you'll get yer heid in your hauns to play wi'.'

A VALUABLE document, a compendium of correspondence sent over the years to various departments of the Western Isles Council, came into the Diary's hands. The following examples highlight the very serious problem of thinking in Gaelic and writing in English:

- I am writing on behalf of my sink, which is running away from the wall.

- The toilet seat is cracked – where do I stand?

- This is to let you know there is a smell coming from the man next door.

- I request permission to remove my drawers in the kitchen.

- Our lavatory seat is broken in half and is now in three pieces.

- Will you please send someone to mend our broken path. Yesterday my wife tripped and fell on it and she is now pregnant.

- Our kitchen floor is very damp, we have two children and would like a third, so will you please send someone to do something about it.

- This is to let you know that our lavatory seat is broken and we cannot get BBC2.

- The toilet is blocked and we cannot bath the children until it is cleared.

- The lavatory is blocked. This is caused by the boys next door throwing their balls on the roof.

- I want some repairs doing to my cooker as it has backfired and burnt my knob off.

- Would you please send a man to look at my water, it is a funny colour and not fit to drink.

- Would you please send a man to repair my spout, I am an old-age pensioner and I need it straightaway.

- I awoke this morning and found my water boiling.

ALSO germane to the subject of

thinking in Gaelic and writing in English is this story from farthest Stornoway. A lady living on the rugged outskirts of said town had an arrangement with her butcher to send her an order of meat on a weekly basis, as travelling all the way into Stornoway for a leg of lamb or two was a wee bit too much for her.

One week, however, she decided she didn't need any meat, as her husband was going to slaughter a sheep for the freezer. Her telegram to the butcher was brief: 'Send no meat. Donald is killing himself.'

STILL on the subject of the Gaelic and the English, a Highland chentleman known to the Diary was explaining to us monoglots how the daily tasks in his household are split between two languages. When he's taking the weans for a nice walk in the park or some other treat, conversation is conducted in Gaelic. When he has the unhappy duty of scolding a child, it is done in English.

THE LAW

The professions, notably lawyers, have been kenspeckle contributors to the Diary's ongoing survey of Scottish life.

GLASGOW lawyer Ross Harper, renowned for his persuasive pleading and witty riposte, also undertook work as a part-time sheriff. Thus he found himself at different times on different sides of the courtroom.

During a case where he had appeared as defence agent, he asked the sheriff to let his client off with a small fine.

'Tell me, Mr Harper,' asked the sheriff, 'what would you do if you were sitting on the bench for this case?'

'I couldn't honestly say, your honour,' Harper replied. 'I have never been presented with such an eloquent plea in mitigation in any of the cases I have presided over.'

ROSS Harper advises young lawyers to finish their speeches to the jury with a piece of purple prose. It may not work, he says, but it is invariably good fun. He quotes one case where he had little to say about the facts of the matter: 'I decided to talk to the jury about justice and waxed lyrical if not eloquent. In conclusion, I held up my hands and said to the jury that as they passed into the jury room I was handing them the crucible of justice, and I made an offering movement with my hands.'

Imagine Mr Harper's surprise when one lady on the jury stood up to collect this crucible.

A MAGISTRATE at Glasgow District Court announced that, although the accused had been found guilty of shoplifting, he was prepared to take into consideration the special circumstances of the case: 'After all, the shop was called Kleptomania.'

SHERIFFS in touch with the lower orders: Sheriff Ewen Stewart is famed on the Northern circuit for his sayings from the Bench and excoriated on occasion by the Appeal Court for using material which is 'irrelevant' or 'based on his own researches'. However, the sheriff remained undeterred, as this quote from him on a case of a child being left unattended indicated: 'From my own experience in life, by nine and a half my friends had taken their tea badge at the Cubs, i.e. prepared the family tea for a week unaided; and I distinctly remember going home from school to an empty house on the servant girls' afternoon off when my mother was out socialising or shopping.'

LORD Jauncey, dispensing justice at the High Court in Airdrie, found himself overruled by a higher authority. The case had reached a critical point and, in order to make progress, his Lordship announced that the court would carry on beyond the normal finishing time.

Up spake a wee wummin from the front row of the jury: 'It's all right for you. But ah've goat ma man's tea tae make.' There was a strained silence while Lord Jauncey considered the situation. Would her man get his tea? Would the woman do some porridge for contempt of court?

Lord Jauncey finally spoke and showed that the qualities of mercy are not strained. He said perhaps the lady juror had a point, and sent them all home in time for tea.

THE reputation of Joe Beltrami, aka The Defender, as one of Glasgow's best-known criminal lawyers, follows him everywhere – even into his place of worship.

Big Joe was attending an Easter service at St Bride's Church in Bothwell. The service included a re-enactment of the Easter story. When it came to the point where Pontius Pilate asks the crowd whether he should let go Jesus or Barabbas, the distinctive Beltrami voice was heard to echo with gusto, 'Free Barabbas! Free Barabbas!'

When Barabbas was duly freed, there was an unscheduled comment from a member of the congregation: 'There's Beltrami got the guilty man off again.'

A WITNESS in Glasgow Sheriff Court was recounting in his evidence how he was on his way to visit 'two chinas'. The sheriff interrupted him in mid-sentence to say he could see no reference in the case papers to any persons of Chinese extraction.

The same sheriff, inquiring about the income of an accused before sentencing him, was told that the poor devil had only £30 a week left after meeting fixed commitments. 'Why, that's hardly enough for a decent lunch,' said his lordship.

AT the Appeal Court in Edinburgh, a man with five aliases failed to turn up. The macer left the court and called him by all five names. He returned to tell Lord Wheatley that 'none of them' had appeared for the appeal. The advocate-depute then asked for a warrant to arrest the man. Lord Wheatley, getting into the spirit of the case, asked: 'Is that for all of them?'

IN a murder trial before Lord Robertson at the High Court in Edinburgh, a pathologist giving evidence wished to demonstrate how, in his opinion, the victim had been strangled. Seeking a model to show how the murderer had grabbed the victim, the pathologist suggested he use the court shorthand writer. Lord Robertson said no, the shorthand writer was not a suitable choice. He indicated that Malcolm, his lordship's macer (legal equivalent of his butler), would do, on the grounds that he was more expendable.

ROSIE Morrison, the colourful and comely advocate, spent three years as a magistrate in the courts of Hong Kong. During her term Ms Morrison was the subject of a complaint by a Chinese male. He was upset because, he said, he could see her breasts through her blouse. Ms Morrison was typically forthright in her reaction: 'My beautiful breasts which have given so much pleasure to so many! I was stunned. I said when they began to show through my tights I might begin to show concern.'

SHERIFFS in touch with the lower orders (contd): An accused in a Lanarkshire sheriff court was giving a long and detailed account of the places where he had been partaking of alcohol on New Year's Eve. He told of various pubs and friends' houses he had visited and added: 'And I had a large whisky at the bells.'

The sheriff interrupted with: 'Tell me, who are these people the Bells?'

A GLASGOW lawyer was making something of a meal of his request to Sheriff Graham Johnston that the sentence imposed on his guilty client should be back-dated to his arrest.

Sheriff Johnston, after sitting through the lengthy, not to say tedious, plea in mitigation, replied that as a special concession he was prepared to back-date the sentence to the beginning of the lawyer's speech.

WHEN the new Glasgow Sheriff Court opened on the south bank of the Clyde in 1986, a number of pubs and restaurants sprang up to provide sustenance to the legal profession. They had suitably legal names, such as Writs and Avizandum. Diary readers came up with their own alternative suggestions for naming a lawyers' pub.

They included Grievous Bodily Arms, Dunplead Inn and Plonkers (this from a lady in the legal profession). Various drinks were suggested, viz: the Penal Colada, the Snowball's Chance (Advocaat and Legal-ade) and the Short Sharp Shock (a sixth of a gill). The winner of the pub name competition was Not Proven's Lordship.

SHERIFF Jackie Stewart of Airdrie proved to be one of the few sheriffs who tried to communicate with young people in their own language, often quoting from pop songs and other areas of popular culture. One youth was released from custody with a warning that the eyes of the law would be on him. If he so much as spat in the street he would be in trouble. 'In fact, just remember that you have Klingons on the starboard bow,' quoth the sheriff.

THE law firm Bird, Semple, Fyfe, Ireland adopted the smart, if impenetrable, new logo, featuring a crescent moon and a sunrise. What does it mean, the legal fraternity asked. One came up with a suitably waspish answer: 'The firm has the sun and the moon, but no stars – and costs the earth.'

DONALD Findlay, QC, is a former director and an ardent supporter of Glasgow Rangers. To his chagrin, his birthday falls on 17 March, St Patrick's Day. Fortunately, his pal, Glasgow solicitor Adrian Toner, who is of the other footballing persuasion, has a birthday on 12 July. An amicable swap was arranged.

LORD Wheatley, the first Catholic lawyer to rise to an eminent position on the Scottish bench, exhibited traits of honesty and sense of humour from his early days. As a young man he worked in the Glasgow law firm of Shaunessy, Quigley and McColl, a firm with strong associations with Celtic Football Club.

Celtic were involved in a Scottish Cup replay which was being played on a Wednesday afternoon. One by one, the senior partners announced that they were leaving for urgent and unavoidable meetings with clients. Just after lunchtime, young Wheatley rose, put on his coat and announced to the office: 'That's me off to Hampden as well.'

LEGEND has it that the town of Stirling once boasted a law firm by the name of Welsh, Robb and Steel. Glasgow firm McLay, Murray and Spence became known by jealous rivals as Delay, Worry and Expense.

ADVOCATES who come through from Edinburgh to ply their trade in Glasgow often have language problems, such as:

Witness: There was a chap at the door.
Advocate: And what was the chap's name?

Witness: So, ah looked at the clock oan the mantelpiece . . .
Advocate: I'm sorry, I don't understand. Who had been wearing a cloak?

Witness: Ah'd jist come oot the Vogue bingo . . .
Advocate: And what was the registration of this vehicle, the Vogue Bingo?

THE traditional Glaswegian slovenly manner of speech can also throw your average Edinburgh advocate. One witness was relating that he had, at the time of an alleged offence, been in his local chip shop purchasing a soft drink and a packet of potato crisps.

What he actually enunciated was that he had been buying 'ginger an'

SAFETY FIRST
PLEASE KEEP YOUR ARMS & LEGS INSIDE THE CAR UNTILL THE CAR STOPS
LIMBS ARE SO DIFFICULT TO REPLACE

criss'. To which the advocate said: 'Can we have the full names of these people Ginger and Chris?'

GIRVAN District Court was the location for this story, of a chap who decided to act as legal adviser to his brother, dispensing with any need for thae solicitor chaps. Hadn't you better get yourself a pen and some paper, he was advised by a court official.

So he asked the police officers in the court if they could oblige with the 'loan' of a bit of paper and a writing implement.

No, they said. As he turned away he called them 'bastards'. This did not go down well with the court. The surrogate legal eagle had even less luck in the afternoon session, when he returned refreshed and was arrested for shouting and swearing. He was fined £40.

As the local paper, the *Carrick Herald*, said on the matter: 'His debut as a "solicitor" wasn't quite in the Joe Beltrami league.'

AND another wee story from the courts . . . A businessman was responsibly but reluctantly performing a spell of jury duty. To his horror, he was nominated to be foreman of the jury. 'No, I can't be foreman,' he said. 'It should be Mr Smith.'

Why, he was asked.

'I'm sitting in the back row and the foreman of the jury has to sit at the front,' he replied.

His fellow members of the jury were considering this dubious legal point when a lady piped up: 'Aye, that's right. That's the way it always is in *LA Law*.'

THE identification parade is a rich source of legal legend and controversy. (Just ask Patrick Connolly Meehan.)

We liked the folk-tale-which-may-well-be-true about the suspect in a robbery case who was in a line-up at the local nick. One of the witnesses asked if she could hear the members of the parade say the words: 'Where's the money?'

This the members of the public on parade duly did. But when it came to the suspect, he didn't seem to understand what was expected of him. He said nothing. 'Where's the money?' barked the policeman in charge.

'It's in the hoose!' said the suspect – or the accused as he soon became known.

THE scene was Glasgow Sheriff Court. The charge was assault by stabbing. The procurator-fiscal's examination of the victim went something along these lines:

'Did something happen to you around October 1989?'
  'Ah wis thingmied.'
'What were you thingmied with?'
'A thingmy.'
'So what you are telling us is that,

in October 1989, you were thing-mied with a thingmy.'

'Aye.'

'Can you tell the court where you were thingmied?'

'Aye. In the what do you call it . . . you know.'

Subsequently, a submission that the Crown had failed to thingmy their case was upheld.

WORTHY of a passing mention is the accused at Edinburgh Sheriff Court who, when asked how he would like to plead, replied: 'Not proven.'

A LAWYER at Glasgow Sheriff Court was trying to persuade the bench that an assault case should be adjourned until a certain witness was able to attend.

The sheriff was reluctant since the case had already been adjourned four times due to non-appearance of said witness. What vital evidence would she be able to contribute, he asked?

'The young lady will testify that she made love to the accused 15 minutes before the alleged attack and she will state that at that time he did not have an offensive weapon in his trousers.'

A DUNDEE court was hearing a case involving a fracas outside a Chinese takeaway. Part of the evidence related to an item of nourishment which had been purchased from the takeaway.

'And what happened to the carry-out food?' the defence lawyer asked.

The witness replied: 'A' e' i' a'.' Thus becoming, possibly, the first witness in a courtroom to utter a full sentence without a consonant.

AN accused in a case at Falkirk Sheriff Court showed some skill as a pleader.

He had been involved in a fight with another youth. Despite the fact that they were both pleading guilty, his co-accused brought in the services of a well-known Glasgow criminal law firm. Our man decided to repres-ent himself.

The Glasgow lawyer duly made a lengthy and eloquent plea in miti-gation. Our man, when asked what he had to say for himself, replied: 'Ah'm jist an erse.'

Both received the same sentence.

THE High Court in Edinburgh was hearing evidence about a fracas invol-ving a number of men who chased their alleged victim into Tony's Café, an Edinburgh chip shop. The man was asked: 'What do you remember about events in the chip shop?'

'I was getting battered,' replied the witness.

THE Airdrie criminal element remember fondly Elish McPhilomy despite her attempts as a depute procurator-fiscal to lock them away. Indeed at the get-together to mark Ms McPhilomy's departure to work in Edinburgh, a well-known local offender turned up clutching an impressive bouquet of flowers. These he handed over while delivering a short speech to the effect that even though the lovely Ms McPhilomy had personally been responsible for an adverse result on each of his last six appearances, he was full of admiration for her. At this point the well-mannered recidivist departed, spoiling the effect of his gesture more than somewhat with his parting shot: 'By the way, I stole the flowers.'

FROM Dumbarton, that unruly legal province on the north-west of the Clyde, such was the volume of work caused by people up to nae good that an annexe had to be opened, consisting of two new courts. The annexe was located through the wall from a public house. Thus justice was dispensed daily in the court to the distant but audible accompaniment of honky-tonk music from next door. In these circumstances, Sheriff John Fitzsimmons was doing his best to maintain the dignity of his court. One accused was found guilty. Sheriff Fitzsimmons asked the defence lawyer to make his plea in mitigation. Just as he was about to do so, the court was treated to a rendition from next door of that old Connie Francis favourite 'Who's Sorry Now?'.

A POLISMAN giving evidence in an assault case at Glasgow Sheriff Court was asked to tell the court what had been said during the affray. He told how one of the accused had shouted to him: 'Away and sook your plums!' The fiscal, understandably, asked the polisman if he could elaborate on what this unusual imprecation might mean. At this point the defence lawyer (no less a person than Joe Beltrami) leapt to his feet with the words: 'Don't answer that. You're not an expert witness. You're not a greengrocer!'

A CHILDREN'S panel was discussing whether or not a child should be taken into care. The lawyer acting for the parents was trying to establish when a certain event occurred. Could they pin down the date by associating it to a birthday or some other notable event? After a moment's thought the wife turned to her beloved and asked: 'When wis it again that you stabbed me?'

A SOCIAL inquiry at Furryboots City Sheriff Court said of the offender: 'He does not seek to excuse himself of responsibility for the offences. In fact, he accepts responsibility for all charges, including those dropped by the procurator-fiscal.'

THE centenary dinner of the XIII Club, a select gathering of Glasgow intellectuals which has a get-together every 13 February, was regaled with a tale from the days when lawyers were gentlemen. Sorry, I'll rephrase that – when lawyers were even more gentlemanly than they are today. The speaker in question was Ron Neil, the

man in charge of BBC Television news and current affairs. He was referring to his father, John Neil. Neil Senior was so proper in his behaviour that, when one day he was accosted by a footpad and relieved of his wallet and gold watch, he pursued the perpetrator shouting the words: 'Stop alleged thief! Stop alleged thief!'

A CASE at Edinburgh Sheriff Court resulted in a most unusual unanimous verdict of not proven. The verdict did not surprise one experienced legal practitioner who remarked: 'It always happens after that film has been on the telly.' That film, it transpires, is *Twelve Angry Men*, Sydney Lumet's gripping tale of how one man of principle convinces the rest of a jury to acquit a man accused of murder on grounds of reasonable doubt. The film had, indeed, been on BBC2 the previous Sunday night.

TWO young criminal types in Ayr swiped a bag containing half a hundredweight of 10p coins from a shop in the Honest Toon. They then made their way to an amusement arcade to spend their ill-gotten gains on the various machines. The extent of their loot excited the suspicion of the manager who dialled 999. The two master criminals spotted the arriving polis and made good their escape. The boys in blue were about to give chase when their attention was drawn to the sound of the photo booth churning out four pin-sharp, self-incriminating pictures of the villains.

THERE was a case in Glasgow involving murder and mayhem, the full details of which need not concern youse gentle readers. A great deal of the evidence had to do with the fact that various miscreants were under the effects of drink and a drug called Temazepam. One middle-aged lady member of the jury was heard to remark to a fellow juror: 'I think I understand it all so far. Except for the bits about the tomato plants.'

ONE cannot accuse Joe Beltrami, the leading lawyer, of not doing his homework. Joe caused some head-scratching in Loretto's, a Glasgow Italian restaurant, when he challenged his lunchtime companions, a team of legal eaglets, to name the river which flows through Florence. 'The Tiber,' quoth one. 'No, no,' said Joe.

'How about the Po?' suggested another. 'Dear, dear,' said Joe (who always says everything twice), shaking his head. 'Everyone knows it is the Arno. The Arno. I'm shocked you don't know. Shocking, shocking.'

As the lunch ended, one of the company furtively approached the Italian restaurateur. 'Go and say to Joe how much you enjoyed as a boy in Florence walking beside the river Tiber,' he suggested. The Italian looked dismayed. 'I cannot,' he protested. 'But it's just a wee joke,' said the lawyer. 'No,' said the Italian, 'it cannot be done.' 'Why not?' asked the lawyer. 'Because,' replied the harassed Italian, 'Big Joe, he ask me just half-hour ago – hey, what ees the river that run through Florence?'

THE common-law widow, if there is such a thing, of one of the victims of a gangland slaying proved a formidable witness when the case came to the High Court. She was asked if her man was of regular habits. She snapped: 'His tea was oan the table at five. If he wisnae there he didn't get it.' Asked if he had any other girl-friends, she smiled grimly: 'He had wan wance.' Pause. 'Why? Are ye gonnie surprise me?'

Another witness poured scorn on the evidence that the murder victim had another lady friend, Miss X. He said: 'He was a big, brave boy – but no way would he have been parked with Miss X outside his girlfriend's house. First, she would have beaten up Miss X, then she would have beaten up the car.'

In the same trial a witness, a hardened criminal, described a fellow villain as: 'Not a very nice person.' Asked for clarification he replied: 'He's a f****** toerag!'

A LEGAL eaglet exhibited a lack of knowledge of the ways of the lower orders when he was defending a citizen charged with recklessly discharging an air pistol. He decided that the only fruitful route for an acquittal was to claim that the air pistol was not a vandal's plaything but was used for hunting. 'What does the accused hunt with the gun?' was the not unreasonable question from the man on the bench. The lawyer consulted his client who could only say that it was a slug gun. 'My client uses that gun to hunt slugs, your honour,' he told an astonished court.

A YOUNG lawyer was appearing at Ayr Sheriff Court for a client who had an appalling record for offences of dishonesty and was about to be sentenced for another. In his attempt to mitigate his client's behaviour the lawyer told the sheriff that virtually all of the accused's previous convictions were drink-related. His client, he went on, had decided to turn over a new leaf and had been attending a local rehabilitation unit. His treatment had been going very well, he told the sheriff, who seemed suitably impressed. Then the lawyer added: 'I would be misleading your lordship if I didn't tell you that there have been one or two hiccups along the way.'

A LAWYER acting for a man on a charge of rape received a visit from the accused's wife. The lawyer had the difficult task of explaining to her that things were not looking too good. He explained that the evidence was pretty strong and her man was facing a substantial jail sentence. 'I know,' she said, 'and, of course, he's done it before.' The puzzled lawyer consulted his files and said: 'Are you sure? I don't see any record here of a previous conviction for rape.' 'Oh, aye,' she says. 'He raped the wumman up the stair.' 'Did the case go to court?' the lawyer asked. 'Oh, no. She didnae tell the polis,' the woman explained. 'We've got awfy good neighbours.'

CHINA Syndrome: A woman was giving evidence against her husband who was accused of beating her up. The defence lawyer, struggling for a line, asked if it was not the case that her husband had suffered a serious head injury and had a metal plate in his skull. 'Aye,' she said, 'but there are times when I think he's got a cup and saucer in there as well.'

FROM Stornoway Sheriff Court we heard the story of a young man who pled guilty to stealing a quantity of frozen prawns, some of which, he admitted, he had sold later at the back door of a local hotel. Sheriff Donald Booker Milburn, who had flown over from Inverness the day before to take the court, duly fined the accused. Then, recalling that he had stayed at this very hotel and further recalling his dinner menu, he

reflected that his connection with the case was closer than merely passing sentence: 'I think I may have eaten some of the evidence in this case.'

THE occasion of Sheriff J. Irvine Smith's retirement caused a flurry of anecdote and memories. The sheriff, for long a terrorist and a humorist in the bailiwicks of Glasgow and Greenock, had semi-retired to Rothesay to be the only law west of Gourock.

A famous client of Irvine Smith's was the late Barney Noone. It is fair to say that he had developed a rapport with Sheriff J. This went as far as poetry. One day, having been found guilty, Mr Noone wrote a message in verse which he asked be passed to the bench. The sheriff read the poetic plea in mitigation and, without hesitation, pronounced: 'Thirty days hath September, April, June, and Barney Noone.'

THE sheriff was famous for his short, sharp custodial method of dealing with chaps who had fallen behind with payment of their fines. In his first such court at Greenock, he was banging away defaulters to such a fine tune that the polisman in charge of the Bar-L bus felt it necessary to approach Irvine Smith in his chambers during a recess to inform him that the vehicle was already full and that there was no more room at the inn. The sheriff casually reached for a copy of the Yellow Pages and handed it to the cop with the words: 'I believe you'll find it under coach hire.'

IRVINE Smith was a hard man when it came to the question of bail. There is the story of the traumatic time when he suffered a heart attack in court. As he was helped into his chambers, he managed to whisper to a court official: 'Tell him bail's refused.'

THE sheriff's uncompromising attitude often elicited a response from the accused. As one chap was being led away for a taste of porridge, he let slip the phrase 'F****** bastard'. Irvine Smith, with his keen hearing, picked this up. Asked to elaborate, the felon claimed it was not a reference to the sheriff. Irvine Smith begged to differ: 'I don't see anyone else in the courtroom who answers that description.'

AFTER having heard a case Irvine Smith asked the accused: 'Have you anything to say?' 'F*** all,' replied the accused in muffled tones. 'What did he say?' Sheriff J. asked the clerk to the court. 'F*** all,' replied the clerk. 'Funny,' said the sheriff, 'I'm sure I saw his lips move.'

LEN Murray, the solicitor, recounts two Irvine Smith stories of a slightly perverse nature. Two homosexuals appeared before the sheriff, having pled guilty to the type of conduct which was then still regarded as criminal. He deferred sentence on them to give them the chance to 'pull themselves together'. The sheriff's penchant for original repartee is further illustrated in the story of the transvestite. He deferred sentence on him, telling him to 'go away and be a good girl'.

HAVING listened to an accused recite his version of events, Irvine Smith leaned forward and told him: 'You are a fecund liar.' 'Oh, no, I'm not,' said the accused. 'I'm telling the f****** truth!'

AN accused, prior to being sentenced by Sheriff Irvine Smith, declared: 'As God is my judge I am innocent!'

Sheriff J. quickly replied: 'He's not. I am. You are fined £50.'

ADDRESSING a businessmen's lunch club, Irvine Smith intoned: 'Gentlemen. You see, standing before you, the Messiah.' A hush fell as the audience began to ponder the sanity of this pillar of the establishment. 'Yes, gentlemen, the Messiah,' he went on. 'Only this morning an unfortunate was dragged before me in court and I heard him mutter, "Oh, it's him, Jesus Christ".'

A CONVICTED wife-beater, having copped a stiffish nine months, protested that he had 'only hit her the wanst'. 'Oh, well, then,' said the sheriff, 'you do not qualify for our quantity discount.'

A LAWYER friend was dining in the Malmaison with Irvine Smith. It was a cold day in the mid-1960s, when the mini-skirt was in vogue, and the legal eagles were transfixed by the entrance of two young women whose skirts would have qualified as wide belts had they been a fraction shorter. Regaining his breath and aplomb, the sheriff dryly remarked: 'If they're not careful they'll get chaps between their legs.'

IRVINE Smith was sentencing a bruiser in the dock to three months. 'Three months?' quoth he, in disdain. 'I could dae that staunin' on ma' heid.' 'In that case, replied Sheriff Smith, 'you can have another three months for contempt of court. Perhaps that will help you find your feet.'

THE LOBEY DOSSIER

ONE of the great highlights – but potentially the greatest disaster – of my career as a diary columnist was the great Lobey Dosser statue campaign.

Glasgow artist Calum Mackenzie came up with the concept of building a statue to the memory of Bud Neill, the cartoonist who entranced readers of the *Evening Times, Daily Record* and *Scottish Daily Express* in the 1950s, '60s and '70s. After the very first mention in the Diary of the plan, it became obvious that Bud Neill was a subject close to the heart of the people of Scotland.

The Diary ambitiously and perhaps foolishly agreed to organise the raising of the £18,000 which it would cost. The stookie is in the form of Lobey Dosser and his faithful two-legged horse, El Fideldo. And this soon involved me in dealing with up to 500 letters a week containing contributions and answering scores of telephone calls.

Fortunately, the letters which flooded the Diary contained, as well as cheques and postal orders, people's rich memories of Bud Neill and his work.

PROFESSOR Alan Alexander of Strathclyde Business School wrote: 'I hope my memory does not deceive me when I remember a Bud Neill cartoon of a barber cutting a customer's hair. I do not recall the caption, but among the small ads pinned to the mirror was a card reading "Budgies Repaired".

'There was a bored clippie in another cartoon, standing on the platform of her car saying: "Awfy quiet the day! Ah wish a cheeky wee man wid come oan wi' six dugs, smoke doonsterrs an' spit oan the flerr".'

ANOTHER memorable Bud Neill Glasgow clippie was captured for posterity, standing on the platform of her caur, all beads, bangles and war-paint, singing:

'I dream of Jeannie wi' the light brown herr.
Wan inside and two up the sterr.'

JACK WEIR, a Glasgow journalist, told how Bud used to give away ball-point pens on which he had printed 'Bud Neill – the funniest man since Rasputin'. Mr Weir's favourite Neill cartoon showed 'the man of the house standing in a doorway, clutching the

good suit-trousers at the waist. Braces dangle from his outstretched palm and the caption reads: "Aw right. Who's took the knot oot ma galluses an' spylt the mechanics o' the hale device?".'

A SIMPLE but side-splitting caption accompanied a cartoon of doctor at a patient's bedside.

Doctor: 'Comfy?'

Patient: 'Govan.'

ALISON McKenzie has a unique memento of Lobey Dosser, the Calton cowboy hero. Her father, Joe McKenzie, a journalist with the *Evening Times*, was a friend of Bud Neill, and he arranged for Bud to fill a page of her autograph book with a special drawing of the sheriff of Calton Creek. In the course of his duties, Joe also found himself back-stage at the Glasgow Empire after a performance of the Roy Rogers show. Being a dutiful dad, he produced Alison's autograph book for an inscription by the singing cowboy.

Roy Rogers spotted the drawing of Lobey Dosser and was so intrigued to hear of the Glasgow cowboy that he wrote his message to Alison on the same page. Alison was pleased at the time, but over the years she has come to regret that her beloved drawing of Lobey has been defaced with the signatures of Roy, Trigger (actually, Roy wrote Trigger's name – the horse had difficulty holding a pen in its hoof) and Dale Evans.

SAM McKinlay, the former editor of the *Evening Times* who first spotted the talents of Bud Neill, wrote from Woking in Surrey: 'Bud was a wonderful man. Quirky, touchy to a fault (his captions were inviolable), very, very amusing when he was in full cry, and with an unrivalled command of the Glasgow idiom.

'A percipient punter once said to him in Sammy Dow's [the *Times* pub]: "Aye, Bud, ye've a rerr lug for the patter." He was not only a gifted cartoonist and something of a comic genius with his choice of names for the Lobey Dosser series, but a shrewd observer of the local and national scene.

'I cherish a drawing of his which I felt ever since it appeared should have been reproduced regularly, rather in the way the *New Yorker* reproduces its famous cover every year on the anniversary of its first appearance. Bud's drawing was of three of his typical Glasgow wifies meeting on a street corner. The caption read: "Mrs Broon, this is Mrs Thomson. Mrs Thomson disney know whit the world's coming to, do ye, Mrs Thomson?"

'I think of Bud every time I come across one of the many stupidities in our jumbled world.'

BUD Neill's surrealism was quoted by James Thomson of Glenrothes when he wrote to mention his favourite Neill cartoon. It showed a large lady, dressed in a peenie, hands on hips and clutching a scrubbing brush, standing in the doorway of a medieval castle with knights in armour galloping about in the background. She demands indignantly: 'Which wan o' youse galoots huz went an' slew a dragon a' ower ma clean doorstep?'

ERIC D. CLARK of St Andrews recalled a pocket cartoon which would have been equally topical today. There had been reports of an operating theatre in a Glasgow hospital closed because of its dirty condition.

Neill had the surgeon asking for: 'Scalpel, forceps . . . wee brush and shovel.'

HOWEVER, while there was a huge response from people of a certain age who remembered and revered the works of Mr Neill, especially the Lobey cartoon strips, there were a number of younger people who asked who or what is Lobey Dosser and just who was this guy Bud Neill.

So, as a service, we provided about 20 things (well, 17 actually) you may or may not know about Bud Neill:

- Bud Neill was born in Glasgow in 1911.

- He may or may not have graduated from Glasgow School of Art.

- He was working as a bus driver just after the Second World War when

he wrote an extremely cheeky letter to the *Glasgow Herald*. A smart cookie called Sam McKinlay, editor of the *Evening Times*, invited him to write for his newspaper. At this point, Bud Neill revealed that he also did wee drawings.

- Bud did a series of pawky pocket cartoons for the *Evening Times* before embarking in 1949 on the Lobey Dosser strip cartoon.

- Lobey Dosser was the sheriff of Calton Creek, a township in Arizona (pronounced Arizon-ey) populated entirely by *émigré* Glaswegians. His arch enemy was Rank Bajin, the accredited local villain, a man who had had the benefit of a public-school education.

- Bud Neill was no respecter of geography, which explains the presence in this Glaswegian cowboy saga of an African chieftain from Yoker.

- Also from Yoker in the Lobey Dosser strip was a character called Fairy Nuff, who wore tackety boots and who, in true pantomime-fairy tradition, spoke only in verse. Her compatriots in the strip included Rid Skwerr, a Russian spy who had defected to the West and had been given a job by the Calton Creek district council as official haunter of the local cemetery, Big Chief Toffy Teeth and Pawnee Mary o' Argyll.

- Bud Neill wrote and drew 20 separate adventures of Lobey

Dosser before becoming thoroughly sick of the character.

• Bud, in fact, killed off his hero in one of these episodes. He also had Rank Bajin reforming and becoming a good guy. But, at the end of the story, he told the readers that it had all been a dream. Whaur's your Bobby Ewing and *Dallas* noo?

• His ambition was to be a writer not a drawer. But, as the inventor of the keelie cartoon genre, he was drawn back to Glasgow humour in his (unpublished) novel *Dan, Dan, the Lavatory Man*, based on the attendant in the public toilets in St Vincent Street, Glasgow.

• At the height of his career, Neill was a megastar, earning big bucks in the 1950s and 1960s. He was a snappy dresser – the first man in Glasgow to wear a zoot suit – and also favoured flashy, hand-painted silk ties.

• Bud was an accomplished player of the mouth organ. He entered a competition for harmonica players at the Pavilion before the war. Larry Adler was the judge and declared Bud a clear winner. Mr Adler offered to fix Bud up with the job of moothie-player in Artie Shaw's band. But Bud preferred to stay in Glasgow, thank God.

• Bud had a pet crow called Ranky. He found Ranky stunned at the roadside in Stepps and adopted him. He rigged up a clothes pole as a perch for Ranky in the back seat of his V8 Pilot motor car. He also took Ranky into pubs where the crow would consume half-pints of beer. Bud himself consumed rather more than Ranky.

• Bud was the supreme Scottish pocket cartoonist, specialising in Glasgow bachles with shopping bags. His words were even more telling than his pictures. He wrote:

Winter's came, the snow has fell
Wee Josie's nose is froze as well
Wee Josie's frozen nose is skintit
Winter's diabolic, intit?

• Bud's technique when drawing a cartoon was 'to start with a neb'. This applied even when he was creating massive, full-colour works such as the Battle of Bannockburn.

• One of Bud's early creations was a Glasgow chap who was to be found hanging around street corners. He was called The Big Yin.

• Bud died in 1970 at the age of 59.

Some correspondents felt that Rank Bajin, Lobey's arch enemy, did not receive the acclaim he deserved. The hooded, fedora'd villain, recalled one lady, had a precise, even scholarly, way with language. Once, urging on his steed (a conventional four-legged one) on some nefarious errand, Rank uttered the memorable threat: 'Forward at an increased pace, horse, or I shall have you painted by Matisse.'

BIG Chief Toffy Teeth was another favourite with readers of the Lobey

Dosser cartoon strip. The chief had a way with words. Once, dealing with a revolt among the squaws of his tribe about discrimination against women on the matter of holiday entitlement, he settled the argument by explaining: 'None but the braves deserve the Fair.'

FROM the bottomless well of Bud Neill humour, Ramsay Armstrong of Forth, Lanarkshire, recalled a pocket cartoon in which a Neillian lady has her small son over her knee raising clouds of dust from his backside with the words: 'I'll teach you tae play peever wi' yer maw's tap set.'

A. TODD of West Kilbride brought back memories not only of Bud but also of one of Glasgow's famous bakeries with a cartoon of the archetypal housewives clutching message-bags. One is saying: 'Peacock's is awfy good for functions so they are. If ah wis functionin' ah wid go there, so ah wid.'

THEN there was Bud Neill's poetry. Avril Stephens remembered (with the help of her aunt Betty Paterson, a Bud Neill *aficionado*) a typical verse from one of the Lobey Dosser strips:

I shot an arrow in the air
It landed I know not where.
I don't care
I've got mair up the stair.

A lesser-known but still beloved piece of Neill verse was entitled 'Spring':

The Snow drop drips;
The crocus croaks;

And in my little windae box
A yelly daffy hings its heid –
It does indeed.
Oh, daff, could you but heid your
* hing,*
Nae bother wad it be tae rhyme
Your heiding hing wi' Spring.

EVEN Bud Neill's fishmongers became involved in the reminiscences with some fond memories of the man. Hamish and Livvy Neill, distant relations of Bud, had an upmarket fishmonger's in Mitchell Street opposite the old *Evening Times* building.

Bud would often pop in for a coffee and chat, usually when he should have been delivering cartoon strips to an increasingly anxious Dr Sam McKinlay, editor of the *Evening Times*.

To avoid the wrath of his editor, Bud would have the drawings delivered by one of the fishmongers. If he suspected that Dr Sam was particularly upset by late delivery of said drawings, a wee parcel of fish was often dispatched as well.

HAMISH NEILL tells that another of Bud Neill's diverse talents was that he was an excellent shot. 'He would bring rabbits into the shop. Normally, rabbits that had been shot would be blasted with shotgun pellets. Bud's were shot neatly through the head with a .22 rifle.'

AS somebody or other said: 'Bud was one of the immortals. It's a pity he's deid.'

BRIDIE McPHERSON

The Diary's search for Glasgow's missing clippie.

WE have to thank the National Museum of Science and Industry in London for some long overdue recognition of the Glasgow tram conductress. The museum had a drama programme in which they said: 'History comes to life with actors/ interpreters inspiring children to learn about such colourful characters as Amy Johnson (*Gypsy Moth*); Thomas Crapper of flush-loo fame; Bridie McPherson, the Glasgow tram conductress; Michael Faraday, the father of electricity; and many more.'

There was, however, one question which sprang to mind: who the hell was Bridie McPherson? We wracked our brains and fully ten seconds later realised we had never heard of Bridie, the famous Glasgow conductress. Other famous Glasgow tram-lore brains were duly wracked but still there was no information on Bridie McPherson.

We asked the museum to cum-oan gettaff and gie us an explanation. A very nice man called Guy Thomas, spokesman for the project, admitted that they had made up the Bridie character. But she was 'based on extensive research into the working lives of women on the trams'.

Bridie's character was 'ebullient, outgoing, extrovert and strong'. (You're telling us, pal, if she was typical of the tramcar breed.) The script which the museum drama project had concocted for Bridie included her having to cope with wee Glasgow drunk men and recalcitrant urchins.

While it was nice to see the Museum of Science and Industry in London keep Glasgow's tramcar history alive, us chaps at the Diary felt there should be some indigenous input. We asked our dear readers to come up with an authentic life story for Bridie.

Details soon emerged of the life and working times of Bridie McPherson, the Glasgow tram conductress.

WILLIAM HADDOW of Pollokshields was quickly into the breach with a story about a group of Glasgow Yoonie divinity students who boarded a No. 3 tram and climbed to the upper saloon which was otherwise deserted. After Bridie had collected their fares they dared to interfere in her domain by turning round all the reversible seats and settling down to read their newspapers, thus giving

SHIEK-MA-TADGERS
(MASSAGE PARLOUR)
7 SCHIPKA PASS, GLASGOW X
PROP. J. BARTON

pedestrians the impression that the caur was trundling backwards. Sensing something was amiss, Bridie investigated and chucked them all off with the ringing rejoinder: 'Wait until yiz come oot as ministers afore ye start pesterin' decent folk!'

M. JOYCE from Eaglesham remembered that Bridie was Amazonian in physique and temperament. She plied her trade on the old No. 7, commonly known as the Yella Caur, which went from Bellahouston to Riddrie. She could often be seen at either terminus changing the overhead trolley rope with her teeth, while counting the money in her cash bag.

BILL Waddell from Cumbernauld wondered if it was the one and same Bridie McPherson who attested in court that her driver, seeing an elderly pedestrian on the track, 'started tae stoap but couldnae go slow fast enough tae avoid a mis-hap'?

MRS D. BROWN from Helensburgh

remembered Bridie McPherson when she took her 'Ha'penny Special' tram ride from Hillhead High School to the Hughenden playing fields on Great Western Road on games afternoon. As the tram slithered to a halt at the stop, Bridie would hang off the platform, hand extended to stop the rush and shout: 'Staun back! Staun back! It's the weans fae the potted heid school gaun' tae play games again!'

THE titan terror of the trams was well remembered by Mrs Alice Forsyth of Inverkeithing: 'Bridie stood five feet ten in her diamond-mesh stockinged soles. Her bosom was of such proportions that Black's of Greenock used one of her brassieres as the prototype for their igloo tents and she augmented her niggardly wage from the Corporation Transport Department through a number of sponsorship deals with the manufacturers of peroxide, Polyfilla and kirby grips, which last she used in vast numbers to secure her clippie's

bonnet, worn folded in half and over the "French roll" below the bouffant hairstyle which added four inches to her natural height.' Mrs Forsyth's favourite memory of Bridie dates back to a wet winter night when she was travelling home to Parkhead. An elderly man, cold and wet and drunk, boarded the tram in the Gallowgate. Displeased at his inebriated presence, Bridie towered over him while he tried to find money to enable him to buy a ticket. Eventually he found a threepenny bit and asked the impatient Bridie, 'How faur kin ah go fur thruppence, hen?' Bridie heaved her bosom and tempered justice with compassion in her rejoinder, 'You may kiss the tips of my fingers and then get aff!'

DOUGLAS Brown from Stranraer recalled an incident when Bridie was going up the stairs wearing a rather tight short skirt which had ridden up a little. A downstairs passenger called out in the face of Bridie's fleshy rear, 'My, the full moon's out tonight.' 'Aye,' retorted Bridie, 'and there'll be a wee man in it tonight.'

THE unflappability of the Glasgow clippie was further well illustrated by Mr T. Hughes of Bellshill, who told of the Saturday-night drunk who boarded the tram at Glasgow Cross and asked Bridie for a fourpenny one to Springburn. 'It's a tuppenny wan fur you,' said the conductress. 'I said a fourpenny one,' he repeated. 'And I said a tuppenny,' insisted Bridie, 'to Castle Street and the Royal Infirmary. There's an axe stickin' oot the back o' yer heid.'

ELLEN JAPP of High Blantyre told how Bridie coped with fare-dodgers: 'She noticed that one man sat every morning and stared out of the window, never offering his fare.' This despite Bridie using her considerable lung power in requesting that passengers tender their cash. Finally it all became too much for Bridie. She stepped off the tram at the next stop, walked round the outside until she reached the window where the man was sitting, held out her hand and mouthed the words: 'Ferrs, please!'

BRIDIE also did a stint on Glasgow buses, where one of her drivers was a West Indian. An old lady stopped the bus to ask if its route took it along Main Street, Bridgeton. Bridie answered in the affirmative. To her great scunnerment, the old lady proceeded to walk to the front of the bus where she asked the driver the same question. He confirmed that the bus did indeed go along Main Street. The old lady climbed aboard to be greeted by these words from Bridie: 'Is that you happy, noo, ye've goat it in black an' white.'

JIM MacDONALD of Drymen related how Bridie was once taken to task for wearing an excess of make-up. The actual words, from a troublesome female passenger, were: 'You've enough clairt oan yir face to make pancakes.' 'Aye, missus, an' you've enough fat oan yir erse tae fry them in,' she replied.

F. CRAIG from Crow Road, Glasgow, was there on an occasion when Bridie was trying to eject a drunk from the platform of her tram. 'Get aff,' she said. 'Aff. O-F-F. Aff.'

DOUGLAS GILCHRIST of Beauly

told how his father-in-law was there the day Bridie took pity on a poor man who was being harassed by unthinking fellow passengers. The man was at the front of the queue waiting to alight from the tram. He was of a nervous disposition, the step was on the high side, and he was waiting for the tram to come to a complete halt before stepping off. The chap had what was called in those days a 'humphy back'. Seeing his predicament and irritated by the abuse he was receiving, Bridie leapt to his defence with a loud bellow: 'Gie the boy a chance. It's no' a parachute he's got in there!'

BRIDIE may have gone to the great caur depot in the sky but her spirit lives in Glasgow transportation circles. In fact, she appears to be working as a station announcer on the Glasgow Underground, or Subway as we prefer to call it. The scene is Hillhead station. Bridie announces that the Inner Circle is out of service and would passengers please use the Outer Circle. (Readers from furth of the city should contact their nearest Glaswegian for an explanation of that last bit.) The passengers dutifully move to the bit of the platform that serves the Outer Circle. Except for one chap who is still hovering on the Inner Circle side. Bridie comes back on the blower: 'Would passengers please note that the Inner Circle is out of service. Please use the Outer Circle . . . Aye, ah mean you!' Embarrassed passenger shuffles over to join the rest, many of them unable to conceal large grins.

MALAPROPAGATION

The Diary, with its abiding interest in the use of language, was pleased to begin a wide-ranging dialogue on malapropism and misspeak.

AMONG items received for the Diary archives were the Collected Pearls of Wisdom of a chap called Bill, recently retired from a certain department of Glasgow District Council.

Bill was fond of saying that since he began in the business there has been 'a lot of washing under the bridge'.

When the time came to go metric, Bill remarked: 'Okay, I'm willing to go metric – 44 millimetres, aye, that's nearly an inch.'

Bill had enough 'savvy flerr' when it came to an office politics to conclude difficult transactions with the words, 'Have you got that in writing – no, well, I didn't say it.'

Bill was a great man for separating 'the dross from the rubble'. After a particularly busy day Bill would claim to be 'fragmented out of my mind' or occasionally 'feeling like a well-skelped rabbit'. Sometimes he 'didn't know if ah'm on foot or on horse-back'.

After such a day, and if the pay cheque was in, he would go to the pub for a few 'Glen Fillets' and would return to say the pub was so busy 'there wasnae room tae swing a dug'.

Bill was never a man 'to kill the fatted goat'. He would talk about his favourite sport of golf and compare his three-wood to his driver. One was like using a rapier, the other a cutlet.

Bill would discuss the news of the day saying wasn't it terrible that story in the paper about the poor cyclist 'who had had his leg decapitated'.

He would always find time to telephone his wife at home, once with the famous words: 'Is that you sitting with your feet on the mantelpiece warming your bum at the fire . . . Oh, sorry, missus, wrong number.'

THERE were obviously a lot more people about like Bill. Joining him in the hall of fame was the manager (anonymous) of a factory in one of the new towns who warned during a dispute: 'Any more trouble and I'll be up these stairs like a ton of bricks.' On another occasion he told the girls in the office he wanted them 'to do the infantry'.

He mentioned once that a colleague had a big, new car with a venereal roof. And said of a noted ladies' man: 'He fancies himself as a bit of a Juan Fangio.'

As our informant wrote: 'That's it

in a nutmeg. I would appreciate anonymity as the man concerned is still going strong and he would not be enamelled about this.'

FROM Carluke came the story of a lady who extolled the quality of the fruit cocktail drinks available at her golf club: 'Nice and fizzy with bits of apple, banana and pineapple topped with a marijuana cherry.'

LOCAL government was a rich source of the pearl of wisdom and malapropism. A councillor in Renfrew district opined that 'this item on the agenda is incontinent'. He also characterised a difficult situation by saying: 'We have buttered our bread and now we have to lie on it . . .'

This councillor also had a knack of handling public meetings. He invited a question 'from the lady at the back. No, not you. The woman beside the wee, fat, baldy man.' Needless to say the wee, fat, baldy man was not pleased and wanted to discuss the matter outside.

ANOTHER Bill-like figure worked in Glasgow Corporation some years ago. His pearls included:

- There are no flies in his ointment.

- He hit the ground with tremendous momento.

- His house was insulated on a top of a hill.

- When you get down to square brass tacks.

- He was illegible to join the club.

THEN there was this woman who went on her holidays to Pompeii. 'You know, the place where the saliva runs down the mountain,' as she told her workmates.

Or the shop steward in negotiations with his employers who said. 'We'll cross that bridge when it rears its ugly head.'

Or the woman from Bridgeton who did the Vermin's Pools every week and was a regular visitor to the Odious Cinema in Rutherglen.

BY far the most impressive submission of acrobatic *bon mots* was the list of 300 sayings uttered over the years by a certain unnamed production manager. (For some reason, most of our contributors on this subject wished to remain anonymous.) This gent's sayings included:

PLEASE TAKE YOUR LITTER HOME

- I went through it with a fine tooth pick.

- It folds up like a banjo.

- Correct me if I'm right.

- Just let him stew in his own goose.

- He jumped in with two feet where angels fear to tread.

- That's me reading between the lines and making five.

- The rose is always redder on the other side of the fence from here.

- We're going down to talk roast turkey with them.

- He's had two runs at the cherry.

The problem was 'with all disrespect' that if the above-mentioned manager found out about this 'heads would fly'.

ALSO worthy of mention was the car park attendant at Glasgow School of Art who guided a lecturer into a space with the words: 'That's right, surr, jist park yer motor up there, paralyse wi' Miss Smith's.'

MR Rikki Fulton wrote to tell us that reading the Diary's malapropisms he laughed so much over his cornflakes that his 'treasure' came rushing to see if he had taken a fit. So taken was Mr Fulton that he has drawn the Diary's series of acrobatic *bons mots* to the attention of his old pal called Josie from the Coocaddens, who was famous for trampolining all over the English language.

Mr Fulton has forewarned to us a letter wrote by the aforeskinned Josie, part of which we reproduce below:

Sir,

I could not believe my ears when I conceived the Diary the other day in which Tom Shields appeared to disride the Glasgow patois. After all us Glaswegians are already impaled with the heavy burden of their ethnic indentification because, admittedly, some of us do not metriculate our words properly and are at times, therefore, slightly incomprehensive. Need I remind you that Glasgow has been defecated the City of Culture for 1990.

For too long Scottish people in general and the Glasgow people in particular have been subjugated to the debilitating situation where they are not understood by the English, which is rich coming from people whose accents have to be seen to be believed.

Yours, Josie.

THE world of medicine provided its usual crock of examples, such as the old lady who phoned her doctor after five days of feeling unwell. Why hadn't she phoned sooner?

'Och, doctor, I've been treating masel wi' thae hot fornications.'

Almost medical was the man described in court as acting 'in local placentas'.

OTHER highlights:

- The lady who wrote her own 'holocaust' will.

- The man whose 'arse didn't know what his left elbow was doing'.

- The employee whose company gave him a 'rail vulture' for his journey to London.

- The union negotiator who could not reach agreement on a certain issue and suggested that it be 'kept in a basement'.

- The tourist asking the distance to a local landmark who was told: 'It's six miles as the cock crows.'

- The football coach who spoke proudly of his centre-half who 'had shoulders like Methuselah'.

WE were told of the Paisley building contractor who became involved in a court action. When asked to comment, he declined on the grounds that, 'It's still quasimodo.' (We think he meant *sub judice*.)

Also the foreman who was determined to catch one of the workers he had long suspected of sloping off the job. The man, however, always came up with a convincing excuse until the foreman declared in his frustration: 'That yin's aye got a lullaby.' And the forewoman whose patience was stretched by underlings constantly asking trivial questions until she told them: 'Just use yer ain transgression.'

In the trade union section we had the shop steward who warned his colleagues to 'keep their feet firmly on terra cotta'. Another steward in the steel industry proclaimed that 'the men are bending their elbow to suit management' but that the employer 'kept going off at a tantrum'. He promised his fellow workers that if they didn't win the dispute 'I'll eat this table without margarine'.

Then there was the chap at a highly charged meeting who shouted at a comrade: 'If you made a remark like that in Russia they would throw you in the Clyde.' Obviously, a pre-Gorbachev story.

THE office tea lady, according to the Diary mailbag, was a rich source for malapropagation. The gems include:

- My daughter's going through a difficult phrase.

- The company has gone bust. It's in the hands of the retriever.

- The doctor's put me on a diet. I'm only allowed that semi-skilled milk.

- A friend who suffers from cloisterphobia.

- A daughter who had spent nearly

24 hours in the labour ward: 'I wish the doctors would just hurry up and seduce her.'

EVEN those of us in the journalism business are prone to malapropagation. We are talking here of a news editor (anonymous) who inquired of a reporter: 'Is this story true or just a false herring?'

During the miners' strike, he asked one of his staff: 'Have you anything up your sleeve apart from the pits?'

When one young cub had his first story printed: 'I'm glad to see the penny's finally gelled.'

He once said to a photographer: 'Get them looking sharp-eyed and pony-tailed.'

He gave this memorable warning

to the male staff before the arrival of a young female recruit: 'Her boyfriend does judo – in fact he's a black dan.'

TRAVEL was a fruitful area with:

● The holidaymaker who went to Dixons to 'get a wee Mintola camera' and then couldn't wait to get to Spain 'to be back among the maracas dancers'.

● The sad story of the lady who went to the Holy Land 'and had all her kroners pinched by a Greek peasant'.

● The visitor to Italy who came back to regale his workmates with the story of the two founders of Rome. 'Remulus and Rolf' – who had been brought up by a wolf.

● The chap who related his moving experience in Jerusalem when he walked down the Via Delrosa.

MORE maladroits: Some political malapropagation came our way. Hugh McMahon, MEP for Strathclyde West, was reported in the Euro Hansard as urging the European Commission not to 'go holusbolus, like a bull at a matador' on the subject of footballers' freedom of contract. Councillor Joe Reilly of Renfrew district was credited with this philosophical contribution to a debate: 'It's a question of dog eat dog and vice versa . . .'

THE polis received a number of mentions for the work of their 'plain-faced detectives' carrying out 'house-to-door inquiries'. Not to mention the time the 'mounted horses' had to take the field at the Scottish Cup final.

IN the field of mixed cliches we have such saying as:

- As happy as a sandpie.

- Above and beyond the call of nature.

- He had a memory like an octopus,

- He was born with a silver lining in his mouth.

- He had another kick at the cherry.

- She was like a lion in a corner shop.

- If you want to stand on your own two feet, take the cat by the scruff of the neck.

- I have plenty of other irons in the frying pan.

- He has struck clover and landed in oil.

- It was like a red herring to a bull.

- It was a minefield of opportunity.

Miscellaneous malapropagisms included:

- The fan who described the Motherwell football strip as 'clarinet and amber'.

- The old lady who predicted bad weather ahead because of all the 'icy-bars' on the weather map. The elderly aunt whose sitting-room wallpaper had 'a gold pattern embezzled on to it'.

- The woman who asked for 'partisan cheese' on her spaghetti. It was probably the same woman who remarked: 'I see they've found that listerine in ice-cream now.'

- The Lord Mayor of Belfast who commented that it would only take one coat of Durex to redecorate the Town House.

- On the same broad theme was the woman who threatened her striking husband that he 'would get his conjuvenal rights when she received a full pay-packet'. Not to mention the schoolboy who described his father in his news book as a 'big balled man'.

OUR delve into the malapropagation mailbag took us to a greetings card shop in deepest, darkest Lanarkshire. A lady had found the wedding card which expressed sentiment she was after. It read: 'Especially for You.' But it wasn't quite right. 'I'd like to make it for the both of them,' she said. 'Do you have a card which says "Especially for Youse"?' Even in Lanarkshire, they didn't.

Also on the wedding theme, we heard of the bride-to-be who was too busy to go out with her pals because she was getting her 'torso' ready for the big day.

A Kilmarnock correspondent told the story of a local woman who was

looking forward to her husband coming home from the army on 'embrocation' leave.

Also mentioned in despatches was the young wife who liked to go on holiday and lie in the sun all day on her inflatable libido.

After three solid weeks of malapropisms one reader accused us of talking a lot of Pifco.

THE malapropism feature extended to cover a whole range of life and language. A reader told how he was being shown some newly acquired paintings by a lady of the Kelvinside variety. He remarked on the Art Nouveau influence in one of the paintings: 'Yes,' she replied, 'I'm very fond of his work.'

THE Malapropagation Mailbag included:

- The lady whose attic has 'a nice wee skylark window'.

- The man who resigned from his job with the words: 'That's the last time I work here and that's it in a nutmeg.'

- The wife who said of her less than perfect husband: 'Look, ah know ma man's no' a plastic saint.'

- The young woman who wanted to marry 'an edible bachelor'.

- The woman who walked farther down the road to get across safely at the 'Presbyterian crossing'.

- The girl whose boyfriend got a job with 'the Customs and Exiles'.

- Two bad apples don't make an orange.

FOOTBALL commentaries were rich to misspeak and malapropagation. Like the commentator (John Greig, actually) who came out with: 'Celtic have taken this game by the scruff of the throat!' In another comment on his erstwhile Old Firm rivals, Greggy said: 'They're behind at the moment but you cannot underwrite Celtic.'

BUT, away from football, how about:

- The US senator who declared his opposition to setting up a 'nuclear suppository' in his state.

- The Glasgow (or was it Edinburgh) councillor who supported a grant for a cultural event because he didn't want the council to be seen as a 'load of Palestines'.

- The Strathclyde regional councillor who, discussing a particularly disastrous episode, remarked: 'What's the point of having a post-mortem on something that's dead?'

EVEN after three months of correspondence, the Diary's exercise in malapropagation showed no signs of falling into a basement.

- There was the conversation in a West Lothian pub on the subject of Mike Tyson, the boxer: 'See thae young guys, the black guys fae the gateau, there's naebody can beat them.'

- There was the chap who was not too pleased with the behaviour of his neighbour's dog which was 'one of those big Dobermann Pensioners'. And the woman who was suffering from 'post-mortem depression' or the lady who had refurnished her sitting-room with 'a mocket suite and eucalyptus wallpaper'.

- A girl at a Lanarkshire church asked by the minister how she was enjoying the youth fellowship, said she disliked 'all the clichés'. Worried that he was not getting across to a young audience, he asked for further details. 'The clichés,' she said. 'All those people who go around together and never speak to the rest of us.'

- An elderly aunt telling her coffee morning chums about the DIY prowess of her niece: 'Maureen is busy now poly-urinating her new wood kitchen cupboards . . .' Maureen, of course, bought her DIY materials at MI5.

- A senior Glasgow district council official commenting on the security for the Pope's visit to Bellahouston Park in 1982, pointed to some nearby multi-storey flats and said: 'It's almost impossible to give complete protection. I mean, just think what a terrorist could do with a Carmelite rifle from that roof.'

- A six-year-old girl, on a wet and windy caravan holiday in Argyll, said as she left with the family for more extremely fresh air: 'Oh, well, once more to brave the elephants.'

- A Glasgow man looked forward to retirement when he would buy 'a wee self-contented hoose wi' a couple o' yon easy-gaun chairs'. All this, of course, before he's 'shuffled off the mortal toil'.

- The man explaining his son's absence from work: 'Jimmy'll be aff fur a couple o' days. He's choked up with the diarrhoea.'

- The angry woman who said of the object of her fury that she 'would have his heid for garters'.

- A chap called Davy who, on hearing of a bereavement, offered his 'heartiest condolences'. To Davy, problems were like 'runner aff a dug's back'. He was often 'blue wi' envy'. Sadly, Davy is now deceased. Or as he might have put it himself: 'Doon in heaven, noo.'

- A lady discussing her daughter's health: 'Our Rose got out of the hospital for Christmas, but she's real poorly. She's got to go back in next week for one of them barrow meals.'

- The middle-aged woman from Springburn who confided to a close friend that her husband's sexual demands appeared to be at an end, because he had become 'impertinent'.

- The radio commentator who, during the latest appearance of Halley's Comet, described it as a 'distinct blur'.

- The councillor who opined during an education debate that Strathclyde region might 'find itself up a gum tree without a paddle'.

- The German businessman who, when giving a talk in English, used the unfortunate phrase 'Early to bed and up with the cock'.

- A chap who boasted about his son's prowess at the swimming baths: 'He can swim like a lintie.'

- A granny who described how an audacious thief stole her purse right there in the street 'when it was pitch daylight'.

- The woman whose friend got a job as a 'vigilante' at last year's Higher examinations.

- A perplexed office manager: 'How would I know what's going to happen next week? I'm not Houdini.'

- An office telephonist responsible for such pearls as:
  'She smells like a tart's brewery.'
  'I'm as dry as a boat.'
  'Don't worry your cotton-headed socks about it.'
  'This behaviour reeks of 1994.'

- The girl, talking about a colleague's many and varied outside interests, who said: 'That man's got a pie everywhere!'

- The chap from Kilmarnock who revealed to his workmates the bad news that he was suffering from 'glocamora' in one eye.

- The young female patient who told her doctor: 'You know how erotic I am with my periods.' Also slightly medical is the story of the gent who had spent a fortune on his girls'

KEEP WELL CLEAR
WHEN WINCHING
IS IN PROGRESS

education and upbringing, and announced to his friends that he had 'very costive daughters'.

- The manager of an unnamed factory in Dumbarton who had been sent on a course on ergonomics and the production line. On his return he received a complaint that a certain procedure was giving female workers severe backache and he announced that he would be 'out to have a right good look at her posterior'.

- The sad story of the young couple who split up 'before the marriage was even consumed'.

- The party that turned out to be a 'damp squid'.

- The lady shopper who liked to go 'bruising' along Sauchiehall Street.

- The councillor who, asked to give his opinion on two candidates for a promotion, said the first 'was a man of a different caliper'.

- The Celtic fans who gave their team 'a helluva barricading'.

- The scout troop leader who told parents there would be a '£5 decapitation fee' for each boy.

- The factory foreman who had continually warned the apprentices about 'all corrugating in the one place'.

- The criticism of a neighbour: 'She thinks she's the Queen's knees.'

- The angry retort: 'That's right, kick the teeth from under me.'

- Agnes from Anniesland who would produce pieces of family gossip with the phrase 'This is without a word of truth'.

- The old lady whose nephew had been involved in a 'fricasee' in a pub.

- The old gentleman who was said to suffer from agoraphobia: 'Y'know,

he's frightened of outer space.'

- The man who, after the General Election, moaned that we were now stuck with the 'quo vadis'.

- The talented wordsmith who described his workplace as being like the 'Black Hole of Kentucky'.

- The woman who complained about the threat to her health from her workmates' 'passion smoking'.

- The man whose favourite song was 'Mairi's Sweating'.

- The man who used to drive along a 'jewelled garageway'.

- The woman who, when requiring help, announced: 'I've only got two pairs of hands.'

- The woman complaining about her new kitchen: 'There's no room to skin a cat.'

- The man who helpfully suggested

to a tourist: 'It's only five minutes' walk if you run.'

- The man who commented on the absent-mindedness of a friend: 'He's got a memory the size of a sieve.'

- The manager who said: 'There's a vulture up there watching me like a hawk!' The same man also said: 'Don't axe your grind wi' me, fella!'

- The proprietor of the small electrical shop who is frequently asked for 'Durex batteries'.

- The Strathaven lady watching scenes on the TV news of the Scottish team returning from Sweden after another magnificent international footballing failure: 'Aye, they sure went out in a puff of glory.'

- The new granny who said her daughter had a forced delivery 'because her pelmet was too small'.

- The old lady at the supermarket checkout who, when paying her bill of £4.18, fetched four £1 notes from her purse and then asked the assistant to 'wait a minute, hen, and I'll gie ye some of this stramash out of my purse'.

- The grandmother who said she wouldn't buy a newspaper with tennis player Billie Jean King on the front because she was one of those 'Elizabethans'.

- The Glasgow office girl who informed her colleagues that she would be preparing for a social engagement by 'going to have her nails manacled and her cubicles pushed back'.

- The rugby player who was tackled by a full-back at the opposition line but his 'impotence' took him over.

- The woman whose boyfriend caught 'fluorosis of the liver'.

- The wee girl who said her mum had just come out of hospital 'after having her second autopsy but they still found nothing wrong'.

- A true story from an epilepsy sufferer who was confiding in a friend about coping with his condition. 'The trouble with being an epileptic is that you become invisible to other people,' he said. 'I know,' his pal replied. 'There is still a lot of astigmatism attached to it.'

- The man training for the Glasgow half-marathon who declared himself 'as fit as a fish'.

- The sage who declared that he was appalled at the cost to the European Parliament of translating their deliberations into all the different tongues and had the perfect solution: 'Why don't they all speak the same language – that eldorado.'

- The schoolteacher confronted with a mountain of paperwork who sighed: 'There goes another Babylonian rain forest.'

- The woman genealogical researcher who had succeeded in finding an elusive forefather in the Register Office where her siblings had failed. She announced: 'It will be a bee in my bonnet when the others see this.'

- The job applicant who said, after a difficult interview: 'I didn't expect the Spanish requisition.'

- The Glasgow lady who opted for some alternative medicine at 'that home of the pathetics hospital in Great Western Road'.

- Overheard in a coffee shop in London:
  Her: 'He's a bit of a dark fish.'
  Him: 'Don't you mean a slippery horse?'

- The salesman who, upon spotting an approaching colleague, said: 'Aye, here he comes. Nae smoke without Punch!'

- The chap who described a devious friend as having 'more faces than the hands of the toon clock'.

- The youngster who had not quite grasped the basics of playground debating skills or even a command of basic swearing. He disagreed with a member of his peer group who, he claimed, was 'talking quiche'.

- The woman who said her brother-in-law had 'never been anything but a snake in the ointment'.

IF YOU'VE EVER WONDERED WHETHER THERE'S AN SDA OFFICE IN EDINBURGH,

Portaloo Solo

HAVE A GOOD LOOK AT THIS POSTER.

SDA (Edinburgh and Lothians office), Rosebery House, Haymarket, Edinburgh.

- The girl who told how a rival in pursuit of her boyfriend made 'a beehive right for him'.

- The neighbour who boasted that her brother had just bought a new car with one of those 'catholic converters'.

- The woman commenting on some newly built houses who said they were 'packed in cheek by bowel'.

- The man who said the after-dinner speaker had 'waxed effluent'.

- The millionaire who was described as an industrial 'magnet'.

- The man who described his associates as a 'henspeckled bunch'.

- The man in the bar who said his

employer was offering him 'a PLO cruise'.

- The girl who said of a financially troubled company that the worst day was when they brought 'the liquidisers in'. Presumably she meant the retrievers.

- The girl who said: 'I know a chap who went to Israel to live on a kebab for two years.'

- The mother who said that a relative had 'cried fox' too often.

- The trade union official at a meeting with the health board who claimed: 'The Sword of Domestos is hanging over our members' heads.'

- The mother-in-law who enjoys a

cup of tea because 'it fair survives you'.

- The Wishaw lady who was discussing the merits of the various brands of lager and asked her daughter if she had ever tasted 'that Castlemilk four X'.

- The woman on her Highland holiday who had a 'panasonic view' of the mountains from her hotel window.

- The old lady on the train to Edinburgh who pointed out they were near Auld Reekie by saying: 'Look! There's the Jenner's Suppository.'

- The man who took a dram every night and slept 'like a Trojan'.

- The foreman in the parks department who had to cope with student summer workers and who often accused them of being 'too smart with your O-levels and your C-levels'.

- The girl whose sister was going into hospital for a 'Bavarian meal'.

- The chap who went to Moscow but found himself totally confused by the 'acrylic alphabet'.

- The gent who said he saw a drunk man 'lying prosperous in the gutter'.

- The young police constable, fresh from training school and anxious to get the full story of a road accident, who asked the hospital doctor: 'This broken leg. Has the victim fractured his tibia or his labia?'

- The woman in the fabric shop who complained she couldn't see the shade of her curtain material because of the 'effervescent lights'.

- The director who warned his staff not to go 'off in a tandem'.

- The man who said his holiday was a 'total fiesta'.

- The lady who waited in her car to join the funeral 'corsage'.

- The lady whose favourite soap was 'Imperial Lather'.

- The woman of whom it was said: 'Every time she opens her mouth she shoots herself in the foot.'

- The teenager who had seen a TV programme on the slimmer's disease: 'Aye, it's terrible that anaglypta nervosa.'

- The RAC man who informed a motorist: 'Your battery's as flat as a dodo.'

- The lady who commented that the man next door had brought a 'Puguenot' motor car.

- The man who was jumped on by a 'Karachi expert'.

- The dear old lady who says her daughter has two dogs: 'One a Corgi, the other a Datsun.'

- The woman who realised she'd mixed up her words and said 'Oh dear, is that me doing a Mrs Malathorp?'

- The salesman who when finalising details of the purchase of a mobile office was told his customer wanted it 'in perpetuity'. That could be a problem, he said. He'd quoted for it being in Yoker.

- The builder who told his boss that he couldn't go up heights because he suffered from 'vertebrae'.

- The manager who arrived at the metallurgy laboratory of a large factory looking for the report on 'the non-ferocious metals'.

- The woman 'who's not in the phone book. She's hysterectomy.'

- The gent who declared: 'It's like getting blood out of a dead horse' and 'You're rubbing blood into the wound'.

- The woman who tired of being taken for granted by her family and yelled: 'I'm fed up being treated like a dormouse!'

- The man who, when asked to perform miracles, chided: 'Do you think I've got a genie I can rub?'

- The local businessman who gave in to yuppiedom and bought 'one o' thae celluloid phones'.

- The chap in the restaurant who informed the waitress: 'We'll just have the soup and the pudding, lassie. We've no time for the intercourse.'

- A shipyard worker, the victim of a practical joke, who vowed: 'I'll get you for that. As sure as God made toffee apples, I'll get you.'

- The Gorbals lady who done good moved to a more highly rated socio-economic area of the South Side of Glasgow. Whitecraigs, even. At a social get-together, the lady was on the fringe of a conversation and overheard one of her neighbours talking about his latest acquisition – a boathouse. 'We've got a boathouse as well,' she chipped in. 'We bought our house 12 years ago.'

- The reader who, after a week of torture on the Cambridge diet had produced no weight loss, was told by her minder: 'Your weight does tend to flatulate from time to time.'

ON the holiday front, there was the man who regaled his workmates with details of how he travelled through France overnight by train 'on a courgette'.

SOME pearls of wisdom just come straight out of the blue. Like the personnel manager who liked to tell applicants who had made the short leet that 'the trees are beginning to thin and your picture's definitely on the piano'.

FROM Stonehaven we heard of a chap whose love life was tangled, to say the least. In fact, as one local **put** it, he was involved in a 'fromage à trois'.

SOME Glaswegians go to great lengths to avoid speaking a' wrang. Occasionally they mangle perfectly good words. Like the woman who had been off work suffering from the bile. Or 'the boil', as she informed her workmates.

MUSIC is a rich source of examples of people what get it wrong. Like the child who sang fervently each Christmas about a 'wean in a manger'. Or the grown-up whose rendition of the Jim Reeves song 'He'll Have to Go' always began: 'Put the jukebox a little closer to the phone . . .'

THE member of a Highland district council who fell out with a trouble-some constituent gave him 'a piece of my tongue' and sent him away 'with his tail between his teeth'.

THE following solecisms are from a larger collection of the pearls of wisdom as uttered by a chap who works in a West of Scotland whisky company. Our informant insisted that the whisky is not a factor:

• I've spoken to every dog and their granny.

• It's an ill wind that blows your granny off a bus.

• Any ship in a storm.

• Old Mother Cupboard.

• Speak now or forever hold your water.

AS good as malapropism, in the Diary's opinion, is when two well-known sayings are combined, such as:

• The woman who 'screamed blue-arsed murder'.

• The politician who warned of 'buy-ing two peas in a poke'.

• The chap who knew a certain secret because 'a wee bird dropped some-thing in my ear'.

NOT quite a malaprop but very close is the story of a young Coatbridge lad who was under the impression for many years that Doris Day sang a number with the chorus: 'Kiss her arse, her arse . . .'

NOT a malaprop but definitely a misspeak is this, attributed to a ScotRail inspector who had been asked to check the conditions in the gentlemen's rest-room: 'Thae toilets ur a pure disgrace,' he reported. 'It's like a shithoose in there.'

MEN AND WOMEN

This section on the subject of men and women is necessarily short. The Diary never majored on sex. We have too many lady readers in Milngavie who might object.

SANDY Ferguson, for many years the urbane barman at the Rogano and Buttery oyster bars in Glasgow, told us he had only one dissatisfied customer in all that time: 'He was a chap who came in and had six oysters because he had heard of their aphrodisiac properties. He phoned later to complain that one of them hadn't worked.'

A YOUNG woman pushing a pram through Kelvingrove Park was engaged in conversation by an elderly lady. The old lady peered into the pram and said: 'That's a bonny wean ye've got there. And whit a grand heid o' hair! Wis the faither rid-heided as well?'

'I don't know,' the young mother replied. 'He never took his bunnet aff!'

THIS is actually a tale about public speaking, but we don't have such a chapter. It's about a golf club where one of the social evenings involved putting slips of paper into the championship cup and asking each member to choose one. Most of the slips were blank but a dozen had a word or phrase written thereon and

the tradition was that the member had to make a five-minute speech on that subject.

One member picked a piece of paper with the word 'sex' written on it. He proceeded to make a witty and knowledgeable speech on the subject. When he got home, his wife asked if he had had to make a speech. 'What was the subject?' she asked. Not wanting to go into detail, he said he had been called upon to speak about yachting. The next day, his wife met the club captain who said her husband had acquitted himself very well in his speech.

'I don't know how he managed,' she told him. 'He knows almost nothing about it. In fact, he's only tried it twice. The first time he was sick as a dog and the second time his hat blew off.'

AN advertisement on the noticeboard of an arts centre in Edinburgh offered an intriguing service: 'The ultimate in personal presents. Beautiful bronze life-cast sculptures.' The gentleman artist providing this service was reluctant to be identified in case the wrong sort of people were attracted but he did say: 'What we offer is a fairly

HEART, St Jude and Blessed Virgin.—P.C.

GRATEFUL THANKS St Jude and St Anthony, Allah be praised.

HEATHER DEVONISH is 18 today. HAPPY BIRTHDAY love from your mum, dad and brother Peter.

standard sculptural technique from which we can produce an exact replica of any part of the body. We do get the odd exotic demand.' The method involves dipping the relevant part into a plaster bed. A polyester model is then made from the mould and finished off in bronze.

The cost, at 1983 prices, of a sculpture you could truly call your own was £30 to £40, depending on specifications.

THIS is the story of a missed opportunity that could have raised awareness of the AIDS threat and made some welcome cash for Strathclyde Region.

Entire buses emblazoned with advertisements have become commonplace on our streets. Saatchi & Saatchi wanted to go one better on behalf of their clients, the London Rubber Company, manufacturers of Durex contraceptives. They wanted to use an entire underground train to get their message across. The whole length of the train was to be painted as a giant condom.

It was a project which would certainly have been eye-catching and potently symbolic. And the advertiser was willing to pay a lot of money – a figure of £1 million was mentioned. The agency approached the Strathclyde Passenger Transport Executive, who run the city Underground system on behalf of Strathclyde Region.

After careful consideration, the PTE bosses declined the opportunity to cash in on the world's first 100-foot mobile condom. The PTE has a strict code on advertising which prohibits messages of a political, religious or sexual nature. In these AIDS-conscious days, television, for instance, has abandoned its ban on condom advertisements. But the PTE could not bring themselves to allow the sight of a huge passenger-carrying condom slipping in and out of Glasgow's Underground tunnels.

The Diary suspects that the ladies of Hillhead and Kelvinside would agree with them.

THIS chap arrives home from work to find his wife rubbing cream into her breasts. It is guaranteed to increase the size of her bust, she tells him. How much did it cost, he asks.

£79. 'Whit?' he exclaims. 'Why didn't you just get a daud o' toilet roll and rub it between your cleavage?'

'Will it work?' the wife asks.

'Well, it's worked for your arse,' the uncouth chap replies.

DEPT of Public House Folklore: We heard distressing details of how a Govan chap was rusticated from his favourite pub. Having discovered that his wife was having an affair, he tracked the philanderer to the pub where he found the man making a phone call. He proceeded to attack him with a machete. The victim suffered severe wounds to his arm. The telephone cable was severed. The attacker was barred by the publican for 'putting the phone out of order'.

THE landlord of a West Highland hostelry was carrying a box of empty bottles into the back yard when he discovered his wife in a compromising situation with a customer. Deeply hurt by this infidelity, the landlord shouted to the man: 'You bastard, you're barred!' As mine host retreated from the scene, he realised that the chap was by far his biggest-spending customer and added: 'For a month!'

DURING the festive season, chaps, emboldened by a sweet sherry or two at the office party, are to be found trying to chat up the temp from accounts. We heard of one Lothario – in Barrhead, of all romantic locations – who has set a standard of sweet talk to which the rest of us can only aspire. 'You know,' he told the chubby but comely object of his desires, 'you don't sweat much for a fat person.'

A Lanarkshire lady of a certain age was on the receiving end of this scintillating patter: 'You know, you're not as old as you look.'

ANOTHER festive-season chat-up line. Diner to comely waitress as she pours cream over his pudding: 'Tell me, dear, what are you and your jug of cream doing later?' Waitress: 'I don't know about the jug of cream but I'm goin' hame to my man.'

OTHER sensitive appraisals of the female sex included:

- 'You're lookin' a million dollars the night, hen. Aw' green and wrinkly.'

- 'Haw, sweetheart, ah love the frock. Did ye huv much bother sneakin' it oot the museum?'

- 'You've got really interestin' eyes. In fact the right wan's that interestin', yer left wan keeps lookin' at it.'

- 'Huv youse two came oot fur a drink an' left Cinders in hersel' again?'

EVEN worse than yur average male's chat-up lines are the discussions they have with their mates the day after a conquest. Like: 'Ah widnae say she was a big girl, but her middle name was Orca and Greenpeace are lookin' for her tae tow her back out to sea.'

WARNING: This joke may upset wimmin.
Question: Why do sumo wrestlers shave their legs?

Answer: So that they won't be mistaken for feminists.

THE ladies' toilet of the Speaker's Corner bar and bistro, Sauchiehall Street, Glasgow, has a vending machine which, for £2, dispenses a package containing two tampons, two condoms and four paracetamol. A handy little something for the weekend which would seem to cover all eventualities.

ANENT the above item on the ladies' toilet vending machine which dispenses an all-encompassing package of condoms, tampons and paracetamol, a former Heriot-Watt student told us that when she was a fresher at said yoonie she was issued with a similarly intriguing juxtaposition of goodies. It was a poke (if you'll pardon the expression) containing a packet of condoms and a pot noodle. For a romantic night just add music, candlelight, champagne and some boiling water.

MERCANTILE MENDICANTS

Ploys used by street beggars become increasingly ingenious.

A BEGGAR in Central Station, Glasgow, cashed in on the Thatcherite principles of self-employment by asking: 'Gies a pound. I want tae start my ain business!'

THEN there was the ruddy-faced, bleary-eyed gentleman who demanded of a passer-by in a Paisley street: 'Hey, pal, gonnae gies 42p so's ah can buy a *Herald* tae look for a job?' Or the more direct approach of a chap in Sauchiehall Street: 'Ur any o' youse bastards gonny gie me f*****' ten pence?'

A DENIZEN of Dennistoun was making his way home from a public house having purchased a fish supper. On Duke Street, he was accosted by a footpad with the words: 'Gies that fish supper or I'll batter your face.' He found it an offer he couldn't refuse.

A YOUNG couple walking along Kilwinning main street were approached by a man carrying an empty petrol can. He explained that his car, which was parked just up the road, had run out of petrol and could they lend him £1 towards a gallon? The man was very grateful and insisted on having a name and address to send the money on to. Walking up the street where the car was supposed to be parked, Mr Dalziel and his fiancee were somewhat taken aback to find no vehicle.

AN Irishman stopped a man in Hope Street, Glasgow. He claimed he was delivering horses to Hamilton Racecourse but had somehow got lost and could he please direct him to the motorway. The passer-by obliged and in return the Irishman advised him to put his life savings on a horse running the next day at Kempton Park. In return for the priceless information he was asked to give the Irishman a silver coin for 'stable luck', and fished out his change. The Irishman quickly picked out two 50 pence coins, touched his forelock, said the statutory 'Good luck to ye, surr', and was gone. Needless to say there was no such gee-gee running at Kempton the next day.

A CHAP, reeking of alcohol, stopped a shopper in Buchanan Street in Glasgow with the curt message: 'Gies tempence [there is no N in tenpence, as you know] for a cuppa tea.' The

PRAY KEEP OFF
THE GRASS
SUCH TRESPASSES WILL
NOT BE FORGIVEN

shopper did so and jocularly added that the coin would no doubt go towards more drink. 'Listen, pal. What I do with my money is my business,' the mendicant replied. Along the same lines is the story of the shnorrer, a Yiddish beggar to you, who knocked upon a door to be told by the kindly but poor lady of the house: 'I'm sorry I don't have anything to give you today, but come back tomorrow.' 'Sorry, lady, I don't give credit,' he replied.

A READER recalled a back-street singer from his childhood days in Cambuslang. One day in an area of the town noted for its Protestant tendencies, the street singer was giving a rollicking rendition of 'Derry's Walls' and being showered with coppers by an appreciative audience. The next day, the same singer had a different song. In a back court of a part of Cambuslang occupied by people of another persuasion, he was delivering, hands clasped, as sweet a version of 'Hail, Queen of Heaven' as you might have heard from Canon Sydney MacEwan himself.

ANOTHER begging victim was visiting a picture house in Portsmouth, when a chap offered to look after his car. A fee was agreed. As he entered the flicks, the beggar approached again and asked if he could have his fee up front 'as I'll be going home in a few minutes'.

'COULD you spare 50p for a drink?' asked a mendicant in the West End of Glasgow. As people walked on, unimpressed, he changed his ploy to: 'American Express, Access, Visa . . .'

ONE Glasgow panhandler's dedication to business overcame his common sense. He was taken into police custody on another matter, and as he was put through the admission process at Barlinnie, the officers noticed a particularly obnoxious aroma emanating from the plaster cast on his leg. Questioned, the chap revealed that the stookie had been on for nearly a year and should have been removed some ten months previously. Why had he not gone back to the hospital? 'It was a great help for the begging,' he revealed. Was he not concerned about the hygiene aspect? 'Well, I did give it two coats of emulsion when it got dirty,' he said.

BUT the prize for ingenuity goes to the Glasgow beggar who would accost clients with the words: 'Haw, chief, for a silly two boab I'll gie ye a bit of information that could save your life!' After the transfer of cash was completed, the mendicant enlightened donors with the words: 'Never take a lift hame in a car fae Edward Kennedy.'

CHIC MURRAY

A STAGE version of the life story of Chic Murray provided the excuse to bask in the memories of the tall droll's comic genius. John Bett, who directed the play, was no stranger to going for the occasional dram with Chic. On one occasion they were enjoying a post-theatre thirst-quencher in a seedy London actors' club. Sitting in one of the warren of dungeon-like rooms, they found themselves sharing it with a chap and his Labrador dug. Chic was telling a long story and kept pausing to gaze at the Labrador. The punchline, although Chic Murray never needed punchlines, was: 'They've got awfy big rats in here.'

CHIC Murray appeared to have a preoccupation with animals. Strolling through the streets of London, he was stopped and asked: 'Do you know the Battersea Dogs' Home?' To which he replied: 'I didn't even know he'd been away.'

Or his comment: 'Just bought the wife a jaguar. Great investment. It bit her leg off.'

One summer day Chic wandered into a pet shop and asked the assistant for a pet wasp. She told him somewhat disdainfully that they didn't stock wasps and, in any case, they weren't creatures that people would want to cultivate as pets. 'But,' said Chic, 'you've got two in the window.'

CHIC described a visit, possibly imagined, to the Olympic Games. He was taking a leisurely stroll in the environs of the stadium when he espied a man coming towards him, dressed in a T-shirt and shorts and carrying a long stick over his shoulder. Chic said: 'Excuse me, are you a pole vaulter?'

'No,' replied the athlete. 'I'm a German. And by the way, how did you know my name?'

A CLASSIC Chic Murray story concerns an attempt to find lodging in a typically welcoming Scottish seaside town. He knocked on the door of a B&B establishment. The landlady opened an upstairs window and asked brusquely what he wanted. 'I'd like to stay here,' he said. 'Well, stay there,' she replied and closed the window.

SOME London-based television people didn't know quite what to make of Chic Murray. Chic was being interviewed on the Simon Dee chat show and the host was trying to put Chic down by repeating his answers, translating the Scottish accent into BBC-received pronunciation.

But Chic had a spot of revenge waiting in the wings. When asked about variety acts he remembered, Chic reminisced about a high-wire troupe 'They were billed as Lunt, Hunt and Cunningham,' he said in his plummiest voice and waited deadpan for a response. The verbal challenge went unanswered. 'Lunt, Hunt and Cunningham,' he repeated with slow emphasis.

The interview ended with Mr Dee, head in hands, face down on the table.

THE word surreal only begins to describe Chic Murray's sense of humour. He took the opportunity, when appearing on the TV comedy quiz show *Jokers Wild*, to push this surrealism to the limit. Asked to discourse on the subject of the seaside, he said: 'I won the pools once, and I said to my mother, "Ma, I've won the pools. What would you like? You can have anything you want." "Oh, son, I'd like to see the sea. I've never seen the sea." So I took her to the seaside, put her on a deckchair and went away. I came back after two weeks and said to my mother, "Well, ma, what do you think of the sea?" She replied, "Is that all it does?"'

ANOTHER joke which mystified the *Jokers Wild* audience. 'Can I have a bar of green soap?' asks Chic of the assistant in a chemist's shop. 'I'm sorry, we only have yellow soap,' she replies. 'That's okay,' Chic reassures

her, 'I've got my bike outside.' It also mystified Diary readers who telephoned in their scores for an explanation. I told them it was an attempt by Chic Murray to question the essential nature of humour. Some of them even believed me.

CHIC was famous for his conversations with his doctor. 'Tell me,' asked the GP, 'are you disturbed by improper thoughts during the night?' 'No,' Chic replied. 'I actually enjoy them.'

'STRIP,' said the doctor. 'Where will I hang my clothes?' asked Chic. 'Just put them on top of mine,' replied the doctor.

'WHAT'S your problem?' asked the doctor. 'I've got butterflies in my stomach,' said Chic. 'Have you eaten anything recently?' inquired the doc. 'Butterflies, actually.'

TALES abound about Chic's ability to while away his daytime hours drinking coffee and distracting the staff in offices where he happened to know the boss. He was a regular visitor to the office of a Glasgow entertainments agency. One summer afternoon, while Chic was there passing the time reading the office's supply of daily newspapers, the work of the office was further disturbed by a loud and persistent bluebottle. There was a sudden bang as a rolled-up *Glasgow Herald* brought the bluebottle's short life to an end.

A deadly hush fell over the office staff who all looked at Chic. His response: 'Sorry. Was it someone's pet?'

Harry Lymburn of the Tait and McLay advertising agency in Glasgow recalled that Chic was no stranger to their offices, mostly to pass the time of day with his pal, the late Jack McLay whom he referred to as the Wee Man.

'On one such occasion, having asked Jean our receptionist if the Wee Man was in, he was told a white lie because Jack was busy meeting a deadline for a client and Chic's visits were known to be anything but short.'

Chic replied that this was not a problem. He would wait for the Wee Man's return. Settled down with a cup of coffee, Chic proceeded to keep the entire front-office staff off their work. Some considerable time later, Jean excused herself, went into Jack's office and explained the situation.

Jack's predicament was that there was no way out of the office without being spotted by Chic. He resolved the predicament by opening his office window and dreeping (good old Glasgow word, there) a full storey into the back garden, climbing the railings, and coming in the front door to greet Chic.

MICHAEL Glancy of Bearsden remembered being introduced to Chic by a mutual friend. Being young and somewhat in awe of the great man, Mr Glancy stumbled for words and could only say: 'Hello, Chic, how are you?' Putting the young man at his ease, Chic replied: 'I'm fine, apart from the odd touch of diarrhoea.'

CHIC, buying an Underground ticket at Hillhead, enquired: 'By the way, is there a buffet car on this train?'

'No, sorry, sir.'

'Well, is there a buffet car on the next train, then?'

'No, sir. There are no buffet cars on any of our trains, sir.'

'Christ, I'll be starving by the time I get to Merkland Street.'

THE Rev. Eric Hudson of Bearsden recalled how Chic related to him the story of his father's funeral. Totally deadpan, Chic told how his mother was a Cherokee Indian (from Greenock) and when his father died she wanted him to have a traditional Cherokee funeral. This involved building a pyre in the back garden and putting the deceased person's dearest possession on to the flames.

So on went Chic's dad's wee dug. After the fire died down and the remains were being gathered together, Chic's mother, he said, picked up a piece of bone. 'Pity the wee dug's no' here,' she said sadly. 'He loved a good bone.'

CHIC on being commiserated with after slipping on an icy pavement and falling on his bahookey: 'Did you slip on the ice?' asked a perspicacious passer-by. 'No, I've got a bar of chocolate in my back pocket and I'm trying to break it,' he replied.

A NEIGHBOUR asked if he could use Chic's lawnmower. 'Certainly,' he replied, 'but please don't take it out of my garden.'

CHIC'S remark as he fell from a bus: 'It's all right. I was getting off anyway.'

CHIC'S aside during a rambling story about how he had spent the day: 'I was making tea in my pyjamas. I must get a teapot.'

CHIC, in a shop buying soap, was asked: 'Do you want it scented?' 'No, thanks,' he said. 'Wrap it up and I'll take it with me.'

'I WALKED into the bedroom – the curtains were drawn but the furniture was real.'

CHIC speaking of a trip to Helensburgh in the days when every chemist's shop had a penny-in-the-slot weighing machine in the doorway: 'It's a wonderfully exciting place is Helensburgh. Full of entertainment. I weighed myself twice.'

CHIC was once standing at a bus stop eating a pie supper when he was joined in the queue by a lady with a small dog. The said small dog, incited by the aroma of Chic's al fresco snack, was jumping up and down attempting to gain access to his pie and chips.

'Would you like me to throw him a bit?' Chic asked her. She replied that her dog would like that very much so Chic picked up the dog and, so the story goes, but we can't believe Chic would hurt a wee dug, threw him a bit.

CHIC went into a butcher's shop: 'Have you got pig's trotters?' he asked the friendly butcher who replied that he had. 'I'll have a pound of mince then, Porky.'

CHIC was driving past a farmhouse when he ran over a cockerel. Conscience stricken, he picked up the deceased bird and knocked on the door. 'I'm afraid I've just killed your cockerel and would like to replace him,' he told the farmer's wife. 'Fair enough,' she said. 'The hens are round the back.'

CHIC often told how he was on a bus in his boyhood Greenock, accompanied by his father. The bus ran out of control, down a hill and crashed into a wall. 'Were you hurt?' his audience would inevitably ask. 'No, but father had the presence of mind to kick me in the face.'

NAE LUCK

The Diary, being the recipient of many a hard luck tale, usually imparted with more than a hint of schadenfreude, instituted the Nae Luck Awards.

WE are all, to some extent, lumbered with public expectations because of the jobs we do. Take the chap who had the embarrassment of being taken off the plane at Glasgow Airport bound for Manchester because he should have been on the plane for London. Mutterings of 'Mastermind? That'll be bloody right!' could be heard from the delayed passengers as the chap walked down the aisle of the aircraft. Nae luck for Magnus Magnusson.

THERE appears not to be much of a future in futurology. That is the conclusion one might reach after studying the career of Mr Robert Underwood, one of Scotland's leading futurologists.

Mr Underwood was a member of the School of Man-Made Future until it closed in 1976. He then founded the Nevis Institute, devoted to examining 'trends in cultural, social, economic, technical and scientific life in Scotland'. After publishing only two editions of its *Nevis Journal*, the institute ran out of money and closed down.

THE Imperial Tobacco Company ran a Cash Snooker competition in May 1981 to promote their John Player King Size brand. Interest in the £170,000 prize was intense. In fact, there were 799,000 winners who each received the magnificent sum of 22p. Many of the lucky recipients decided to keep their jobs and live the same modest lifestyle.

RANGERS fan George MacDonald was so annoyed by his team's poor form in season 1983–84, he threw away his £45 season ticket after only a third of the games had been played. It was found by a Good Samaritan who posted it back to him.

HERR George Binder sent a mailshot to sundry Scottish households promoting the north-west German state lottery. The weekly prize of one million marks was quite enticing but Herr Binder kind of spoiled it by adding: 'It is not just the high prize amount that is so attractive but also the great number of fat prizes and the fat chance of scoring one or more.'

A RADIO Clyde car left in the car park at Parkhead by commentator Ken Robb was broken into. Nothing was stolen, not even the radio. But the bad boys who broke in did change the channel from Clyde to Radio 1.

THE Government published a brochure to show that the National Health Service in Scotland was in good hands under the Thatcher regime. The design on the cover of the glossy, full-colour brochure featured a reading from a cardiograph. Unfortunately for a publication which purported to portray a healthy health service, the cardiograph reading showed, in fact, an atrial flutter, a sign that the patient was not at all well.

A NAE LUCK award went to BBC Scotland, who broadcast on BBC2 a performance of Berlioz's *Te Deum* from Kelvingrove Art Gallery as part of their contribution to Glasgow's Year of Culture.

A viewer who by chance had left running the Ceefax subtitle service on his TV set was intrigued to find flashing on to the screen during the *Te Deum* such phrases as: 'I can't stand any more of this . . .', 'Who ordered the bacon and eggs?' and even the information: 'Toilet flushes'.

The technical hitch on this occasion was that BBC2 viewers in the rest of Britain were watching the *Mosquito Coast*, a film starring Harrison Ford, and there was no way of Scotland opting out of the Ceefax subtitle facility.

THE Berlin Wall was a potent symbol, so you can imagine the excitement when Strathclyde Regional Council's architects department

Pan ar gau, mae'r cyfleusterau
toiled agosaf yn
Pwll Trochi Troed Rhodfa Mor,
Craig-y-don

When closed, the nearest toilet
facilities are at
Craig-y-don Promenade
Paddling Pool

received a chunk of it through the post.

A parcel addressed to the chief architect of Glasgow, Strathclyde, arrived at the region's HQ containing a chunk of concrete mounted on a tasteful wooden plinth. An accompanying letter, from the Architekturministerium Ostberlin to the Lieber Kamerad Direktor said that the bit of concrete was a bit of the Berlin Wall.

It continued (in bad English): 'We think hopefully that such a small peace of the Demolition may part of a new bridge between East and West begin, and that our Ministeries may soon be joined in a new Spirit of Co-operation as I am sure you will agree that the Architekts must be seen to be the Leaders of the Renaissance. I look forward to perhaps one day you meeting.'

Mr J.C. McDougall, Strathclyde's director of architecture, was touched by the gesture and wrote back saying that, as president of the Chief Architects of Scottish Local Authorities, he would transmit the message from East Berlin to his colleagues all over

Scotland. He added that he was grateful for the sample from '*Die Mauer*' which he would keep for display in his office. He also duly wrote to the Royal Incorporation of Architects of Scotland and to the Glasgow Institute of Architects, spreading the word of the glasnost news from East Berlin.

Then, as Mr McDougall examined the letter further, some doubts began to set in. Why was the crest of the East Berlin architect department the same as that of the Royal Incorporation of Architects of Scotland? Then there was the date of the arrival of the package – Monday 2 April. One day after a well-known day of fun. The signature on the letter was then examined closely: Floda Reltih. An unusual name, even for a German, and what a coincidence that backwards it spells Adolf Hitler.

Yes, one of the better April Fool stunts. And executed with an architect's eye for detail.

DEFINITELY in line for the Diary's Nae Luck Citation was an unnamed Scottish soldier in the 7th Armoured Division, over in Saudi Arabia during the Gulf War.

Before his unit was despatched to the Gulf, the soldier managed to get along to his local tattooist for an appropriate image to be etched on his forearm.

He was quite proud of his tattoo, featuring as it did a drawing of a fierce rodent above a popular generic title commonly used to describe our brave lads out in that hot, sandy hell.

The squaddie is not the only one to sport such a tattoo but he was singularly unfortunate in selecting a tattooist whose spelling was suspect. Thus he was forever condemned to be a Dessert Rat.

A BRIDE-TO-BE, after much thought, chose to proceed to the altar to the tune from the film *Robin Hood, Prince of Thieves*. This tune, which you may have heard, is the romantic 'Everything I Do, I Do It For You', by Bryan Adams. The person in charge of the wedding music, being of a different generation, got it slightly wrong. The bride was not impressed to be confronted by the strains of an earlier hit (Gary Miller, circa 1956) with the stirring but decidedly unromantic lyrics: 'Robin Hood, Robin Hood, riding through the glen . . .'

PROFESSOR Neil Brooks, a neurosurgery expert at Glasgow University, was booked to give a talk to staff and clients at a day centre in Shettleston on the topic of memory loss and lack of concentration. He failed to turn up because he had forgotten to put the engagement into his diary.

DAVID McNiven, musician of 7:84 and Wildcat fame, told how many years ago he had found a pair of tarnished candlesticks in a bin in Dennistoun. He gave them as a present to a chum. Mr McNiven recently had cause to visit this chum in his new, recently purchased, bijou country retreat. 'It's all thanks to you,' the chum explained. 'Those candlesticks were Charles Rennie Mackintosh and became very valuable. In fact we bought this house with the money they fetched.'

A BUS driver taking a party on a coach tour of the Scottish Borders was invited to join his grateful passengers for high tea. As orders were taken for steak pie, gammon or chicken, the driver piped up: 'Can I have a cheese salad please, as I do not believe in killing animals for food.' This remark was met by a stony silence. The party he was driving were retired butchers and their wives on an outing organised by the ancient Incorporation of Fleshers of Glasgow.

A NAE LUCK Oscar to the Scottish Television cameraman who was sent to the Possil housing scheme in Glasgow 'to get background shots for a programme on the drug problems. The cameraman misheard the instructions. After a day risking life and limb filming in those mean streets, he returned with definitive footage of the Alsatian and sundry other dugs who roam the range up Possil way.

A SOLDIER in the Royal Scots was out in the desert a few days after the Gulf War ceasefire. There was still the odd alarming bang and thump as shells and other bits of ammunition were disposed of. Our man duly heard a loud bang. Then he noticed a three-legged camel hirple on to the horizon. Poor thing has lost a leg on a landmine, he thought, before fixing it in his rifle sight and humanely consigning it to the next world. Enter, stage left, an irate Bedouin who had been in pursuit of the camel. The very same camel that was always escaping and one of whose legs he had hobbled up so that it couldn't run away too far.

THE NAME GAME

When the Leyland truck company merged with the Dutch firm DAF, it took less than a morning for the rumour to spread around the Leyland Glasgow factory that the new set-up was to be called, with overtones of redundancy, Ley-DAF, This is the sort of stuff, folks, we spent 12 years gathering in our Name Game section of the Diary.

SIR COLIN CAMPBELL, the portly chairman of James Finlay, the Glasgow company much pilloried by pressure groups for their activities in Bangladesh and other parts of the Third World, is known as Sir Cumference.

BUFF HARDIE, a member of the hilarious *Scotland the What?* comedy team, is one who confesses to having a diabolical memory for names.

On one occasion, he was greeted after a show by an acquaintance whose name he had forgotten. He was about to come clean and apologise when the man said: 'Don't you remember? Stewart Park?'

'Yes, of course,' he lied. 'How are you, Stewart?'

'No, no. Stewart Park was where we played football as boys,' came the reply.

IN the bad old days of trade union abuse of power, there was a Glasgow docker who had the nickname High Noon. He was so called because he was wont to exclaim to his workmates during elevenses: 'Tae hell wi' this, I'm shootin' at twelve.'

ONE of the great double acts in the history of the Labour movement was James White, MP for Glasgow Pollok, and Ian Campbell, MP for Clydebank. Before they retired in 1987, after many years at the Westminster coal face, the pair were inseparable. So much so, they were nicknamed 'Semmit and Drawers'.

Fortunately, the 1987 intake of Scottish Labour MPs included another great double act: Jimmy Wray and Jimmy Hood. They were both dapper dressers and looked for all the world like prosperous car salesmen. They quickly attracted a

EAST ANGUS CONSERVATIVE ASSN.

MEAN MACHINE

number of nicknames, including the Two Jimmys and The Wray Twins.

A NORTH of England constabulary boasted a famous but shortlived name for its version of a special patrol group. It was called the Fast Action Response Team. The acronym alone fairly put the wind up local criminals.

MEANWHILE, the team set up by Strathclyde Police to deal with ice-cream van drivers who played their jingles too loud or were too liberal with the tooting of their horns was nicknamed the Serious Chime Squad.

THE Scottish Office unit set up to deal with the problems of the travelling people was given a shorter and altogether snappier name by staff at New St Andrew's House. They called it the Tink Tank.

THE Renault car company had a successful advertising campaign in which owners of Renault 5 models gave their vehicles pet names. Renault suggested such names as Speedy Gonzalez or Gordon (after footballer Gordon Strachan), who takes corners well! Inevitably, one owner, less than happy with his Renault 5, christened it Rusty.

NAMES of Chinese and Indian food establishments can often be uncannily accurate. A Chinese takeaway in Dundee is called the Tak Awa. An Indian eating house in Rutherglen was ominously titled Curry Fever.

ANOTHER suitable trade name was: M. Pyre (Builders) of Glasgow.

A DIARY reader sent us this list of his favourite (genuine) company names in the Hong Kong phone book: The So Kee umbrella company; the Lee Kee shoe factory; the Hung Fat brassiere manufacturer; and the Wing King optical company.

GENERAL Accident had an agent in Sabah (what used to be British North Borneo) called the Fuk Hing Garage and Automobile Service.

A EUROPEAN agency to promote multilingual broadcasting was titled Broadcasting Across the Barriers of European Language. Or BABEL for short.

THE Ubiquitous Chip restaurant in Byres Road, Glasgow, is a constant source of confusion for the many visitors to the city. One official of the European Parliament visiting Glasgow (to study urban decay and poverty) spent all evening trying to find a place called the Ultimate Chip. Dame Edna Everage in his Glasgow stage show referred to it as the Promiscuous Chip. Glaswegians sensibly just call it The Chip.

THE strong ale made by Robinwood brewery of Todmorden, West Yorkshire, is called Old Fart. Topers will be relieved to hear that it is 'additive free'.

BUT surely only in the West of Scotland would you find a public house called the Duke of Schomberg, after a German soldier of fortune who fought and died for King Billy at the Battle of the Boyne 300 years ago.

THE company slogan of Durex Products Inc., of Luck, Wisconsin, USA, is 'Working to be the best, not the biggest'. We should add that this Durex is not in the same business as the British Durex, but makes mining equipment.

FINALLY, a few choicely named individuals:

● The manager of the Saudi Arabia office of China Airlines was a Mr Peter Pan.

● The author of *A Catalogue of Everything Israeli* is Josephine Bacon.

● Oban boasts a lawyer by the name of Robin Banks.

● A lecture at Glasgow University on the subject of Black Sheep was delivered by a Dr Woollen.

● Partick Thistle had a full-back duo called Dinnie and Kerr.

● The Ugandan Deputy Minister for

Trade and Industry who visited Scotland in 1989 was called Mr Aggrey Suit.

● A member of the staff at the Royal Observatory in Edinburgh is one Dr A. Heavens.

● The deputy director of the National Center for Earthquake Engineering in Buffalo, New York, is a Mr Ian Buckle.

● The director of the National Fish Bureau of the Netherlands is one Robert Carp.

● Managing director of the British Beef company is a Mr Jeff Steer.

● Organiser of a conference at Strathclyde University on global warming was one Valerie Flood.

● Head of the Scottish Development Department's rural affairs division is a Mr Richard Crofts.

● Appeals co-ordinator at Edinburgh

Zoo is Mrs Isobel Beevor. A hard worker, we're sure.

- Writing on the subject of slimming in the magazine *Treating Overweight* was Dr Lean, of Glasgow University's department of human nutrition.

- Castle Douglas down in bonnie Galloway boasts a dental surgeon in King Street by the name of Aitken Grieve.

- A firm of property developers were spotted in Cumnock, Ayrshire, by the name of Steele and Cosh.

- The organiser of a conference in Newfoundland on the subject of 'Training for Survival and Rescue at Sea' was a Captain Drown.

- Author of an article entitled 'Going for a pint, girls?' in *The Dear Green Pint*, CAMRA's guide to Glasgow's real-ale joints, was one Ellen McSwiggan.

- A number of British Airways passengers have been in touch to tell us of a little discovery they made while stuck far longer than planned on the Shuttle. They whiled away the extra hours reading *High Life*, the BA magazine, where they found the fascinating information that the airline's head of planning was a Mr Rod Muddle.

- A Diary reader sojourning in Malmesbury, Wiltshire, reported that a local coffee shop is owned by one Jill Eatwell. Then there was the chap in the Inland Revenue enforcement section in Edinburgh with the biting name, Mr I. Bark.

- The chap given the task of explaining to the shop assistants at Harrods that times were tough and there would have to be a wage freeze was a Mr Bollinger. Not 'Champagne Charlie' but plain Peter Bollinger.

- Harland and Wolff of Belfast is building six ships specially designed to carry ore and coal around the difficult waters of the Cape of Good Hope. They are to be called Capesize-class ships – not a very safe-sounding name, especially when pronounced in a Kelvinside or Morningside accent.

- A fast-food chain specialising in French fries (a chip shop to youse) in Saudi Arabia rejoices in the name Badkook and Sons.

- The British Wellness Council launched National Condom Week (slogan: Slip into Something Safe and Sexy) and took the sensible precaution of appointing as Condom Week press officer a lady called Emma Cox.

- Vacancies were advertised for store detectives by HMV, the high street music chain. Aspiring crime-stoppers were asked to apply to a Mary Cotmore.

- *The Engineer* magazine reported that the flushing toilet, as invented by Thomas Crapper more than 100 years ago, is to be superseded by a new toilet, the Somerfield solid-state syphon. But, as *The Engineer* points out, it will not be the same: 'That's a load of Somer just doesn't have the right sort of ring to it, does it?'

- For no particular reason at all, we would like to inform you that in the town of Wallington, Surrey, there is a street by the name of Senga Road.

- The manager of the British bob-sleigh team for the 1992 Winter Olympic Games was one Colin Snowball.

- In Tanah Rata, Malaysia, there is a takeaway food store called the Chip Fatt Shop.

- Manager of Kelvingrove Park, Glasgow, is a Mr Jim Chestnut.

- Winner of the Financial Director of the Year award 1992 was a Mr Brian Fidler.

- One of Washington's leading claims lawyers is Phyllis Outlaw.

- Scottish Enterprise sponsored a symposium on Sewage Sludge Disposal, The Commercial Opportunities, at which a lecture on the topic of 'Existing Scottish Disposal Arrangements' was delivered by Dr Mike Heap of Lothian regional council.

- A chap ordained to appear at Stranraer Sheriff Court on a charge alleging assault was one John Brawls.

- By deciding not to use her husband's name, Baroness Lynda Chalker has deprived the House of an interesting name. She is mairrit

oan to one Clive Landa. So she could have been Lady Lynda Landa.

- Head of religious education at BBC Wales is one Mair Pope.

- Mother India Café, Glasgow's original low-cost restaurant offering traditional home cooking from the subcontinent, occupies premises previously called The Bad Ass Club.

- The Howard Committee for Penal Reform has a member by the name of Francis Crook.

- A lecture to the Geological society of London titled 'Explosive Volcanic Eruptions' was given by Dr Steve Sparks of Cambridge University.

- German tourists are famous the world over for their aggressive attitude. So it is perhaps not surprising that a London company offering package holidays to Germany should be called GTF Tours.

- The picket lines at strike-bound BBC headquarters in Glasgow were crossed by a gent by the name of Mr Pidgeon. Justified or not, he was henceforth referred to as Scabbie Doo.

- The leading firm of undertakers in Cape Town rejoices in the name Human and Pitt.

- The chap appointed as consultant to the project to recover the con-

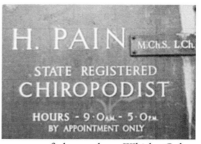

tents of the sunken *Whisky Galore* ship, SS *Politician*, was a Mr Davie Jones.

- The director of the Derbyshire Centre for Integrated Living is Mr Peter Pine-Coffin.

- Who could resist a makeover at the Hackett Beauty Centre, London?

- The Events Suppliers Association appointed a new chairman, Mr Cliff Ball of the Humping Company.

- Hero of the hour when fire broke out at the Myreton Motor Museum, Aberlady, was the curator, who alerted the fire brigade, and then contained the flames. He is a Mr Match.

- A Mr J. Mycock holds the position of controller of small parts at Rolls-Royce, Derby.

- The vicar of the Church of St James in Devizes, Wiltshire, is the Rev. Tim Pape.

- The author of the American edition of the *Illustrated Encyclopaedia of Sex* is Dr A. Willy.

- Ross Perot, that awfy nice wee billionaire who ran for the US presidency in 1992, had a campaign manager called Orson Swindle.

- We were intrigued to hear that Paisley has an eating establishment by the name of Café Borgia. As in: 'Hello, my name is Lucrezia. I'm your waitress for tonight.'

- An Edinburgh establishment goes by the name of the El Paso Driving School. We are less certain of the allure of the Edinburgh restaurant which boasts the name Pancho Villa's Dry Boak Gulch.

- The Diary reported the missed opportunity of Dumfries and Galloway police to have the street hosting their new HQ named Annapolis Street, after the Doonhamers' twin toon in the United States. An appropriate alternative name for the new thoroughfare to the cop shop might have been Letsby Avenue.

- Executive producer of the BBC programme *A Secret World of Sex* was one Sam Organ.

- The threat that some of Scotland's regiments may be amalgamated with their English counterparts

raised the vexed question of what these hybrid units might be called. The Duke of Wellington's Regiment might merge with the Royal Green Jackets to become the Royal Green Wellingtons. The Royal Electrical and Mechanical Engineers could join forces with the Argyll and Sutherland Highlanders and be known as the Royal Electrical and Mechanical Highlanders. The Lancers and the Royal Army Dental Corps appear, on the face of it, to have something in common. They could become the Dental Lancers. The Army Legal Corps will no doubt join up with the Parachute Regiment to form a corps of crack solicitors who can drop behind enemy lines and sue people. Crossing the geographical boundaries we could have the King's Own Scottish Kent Yeomanry. It is surely only a matter of time before cutbacks force the army to form alliances with outside agencies and even private enterprise. Thus the Boy Scouts and the Queen's Own Highlanders could form the Boy's Own Highlanders. The Guards Division could save money by amalgamating with Group 4 to form the Group 4 Security Guards regiment.

PEOPLE

The following are some notes and anecdotes on people who did not fall readily into the other categories of the book.

ONE of Scotland's great characters was the late James 'Solly' Sanderson, sports journalist and doyen of the Radio Clyde phone-in. His highly personal style of prediction and controversy attracted a large following. So much so that an advertising agency decided to use his character in a series of radio adverts. They approached the comedian Allan Stewart, who did a very accurate impersonation of Solly. Mr Stewart said it would be no bother and quoted a price of £200. At this point the agency had second thoughts. They approached Solly and hired him to be himself for only £50.

COLIN BELL has been hosting a morning discussion programme on Radio Scotland for more years now than we care to remember. He does it in his own inimitable, abrasive and robust style. So much so that his first series, *Taking Issue with Colin Bell*, soon became known as *Taking Exception to Colin Bell*. His second, and current series, *Head On with Colin Bell*, quickly became known as *Sticking the Head on Colin Bell*. Which is what many guests and listeners often wish to do.

WE could fill a whole book with stories about Mick Broderick, singer and bodhran player with the Whistle-binkies, but we will not pre-empt the big man's own memoirs. A shipyard worker, he found himself pursuing his trade in New York at the time of the Watergate affair. He was sitting in a bar where everyone was watching with quiet reverence their President assure the nation there was no truth to the *Washington Post* allegations of corruption and criminal activities. 'There will be no whitewash in the White House,' intoned Mr Nixon.

'Bloody liar,' intoned Big Mick, starting a bar-room brawl of the type usually only seen in bad western B movies.

We will leave Mick to tell the world his other stories, like the pimp in Harlem who tried to buy the Mickey Mouse clock Mick had bought for his auntie.

We will tell you, however, about Mick and the time he left a recorded message with a parrot. Mick had been for a few jars and decided to go for a few more with his pal. He went to fetch his chum at his flat in Byres Road. The chap wasn't in. Undeterred, Mick lifted the letter-box, saw the mate's parrot and shouted repeatedly: 'Polly, tell Jim I'll meet him in the Cutlers at five o'clock.'

Jim duly turned up at the pub at 5 p.m. 'Did Polly give you the message?' Mick asked.

'No,' said Jim, 'but the old lady next door told me a long story about a wild man shouting a message through the letter-box to the parrot.'

ALAN HICKEY is a travel writer with a difference. He is author of a tome called *Europe on Ten Litres a Day*. The ten litres is a reference to alcohol and, yes, Mr Hickey is an Australian. The Diary met up with him when he was in Glasgow to research the new edition of his bevvy bulletin. He said: 'While other guides give you all the bullshit about what historic houses and art galleries to visit, my book tells you where to get the best and cheapest pint of beer afterwards.'

Mr Hickey was impressed by Glasgow. He told us the only other place in Britain to match Glasgow was Haworth in Yorkshire 'where those Bronte sisters used to hang out. I had a beaut of a time there for months drinking beer and watching television.'

He took up the onerous task of chronicling the world's beers and bars in 1974: 'I was sitting on a beach in Goa sharing an ice-box full of beers with this Irishman. He suggested doing a guidebook called *Globetrotting on Ten Litres a Day*.' Mr Hickey doesn't know what happened to the Irishman but he has been an itinerant author ever since.

He practises what he preaches and consumes at least ten litres a day. When we spoke to him he was having a quiet Sunday. He had had a few pints of lager and was heading off to write up his notes in his hotel room. 'I've got a couple of litres of Furstenburg and a bottle of nice wine that I remembered from Cyprus,' and which he had discovered in a Great Western Road off-licence. 'I've also got a bottle of very strong Swiss ale that I found in a pub in Hope Street. I'll pop out later for a few glasses of Guinness and Tennent's 80 Shilling Ale.

'I will be telling my readers Glasgow is the place. The tourists normally go to Edinburgh, but all it's got is that bloody castle.'

THE Diary met Kayah Thet at the Easterhouse Festival in 1983. He was

a merchant navy navigator from Rangoon, Burma, who had settled in Glasgow 14 years before. Joe, as he preferred to be known, was a fully naturalised Easterhouse citizen with a council house, a wife, two weans, and a Giro from the government every fortnight. What kind of job would he like?

'I want to be a racing tipster on the *Daily Record* like Garry Owen. I can do that job.'

How does he enjoy living in Easterhouse?

'It's no problem. And, by the way, it's nice to be nice.'

POLITICS

Politics, from its highest to its lowest manifestations (the House of Commons to, for instance, Largs Community Council), exercised a fascination over the Diary.

A GROUP of anarchist students at Paisley College were faced with a dilemma. If they formed a society with 16 or more members they would qualify for a £200 grant from the college student body. Swallowing their anarchist principles they formed the Paisley College of Technology Anarchist Society.

The next hurdle was that, to qualify for the cash, the society had to have a constitution. Anarchists are not too hot on constitutions but a solution was found. With a piece of political sleight of hand, they borrowed the constitution of the Sports Society and added a final clause which stated that no member was bound by any of the previous clauses.

GREAT political issues of our times: During a debate in 1982 on the Civic Government Bill, a small schism appeared in the normally united faction of Scottish Conservative MPs. Albert McQuarrie, MP for Buchan, moved that every dog over one year old must 'have a permanent identification by means of a code number which will be indelibly marked on the inside thigh of the dog. The code number would be the identification

mark for the life of the dog and the number shall be inserted on the dog licence.'

His colleague, Mr John Corrie, MP for Cunninghame North, put forward a counter proposal that every dog 'shall carry a permanent identification on its left ear placed there by the breeder, with indelible ink'.

While the identification idea has obvious merit, both suggestions as to the location of the number carried disadvantages. Looking in a Labrador's left ear could be almost as unpleasant an experience as inspecting the inner thigh of an unco-operative Alsatian.

Update: Both suggestions were rejected and both MPs lost their seats in the 1987 General Election.

IN the 1983 General Election, Mr Kenneth Hill won the award for the most reticent candidate. Mr Hill, who lived in London, told the Diary that he would not be coming north to campaign in Glasgow Shettleston where he was standing as British National Party candidate. Why not? We asked. 'Pressure of business.' What kind of business was he in that was more pressing than a General

Election? 'I am in the cleaning business,' he replied. What kind of cleaning? 'Windows.'

Then Mr Hill came clean himself. 'We have active candidates and inactive candidates in the party. I am an inactive candidate. I will not even have time to help in the campaign down here in London. My name has been put forward with others so that the party will qualify for time on television.'

ROY JENKINS, before he was a lord and when he was fighting the Glasgow Hillhead seat in a by-election, went a-wooing voters at the university. A professor raised the topic of the number of Gaels in Partick. 'Oh, but the weather is much better at the moment,' replied Jenkins, who won the seat and subsequently became more *au fait*, as they say in Gaelic, with the Partick Highland situation.

AS early as February 1984, there was a campaign for a Scottish Assembly. And they had a plan for disposing of the 21 Tory MPs in Scotland. Of these 21 seats, 20 were held by a minority vote. If the opposition parties got together they could unseat all but one of the Tory MPs.

This is where the plan began to fall apart. The only Tory MP left in Scotland would be Bill Walker, in North Tayside. Despite the loss of seats in Scotland, Mrs Thatcher would still have won in the UK – and Bill Walker would have been Secretary of State for Scotland.

The plan was not proceeded with.

ESSENTIAL reading in any new

edition of *Who's Who?* was the entry under hobbies by Sir Nicholas Fairbairn, MP for Perth and Kinross. In 1977 he listed his favourite pursuits as 'bunking and debunking'; in 1980 it was 'giving and forgiving'; in 1983 'being blunt and sharp at the same time'; in 1984 'philanthropy and philogyny'. It has to be said that the entry for 1981 is a puzzling one – Sir Nicholas apparently lost his interest in the fair sex in favour of 'the cure and eradication of British tick fever'.

SIR Nicholas Fairbairn turned in many bravura performances at the Commons. Like when he livened up an otherwise dull 1987 debate on devolution by informing the House: 'There are ten times as many Scots in Holland than there are in Scotland.' When parliamentary colleagues interrupted, he continued: 'Opposition Members who say "Havers, man" should consult the telephone directory for Schravenhagen to ascertain the number of MacKays who are living in that area.'

The Diary did not have the research resources to establish if Holland (population about 15,000,000) really did have more Scots than Scotland but we did have a look at the telephone directory for Schravenhagen, or The Hague as others call it.

It contained three MacKays. It also listed a further 18 Makaijs, Mackaays and sundry other spellings. We cannot say, however, if they are real MacKays.

THE June 1984 Euro elections featured two lady Tory candidates with suitably European names – Patricia de Seune and Jacqui Lait. Ms de Seune, contesting Strathclyde East, used her name in her election slogan: 'De Seune the better.' The Tories in Strathclyde West thought about using 'All the way with Jacqui Lait' but dismissed it on grounds of sexism, plumping instead for 'Jacqui's best for Strathclyde West'. Neither was elected.

ONE of the matters of major importance discussed at the European Parliament was whether MEPs should be issued with a 'distinctive sash' (like those worn by French mayors) so that they would be easily recognisable at official functions. The design would be a circle of ten gold stars on a blue background. Janey Buchan, the no-nonsense MEP for Glasgow, said she had no objection to Euro sashes. But she did suggest one amendment – her fellow MEP Ian Paisley, no stranger to sashes, should wear his tied round his mouth rather than across his chest.

ONE Scottish MEP took too kindly to the European ideal and studied a number of foreign languages so that he could converse with his various colleagues at the European Parliament. He missed no opportunity to practise. Dining in a Strasbourg restaurant, he was asked how he would like his coffee. '*Avec lait,*' he replied. The waiter did not understand, so the MEP elaborated: '*Lait. Le produit de vaches.*' Or milk, as the waiter finally said.

MRS Thatcher, on a tour of hostile territory in Glasgow city centre in September 1987, encountered artist John Taylor. Going about his lawful business, carrying a large canvas to his studio nearby, Mr Taylor found himself caught up in the street circus which surrounded the Prime Minister.

The Iron Lady pounced on him. 'Do you work here?' she asked.

Mr T replied that he was indeed on his way to his studio. This required a great deal of self-restraint since Mr T is an ardent CND supporter and his politics occupy a totally different part of the spectrum from Mrs T's.

'Can I see your painting?' she asked.

'No,' he said, making off before being captured for posterity fraternising with the enemy.

BELIEVE it or believe it not, life can become tedious for our MPs down at Westminster. It was boredom, and not malice we are sure, that led one to aver that it was his intention, nay ambition, when Cecil Parkinson was

speaking to interject anonymously: 'Show us your willy!' This, being unparliamentary language, would be followed by the usual cries of 'Withdraw! Withdraw!'

DURING a House of Commons finance committee debate on the poll tax, Labour MP Brian Wilson complained that three Conservative MPs were reading books. The chairman ruled that books should not be read unless they related to committee business. Mr Wilson pointed to the Honourable Member for Crawley, Nicholas 'Bunter' Soames, with the words: 'He's not reading it, he's colouring it in . . .'

DUMBARTON is not fertile territory for the Conservative Party, as an advertisement for a secretary for the local party office indicated. The applicant 'must be a Conservative supporter and capable of working alone'.

BRIAN Wilson's winning of the Cunninghame North seat for Labour coincided with the publication of his book to mark the centenary of Celtic Football Club. Former Labour Party leader Michael Foot had seen a review of Brian's book and dropped him a note. Mr Foot said that he too had recently had a book published and suggested that both authors should swap copies of their respective works. Mr Foot's book was called *The Politics of Paradise*. Nothing to do with boardroom struggles at Parkhead, but a study of Lord Byron.

THE Diary suffered from an outbreak of political Light Bulb jokes in December 1989, in the wake of the Jim Sillars Govan by-election victory:

- How many Scottish Labour MPs does it take to change a light bulb? Scottish Labour MPs don't change anything.

- How many Scottish Conservative MPs? None. It's Conservative policy that the light bulb should learn to change itself. (Or, how many Scottish Conservative MPs after the next General Election? Both of them.)

- How many Scottish Liberal Democrat MPs? Sorry, we're too busy changing the party name.

- How many Sinn Fein MPs? Two; one to change it and one to claim responsibility.

- How many Democratic Unionists? Party spokesman Dr Ian Paisley said: 'Change a light bulb? Never! Never! Never!'

- How many National Front MPs? 'We don't want to change the light. It's white, innit?'

- And back to the chap who started it all with his Govan win: How many SNP MPs? Only one but he would have to ask his wife how to.

TOMMY McAvoy, Labour MP for Rutherglen, was sent a copy of the Bible by a Northern Ireland fundamentalist religious group, to mark the 300th anniversary of the Glorious Revolution. The Bible was adorned by a full-colour illustration of a chap on a white horse who used to be king of Great Britain. (Yes, his name was William and he was Dutch by birth. That's it. No more clues.)

Mr McAvoy, an FP of St Columbkille's Secondary School, appreciated the gift but passed it on to some people who liked it even more. His local Orange Lodge.

JOHN Home Robertson, Labour MP for Berwick and East Lothian, wrote to the Leader of the House of Commons on the vexed subject of English Tory MPs hogging the limelight at Scottish Question Time.

This letter, as is the usual practice, was sent to some faceless civil servant to concoct a reply that would cast the Government in a good light while assuring all and sundry that the principles of democracy were being upheld to the highest standards.

Unfortunately, by some slip-up, instead of receiving the usual anodyne reply, the Labour MP was sent a draft copy written by a civil servant and an accompanying note in the best traditions of the Civil Service.

The note, from a Scottish Office official to his Whitehall colleague began: 'I enclose a self-explanatory suggested form of words which deliberately avoids commenting on the figures he quotes (which are probably correct) . . .'

Yes, Minister, truth is stranger than fiction.

GUESTS at a cocktail party in Edinburgh Castle had an opportunity to see Mrs Thatcher in action socially. Herself and Denis were among the guests at a Scottish Office drinks and canapes bash to honour Scotland's Grand Slam rugby team.

Mr Thatcher, a former rugby referee, was in his element. Gin and tonic in one hand, cigarette in the other (even though it was a No Smoking zone) he was fairly enjoying the crack, as they say in Dulwich.

Then She Who Must Be Obeyed appeared, tapped him on the arm, and turned away. That was the wordless indication that they were offski.

'Duty calls,' Mr Thatcher told the small group he had been talking to.

This left the problem of what to do with the cigarette and gin and tonic.

There being no ashtrays, Mr T popped his fag-end down the muzzle of a nearby cannon, producing a nice little smoke effect in the process. The remainder of the gin and tonic he poured into some fake shrubbery which had been imported for the occasion.

Denis is a brave man if he does that sort of thing at home.

THE scene was one of the packed TV lounges of the House of Commons during the World Cup semi-final between England and West Germany. The game went to a penalty shoot-out. There were three Labour MPs in the lounge, all Scots – Messrs Dewar, Maxton and Wilson.

The assembled Tories greeted each German goal with collective groans and each England goal with great hurrahs. A deathly quiet fell over the room as Pearce and Waddle missed their penalties. At which point Brian Wilson, the Honourable Member for Cunninghame North, was heard to say: 'Of course, it's the taking part that's important.' There was no reply.

A NATION ONCE AGAIN: Scotland's Members of Parliament were urged to wear the kilt every day to their work. A letter to all Scots MPs said: 'We look to you, the elected representatives of the homeland Scots, to fulfil essential leadership roles in those matters of Scottish heritage and culture which are of special interest to us . . . Therefore, on behalf of the homeland Scots, all expatriate Scots, and all descendants of Scots to the nth generation, I respectfully suggest that you and all other MPs who represent Scottish districts, begin wearing Scottish national dress on a daily basis . . .'

The writer of this letter (yes, he was an American: one Curtis Hall of Cypress, California) said the benefits would be threefold:

'It will affirm in the strongest possible way the modern validity of Scotland's historic traditions and societal values.

'It will electrify the imagination and enhance the pride of Scots everywhere.

'It will instantly magnify your image as a leader of perception, maturity and character.'

What a great idea. We look forward to seeing Donald (Dewar) without his troosers, electrifying imaginations and magnifying his image at Parliament.

THE extreme fiscal caution shown by MP John Smith led to an outbreak of jokes in honour of the now deceased eminent Labour politician. It was apparently suggested to Mr Smith in the tearoom at the Blackpool party conference that it was his turn to buy the coffee. He agreed that he would do so 'as soon as the resources became available'.

THE programme to root out male chauvinism in the People's Party has a long way to go. A detailed and laudable action plan was formulated to increase the number of women MPs and female party office-bearers.

This action plan was presented to a meeting of prospective parliamentary

candidates at a Labour Party conference briefing session in which the MPs of tomorrow were being taught parliamentary and diplomatic skills.

One of the candidates showed he had not yet caught on by referring to the paper on women's equality as being 'as useless as tits'. This caused a sharp intake of breath all round and general pondering on exactly what he meant by this unfortunate simile.

The Diary was later to establish that the full text should have read 'as useless as tits on a front-row forward'. The candidate, you may not be surprised to hear, was a Welshman.

ONE of the proud banners of the Scottish Constitutional Convention is the commitment to fair representation for women. Imagine, therefore, the shaking of heads which accompanied these remarks by Mr Harry Ewing, the Labour MP and joint chairman of the convention, at the close of a meeting.

Mr Ewing thanked convention administrator Bruce Black for his sterling work and also 'the lassies in the office who did the typing'.

A FEATURE of the intense security at all Tory Party conferences is the team of policemen who have to check every drain and sewer in the vicinity and seal off the manhole covers. At a conference in Aberdeen, the cop whose task it was to spray yellow paint on the manholes, indicating that they had been checked, became exceedingly bored. As he waited to mark yet another drain, he spotted a dead cat. As a joke on his colleagues, he went ahead and added a set of yellow stripes to the corpse of the unfortunate deceased black pussy. Merry jape all round. But with so many manhole covers to paint, he forgot to go back and remove the feline cadaver from the public gaze. Thus it was that the local police station received a telephone call from a distressed elderly lady who had been out walking her dog when she discovered what she described as evidence of satanic rituals in the vicinity of Aberdeen conference centre. The cop involved inevitably became known as Garfield.

JIMMY Allison, the former Scottish Organiser of the Labour Party who retired early after less than gracious treatment at the hands of the party organisation, keeps active in the party and was canvassing in a Monklands council by-election. While the Labour activists were chapping doors, one householder said: 'I'm not voting Labour after what they did to Jimmy Allison.' The canvasser attempted to retrieve the situation by pointing out that Jimmy was still doing his bit for Labour just a couple of streets away. The potential voter thought for a moment and replied: 'Well, he must be daft then. I'm still not voting Labour.'

LORD James Douglas-Hamilton, the Edinburgh West Tory MP, is dreadfully nice and all the better for being a wee bit eccentric. It obviously runs in the family. Lord James, in his capacity as Scottish Home Affairs Minister, received a letter from Haddington bemoaning the breakdown of law and order in those parts. The letter went into some detail on vandalism, hooliganism and other patterns of behaviour not normally associated with that peaceful burgh. The letter received the minister's utmost and rapid attention. And so it should have. The letter was signed simply 'Mummy'.

LORD Fraser, even though he was then the Lord Advocate, had to go through the annual conference secu-

rity rigmarole. Realising, somewhat late, that he would have to submit two passport photographs, he rushed to his local post office in Edinburgh. He inserted his £1.50 in the machine, pressed the button, and confidently awaited his four passport-sized pics. Out from the machine popped a postcard-size photograph of Edinburgh Castle with his physog inset in a corner. Examination of the machine showed that he had pressed the wrong button. But it could have been worse. Another option was to have his face on a tourist souvenir photograph of the Loch Ness monster.

DONALD DEWAR once came top of a poll of most romantic MPs conducted by House of Commons secretaries. Donald, who often comes across as a deeply serious man, was described by the secretaries as a Heathcliff-type figure. But Mr Dewar did not live up to this romantic reputation when, during a meeting of the Scottish Constitutional Convention's executive, it was decided that the next meeting would be on St Valentine's Day and he asked, 'When's that?'

JOHN CORRIE, the Conservative candidate for Argyll at the 1992 General Election, had a wee gem of a campaign leaflet. It began: 'John Corrie was Member of Parliament for North Cunninghame until boundary changes altered the seat.' In other words he lost it to Labour. It went on: 'In 1979 he was awarded the Wilberforce Plague for humane work.' Actually, it was plaque. Finally, the leaflet gave a persuasive reason why Mr Corrie was the man for this rural seat: 'He was Scottish Shearing Champion in 1959, shearing 221 sheep in nine hours.'

THE *Shetland Times*, in their excellent coverage of local boy Norman Lamont's first Budget, reported that his maternal grandfather, Charles Hughson, lived in a croft called Loot.

ONE of Lord James Douglas-Hamilton's ministerial tasks was to declare open the Dundee Advice Centre for Education and Training, a new joint effort between Scottish Enterprise Tayside and Dundee College of Further Education. As the Scottish Office announced at the time: 'The Minister will be presented with an honorary Scotvec module in public speaking.' Stick that in your CV, Jimmy.

FULL marks to the English politician who wanted to send a message to David Blunkett, the Sheffield Labour MP. Taking full cognisance of Mr Blunkett's impaired sight, the man had the letter specially typed in Braille . . . and then sent by fax.

SIR David Steel's memoirs, in which he recounted his adventures in Russia as a student, provoked from another source a tale about the trip which hadn't made it into the book. The Boy David was to address the hosts on behalf of the Scottish students at a dinner on the final evening. He spoke no Russian but decided to make an effort. He scribbled down two words he had seen on lavatory doors which would enable him to begin his speech with the Russian for 'ladies and gentlemen . . .' This he did and received tumultuous applause. Later that evening he was to learn that the English translation for his words was 'toilets and urinals'.

ONE of the sports at Glasgow City Chambers over the years has been spotting the cooncillors and officials with the biggest appetites in the official dining-room. One tribune of the people – seen consuming the soup, melon balls, a mountain of cold meat, a hot dish, and two puddings – rapidly became known as Two Dinners. Another, observed working his way through seven portions of haddock, was christened The Fishermen's Friend.

ONE of the legends of local government in Scotland is Mr Charles Horsburgh, clerk to the Glasgow licensing board. He is famous for putting publicans through the hoops as he enforces the licensing laws to the letter. Take the case of Granny Black's pub, which decided to add their bit to the yuppification of Glasgow's Merchant City *arrondissement* by putting a smart black-and-gold canopy on its façade.

Yes, says Mr H; but under the Act, the pub must lost its existing afternoon licence and close between 2.30 p.m. and 5 p.m. because the canopy changes the appearance of the premises.

But surely the canopy is outside the building and not part of the licence, argue the pub's lawyers. No, the canopy is attached and must be licensed, says Mr H. Oh good, say the pub owners, now customers can sit under the canopy and enjoy continental-style pavement service. No, says Mr H, the pavement is not licensed, only the canopy. The customers could drink on the canopy but not under it.

The owners decided not to proceed with the idea of a canopy.

A NUMBER of cooncillors, from Greenock so the story goes, were on a social outing, or a 'bus run' as it is more properly called. On the way home, the treasurer of the outing announced that there had been a miscalculation and there was a deficit of £15. What was to be done, he asked the good men of the cooncil.

One chap had no doubt: 'I move we give the £15 deficit to the driver.'

We think this may be the same cooncillor who made the famous statement at Greenock Corporation: 'Allegations have been made about me. And I know who the alligators are.'

A GLASGOW Corporation cooncillor was on civic duty at the City Chambers. He had two functions to attend. The first was to hand out commemorative badges to bus drivers and conductors who were leaving the Corporation's employ. The second was to greet a dozen television executives from African countries who were on a course at a Glasgow college and were being entertained to a civic dinner in the Satinwood Suite of the Chambers.

As usual, on both these occasions the civic hospitality was lavish and by the time he was wheeled in to meet the African TV people, the cooncillor had partaken too well of the Chambers' wines.

The Africans were bemused and their college hosts stunned to see the cooncillor hand out commemorative bus badges with the words: 'If it hadnae been for people like you, Glasgow's transport system would huv ground to a halt years ago.'

THE scene is Dundee Trades Council, where a discussion is taking place on ways to broaden the appeal of the May Day rally. One member proposes that the Vegetarian Society be invited to set up a stall. This is vetoed by the chairman, obviously a carnivore as well as a Stalinist, with the wonderfully Dundonian statement: 'If the vegetarians take over we'll end up as a banana republic.'

IT was not often that the Diary ventured into the world of community councils. But we were prepared to make an exception in the case of the December meeting of Largs Community Council.

The good burghers of the jewel of the Clyde were discussing the manner in which the local district council was spending cash from the Common Good Fund. As the community council minutes put it: 'Councillor Boyd stated that our district councillors were throwing the money about like drunken sailors in Singapore, and when questioned about this analogy she confirmed having knowledge and experience in this area.'

QUOTE, UNQUOTE

A close cousin to Apocryphal Tales, Quote, Unquote is a category which allows the Diary to practise shameless plagiarism of other people's bons mots under the guise of claiming they provide a wry insight into society.

QUOTE from a public relations official at a Scottish New Town on being questioned by a news reporter: 'I'm sorry, I don't think I can be sufficiently vague on that one, so I'll just have to make no comment.'

ROD Hull, keeper of the infamous Emu, asked at a press conference to publicise his show at the Pavilion Theatre if his violent puppet had plans to wreak havoc on Glasgow, replied: 'I think someone already has.'

PROFESSOR J.L. Prattis of Carleton University, Ottawa, Canada, carried out a study into 'industrialisation and minority languages' on the Hebridean island of Lewis. One of the reasons the professor gave for the fact that Lewis folk had stuck to Gaelic was 'Isolation – this refers to the distance from interference by the dominant language group and can be operationalised in terms of geographic and communication criteria'. Or, to put it another way, Lewis is separated from the mainland by the Minch.

'BANK robbery is primarily an urban crime' – sociology lecturer at Strathclyde University.

'I WILL tell you why top civil servants are called mandarins. They are small, fruity, and give you the pip.' – Sir William Kerr, then Permanent Under-Secretary of State at the Scottish Office.

A ROYAL visit to Glasgow by the Duke of Edinburgh progressed so smoothly that HRH found himself at the Pollok House estate 45 minutes ahead of schedule. There to greet him was Bailie John McQueenie, chairman of the civic amenities committee. Bailie McQueenie asked HRH if he would like to see round the Pollok House gardens.
'I don't want to detain you and your staff,' Phil replied.
'That's all right,' the Bailie said, 'my wife isn't expecting me home till half-past five.'

COMEDIAN Arnold Brown, now based in London, said he was appalled at the deprivation he had seen on his return to his native city of Glasgow: 'Did you know there is a waiting list of two years to vandalise a telephone box in Easterhouse?'

'ONLY a fool would attempt to

predict the result of an Old Firm game. I think it will end up a scoring draw.' – Hughie Taylor the legendary sports writer of the *Daily Record*.

PRESIDENT Reagan on his defence policy: 'First we get all the wagons in a circle . . .'

STRIKING miner with collecting can outside Celtic Park during the 1984 pit strike: 'Ian McGregor's an Orangeman! Support the miners!'

SIR Graham Hills, principal of Strathclyde University, said in an annual report: 'The consequential decouping of the optimisation of our human resources from that of our salaries bill dispelled the prospect of financial disaster.' What he meant was that a number of staff had transferred to part-time work and the university did not have to enforce redundancies.

DOUGIE Lauder, from Nitshill, Glasgow, a contestant in a Pub Patter competition: 'Our family were so poor, we got our clothes in an army surplus store. Okay, I know a lot of families did but how many of you went to school as a Japanese general?'

STREET trader selling bunches of green grapes outside Celtic Park: 'Eat the colours!'

THE Diary was invited to be a judge at a talent competition in the Casbah Bar as part of the Easterhouse Festival. The compère introducing the judging panel said: 'And this is Tom Shields, a famous journalist with the

Glasgow Herald.' This was greeted with silence. 'The *Glasgow Herald.*' Still silence. 'You know, the newspaper. No' wan o' the wee yins. Wan o' thae big kind ye canny read in the toilet.'

A LADY, actually a deaconess of the Church of Scotland, replying to a particularly sexist Toast to the Lassies at a Burns Supper, opined that men were no longer as romantic as they were in Rabbie's day: 'I received an obscene phone call last week, and even he needed some prompting.'

THE scarred relationship between police and the mining community took some time to heal after the picket-line battles of the miners' strike. At the 1985 Scottish Miners' Gala in Edinburgh, Mick McGahey, doing his MC, had to broadcast the fact that there was a lost child in the police tent. 'Could someone please go and get the child free immediately,' was how he put it.

ERIC Clarke, of the Scottish NUM, during a BBC Scotland interview, maintained the trade union movement's proud record of mangling the English language. Asked to comment on the Labour Party's proposals on trade union reform, he replied it was 'good in parts, like the parson's nose'. The recording was stopped while a BBC person asked if he meant it was good in parts, like the curate's egg. Unabashed, Mr Clarke replied that he knew it had something to do with ministers.

A COMMENT from the newsletter

SAND KEY PARK REGULATIONS

. ALCOHOLIC BEVERAGES PROHIBITED
. NO PETS ALLOWED ON BEACH
. CHANGING CLOTHES ON BEACH IS PROHIBITED
. NO OPEN OR GROUND FIRES
. PROPER SWIM ATTIRE REQUIRED
. SWIM ONLY IN PROTECTED AREAS
. PARK IS CLOSED AT DARK

HAVE A NICE DAY

of the Civil and Public Services Association, on the subject of a new staff assessment system: 'It's a vicious circle and it's the members who are at the sharp end.'

'PARASITE MARRIES SCROUNGER' – Heading from the *Socialist Worker* newspaper on the occasion of the marriage of Prince Andrew to Sarah Ferguson.

IN a greengrocer's in Byres Road, a university lecturer is causing a small scene. In accordance with his anti-apartheid principles, he refuses the South African oranges he has been offered. The West End lady behind him in the queue chimes in: 'I do so agree. All those black fingers . . .'

A MALE colleague of a female journalist famous for her striking skin-tight jeans, worked up the courage to ask her: 'Tell me, how do you get into those jeans?'

'You could try a couple of gin and tonics for a start,' was the withering reply.

A ROOFTOP protest was in progress at Perth Prison. The men on the roof, not content with ripping off slates from the historic building, began to demolish the battlements. As the first chunk of masonry crashed into the prison yard, a member of the local press remarked: 'That's him in trouble now. This is a listed building and Perth Civic Trust will have him.'

OUT of the mouths of babes . . . a colleague of the Diary was attending a routine press conference at the site of the Glasgow Garden Festival. The occasion was the announcement of 18 jobs – YTS jobs – being created by Glasgow parks department. The *Herald* reporter, interviewing one of the youths who had been wheeled out for the media, asked if he was into gardening. 'No, not really,' the boy replied. How did he end up in this job, then, the reporter continued. 'I got the job through my dad. He knows somebody in the masons,' the youth added, to the embarrassment of nearby officials. We presume the lad meant somebody in the stonemasons' department at the council.

GRAFFITO on the wall of a toilet in Glasgow University: 'If President Reagan doesn't tell lies, why do they keep cutting bits off his nose?'

STRATHCLYDE Region readvertisement for the post of Director of Water: 'The regional council wants to be certain that it has fully trawled the pool of talent at the highest level of water supply . . .'

No, we do not have any similar advert for the post of Director of Sewage.

SAM McCluskie, the plain-spoken leader of the National Union of Seamen, speaking on radio about some aspect of a long and difficult pay dispute: 'I'll jump off that bridge when I come to it . . .'

ASKED why there was no street in Dublin named after the Republic's first Prime Minister, Eamon De Valera, an Irish political observer said: 'Well, you see, there's no street long enough, or narrow enough, or crooked enough.'

OVERHEARD on the Edinburgh Shuttle: Scottish Office Minister Lord James Douglas-Hamilton chatting with a Civil Service minion: 'And where do you live?' The civil servant

replied that he lived in a certain street in the New Town in Edinburgh. 'Very nice,' said Lord James, 'and where do you live at weekends?'

'PLEASE do not wander about during dinner and, gentlemen, please keep your jackets and ties on during dinner. Please sit down and do not talk during speeches. It is not only very bad manners but lets both you and the school down in front of the many guests attending. Please do not smoke until after the Loyal toast.'

Details from a letter by the chairman of Gordonstoun School Association to former pupils attending the 1988 annual dinner.

WHEN Rangers FC formed a professional basketball team, the captain, a Mr Jim Morrison, was invited to sample the Gers match-day hospitality in the Premier Club. He was heard to remark afterwards: 'A really nice place the Premier Club but I've never had so many funny handshakes in my life.'

OVERHEARD in a Newton Mearns coffee chop, a lady is relating to her friends a rather nasty experience on a bus. 'This man sat down beside me. Then he put his hand up my skirt. You know the Jaeger one with the pleats . . .'

FROM a BP brochure explaining why they had decided to make more use of the colour green in their corporate identity: 'It not only differentiates BP from its rivals but if used in conjunction with certain styles creates a feeling of freshness, an impression of foliage, even of paradise.'

'MY wife can't stand the Scottish Liberals or Scotland and when she comes to power she'll see that they are soundly defeated.' – Denis Thatcher in South Africa in 1964, quoted by Ben Coutts in his autobiography *From Bothy to Ben*.

MINE host of down-to-earth Glasgow pub to chap who has ordered a Perrier: 'This is a pub, son. We don't sell water.' The customer orders a gin and tonic and asks for a slice of lemon, to be told: 'Whit d'ye think this is, Malcolm Campbell's?'

THE incredulous family of an 89-year-old bachelor who had announced his engagement to a young woman asked him two questions. Was it true? And would he be moving house? His answers were: Yes. And yes, we want to be nearer the schools.

GREAT BOOK REVIEWS OF OUR TIME: A critic writing of the memoirs of Dr Henry Kissinger, eminent US statesman, said: 'I do not know whether Dr Kissinger is a great writer, but anyone who manages to finish this book is certainly a great reader.'

AN oft-repeated, but worth repeating, story is that when God was creating the British Isles he started with Scotland and was busy installing beautiful mountains, breathtaking glens, salmon-filled rivers and all the rest of the glories that are Scotia, when one of the angels asked Himself if perhaps He was not going over the top in the provision of amenities to Scotland. 'Perhaps,' he replied, 'but wait and see who they are getting as neighbours.'

A YOUNG lady in a Stirling hairdresser's, to her customer who was a musician in the Scottish National Orchestra: 'Are ye no' workin' the day?' Snip. Snip.
'Well, I work mostly in the evenings.'
Snip. Snip. 'Really? Whit is it ye dae?' Snip. Snip.
'I'm a member of the SNO.'
Snip. Snip. 'Och, I dinna ken onythin' aboot politics.' Snip. Snip.
Update: Since then, perhaps in search of an identity, the SNO has changed its title to the Royal Scottish National Orchestra and then to the Royal Scottish Opera.

AS you would expect when a local legend is in hospital, Sydney Devine received special treatment when he was in the Western Infirmary, Glasgow, for a heart bypass operation. This even extended to the nurses singing Tiny Bubbles In Your Drip as they wheeled Steak and Kidney into the operating theatre.

FROM the synopsis of Glasvegas, a musical play created for Mayfest 1989 by Borderline Theatre: 'Glasgow, where some are born great, some achieve greatness and some are still throwing spears at buses . . .'

AMERICAN lady in Edinburgh at Festival time, surveying hundreds of people queuing for tickets at the

Tattoo office: 'Oh, my goodness, look at all those people waiting to be tattooed.'

A MAN sitting at his wife's death-bed is asked: 'Hamish, grant me a last wish. Promise me you'll sit in the same car as my mother on the way to the crematorium.'

'Okay, if it makes you happy,' he replies, 'but you know it will spoil the whole day for me.'

THEN there's the tale of the man who could no longer put up with his mother-in-law. He went to the chemist and asked: 'Can I have some arsenic for my mother-in-law?'

'Do you have a prescription?' the chemist asked.

'No, but I've got a photograph.'

THE eminent cartoonist Malky McCormick is also something of a philosopher. He presented these great imponderables of life to the Diary:

- Why is there only one Monopolies Commission?

- How do they get Teflon to stick to non-stick frying pans?

- If Karen Carpenter had eaten Mama Cass's sandwiches, would they both still be singing today?

ON the familiar theme of rampant inflation we heard of the old chap who, on his way home from the pub, decided that a poke of chips would be just the thing.

'That'll be 45p,' said the girl behind the counter.

In the eye

I HAVE distorted vision in the right eye. Could the cause be something in my stomach?

No – it's something in the eye! Do seek your doctor's opinion.

The old boy looked at the four florins and single shilling in his hand and said: 'Nine bob? I can remember when you couldnae carry nine bob's worth o' chips, never mind eat them.'

THIS conversation was overheard on a Glasgow building site shortly after the release of Nelson Mandela:

'Jimmy's no' goin' tae South Africa.'

'Ah thought he was gonny be oan £10 an hour.'

'Aye, but they've let that Idi Amin oot and it's buggered up the whole thing.'

THE setting for this story is a bar in Glasgow's smart Princes Square shopping centre. A would-be man about town, well past his sell-by date, is attempting to make conversation with a young woman.

'Where do you work?' he asks, in an Oscar Wilde kind of way.

'Déjà vu,' she replies.

'Is that a new shop?'

'No.'

'A restaurant?'

'No.'

'A bar?'

'No. Just the feeling I get when I'm speaking to you. I told you a fortnight ago. You've obviously forgotten. It was the night you said you'd phone me to arrange to go out for dinner and never did.'

TWO elderly women on the 57 bus in Glasgow. 'How's your man?' asks Betty.

'Deid – last Wednesday,' replies Sadie.

'Away tae hell,' says Betty, taken aback by this sad news.

'Aye,' says Sadie, 'last Wednesday.'

AN AA person warning Radio Clyde listeners about traffic jams, one day alerted drivers to a half-mile tailback at the Charing Cross underpants.

THE Scots have a cheery way of welcoming German tourists to these shores. The German in question was upstairs in a bus in Edinburgh. He remarked loudly that smoking was such a disgusting habit. This comment was obviously aimed at the elderly gent in a bunnet who was smoking a pipe. The smoking bunnet replied: 'The effan smoke didny seem to bother yiz at Auschwitz.'

A PUBLIC inquiry at the City Halls in Glasgow heard an application by a mining firm who wished to operate an open-cast mine on the outskirts of Easterhouse. One of the concerns voiced by anxious locals was that 'settlement ponds' which would have to be dug would pose a danger to children in the area. No problem, said a company spokesman. A wall-and-chain-link fence 17 feet high would be built round the ponds. 'You don't ken the weans frae Easterhouse,' was the comment from one of the locals in the hall.

GLASGOW continues to welcome tourists in its own peculiar way. An English chap was overheard in the bar of the Boswell Hotel enthusing about the selection of real ales on tap. He was particularly impressed by the McLay's. 'Where is McLay's from?' he asked the barman. The barman, obviously enrolled in the Chic Murray school of humour, replied: 'By the look of you, from Paddy's Market.' Laughter from locals, bemused look from tourist.

GREAT Tannoy Announcements of Our Time. During a speedway match in Peterborough involving Glasgow Tigers, the following information was broadcast: 'Would the driver of the yellow Vauxhall Nova in the car park please note that his Alsatian dog has just switched the windscreen wipers on.'

RICHARD STOBBS of the Mount Florida Community Council commenting on the subject of football fans' misbehaviour in the vicinity of Hampden Park on big match days: 'Our gardens are constantly being used as toilets and litter bins. I personally have had my fill . . .'

NOTICE in the bulletin of the Sacred Heart Church in Carndonagh, County Donegal: 'Cemetery Blessing. The annual ceremony of blessing the graves in the cemetery will be held at 5 p.m. on Sunday, 18 August. Please ensure that your grave is neat and tidy for the occasion.'

GREAT Tannoy Announcements of Our Time II: A dreary Monday morning on the Glasgow Underground at Govan was greatly enlivened by the following announcement: 'Would driver Singh please phone control and we'll tell him where his train is.'

EILEEN McCallum rose even higher in the Diary's estimation when she accepted her award as Scotland's actress of the year at a BAFTA Scotland ceremony. In her wee speech after receiving her Baffie (or whatever they're called), she said: 'Oh dear. If I knew I was going to win, I would have bleached my moustache.'

MIDLOTHIAN District Council took advertising space to inform their poll tax payers: 'Because of its official opening, Midlothian House will be closed to all members of the public on Friday, 22 November.'

OVERHEARD in a BBC canteen: 'Me pretentious? I used to be but I'm not *maintenant*.'

QUOTE from an Edinburgh legal chap envious of the $250,000 fee earned by an American lawyer for a trial: 'Och, it would take a Scottish solicitor a year to defraud a client of that amount of money.'

THE proliferation of forgeries of Bank of England £5 notes led to a degree of caution in retail premises. Thus this conversation between two check-out operatives in Safeway in Paisley in which the first (holding out a Bank of Scotland fiver to her colleague) asked for advice as to its authenticity. Second operative: 'Aye, that's okay. It's the wan wi' the wumman's heid we don't take.' The wumman she was referring to was none other than our own dear Queen.

DEPT of We Know What They Meant: The HMSO publication entitled *Sexual Harassment in the Workplace* advises: 'If a complaint is upheld you may need to separate the parties involved.' But hopefully not with a bucket of water.

THE Diary does not normally endorse graffiti but we were prepared to make an exception in the case of a wee inscription in a lift at Mercantile Chambers in Bothwell Street, Glasgow. The offices of the Prince's Scottish Youth Business Trust are in the building. The Prince of Wales himself had visited and, by chance, the lifts had just been refurbished. The brown paint in one of the lifts had been scratched with the message 'HRH was ER'.

SIGN spotted attached to a defective turnstile at Cowcaddens Underground station in Glasgow: 'Broke – As in Not Working.'

DEPT of We Know What They Meant II: A customer phoned a mail-order company and gave his address as 'Smith – seven oblique four Castle Wynd, Edinburgh'. He duly received a parcel address to 'Smith, 7 O'Bleak 4, Castle Wynd, Edinburgh'.

A COMPANY called Adams Rental advertising in the American magazine

TV Facts: 'Now renting Diamond Engagement Rings and Wedding Bands – No Long Term Obligation.'

ADVERT for La Florida restaurant in Tenerife: 'Due to popular demand, Sunday lunch is now served on Wednesday nights.'

OVERHEARD in the John Menzies shop at Glasgow Airport. An American lady is holding aloft a tartan-bedecked tin labelled 'Nippy Sweeties'. She asks the shop assistant: 'Hi! Can you tell me what these taste like?' To which the shop assistant helpfully replies: 'Ah'm no awfy sure, but ah think they taste something like Soor Plooms.'

BRITISH Home Stores, seeking for its store at the St Enoch Centre, Glasgow, an 'intimate-apparel manager' placed an advert stating that 'applicants must possess a hands-on approach'.

THE more all-seater stadiums proliferate, the less fun there is to be had on a sporting day out. Ask the Murrayfield debenture-holder who found the two seats behind him occupied by two women who gossiped all the way through a Scotland-Ireland match. Try as he might, he just couldn't concentrate on the game as one of the ladies told in some detail how her husband was having an affair with his secretary. All hope of paying attention to the game went out of the window when he heard the words: 'And honestly, I don't know what she sees in him. I haven't had an orgasm for six years.'

LORD James Douglas-Hamilton, the former Scottish Office roads minister famous for the common touch, asked as he was being driven along an Edinburgh street in the back of Scottish Office limo: 'Tell me. What exactly is a bus lane?'

OVERHEARD in a Maybole pizza parlour: 'Give me a big pizza with the trimmings.' 'Do you want it cut in four sections or eight?' asks the guy behind the counter. 'Better make it four. I don't think I could manage eight.'

DEPT of We Know What They Meant III: The menu of an Italian restaurant in Cork bears the slogan: 'You will not get better.'

MYSORE, India, has a restaurant which boasts that its food 'will make more than your mouth water'.

THE *Co-operative News* carried a news story headed 'Funeral Directors Celebrate' which told us that one of their divisions is 'reporting strength in depth in the funerals department'.

GREAT Pub Observations of Our Time: 'I wouldnae say the service is bad in this place but you could get a drink quicker in the Betty Ford clinic.'
   'I wouldnae say it's a rough pub but at drinking-up they send in Kate Adie to collect the glasses.'

OVERHEARD while filing out after a bowling club dance. First genteel lady: 'Did you see the eclipse of the moon the other night?' Second genteel lady: 'I didn't actually see it but I heard it on the radio.'

TALES of the Unexpected. An advertisement in the Borders weekly newspaper the *Southern Reporter* forlornly advised: 'Due to an error an evening of clairvoyance will NOT be held tonight in the Foresters Arms, Jedburgh.'

AN outbreak of humour at Fife Regional Council, where they were discussing statistics in the chief constable's annual report. Councillor Tam Dair remarked that he always looks at the bottom of the statistical tables first and added: 'Mind you, I am a Cowdenbeath supporter.'

SEE Glasgow? See culture? The Diary normally shuns toilet talk but was impressed by the following conversation in the gents at (where else) the Centre for Contemporary Arts in Sauchiehall Street after a show of avant-garde theatre.
Man at first urinal: 'Spirituality is still an important element in society . . .'
Man at second urinal: 'No, I doubt the relevance of spirituality in life today . . .'
Voice from second cubicle on left: 'Surely first of all you have to define spirituality . . .'

AN EXTRACT from a letter sent by a Strathclyde education official to the headmaster of St Ambrose High School in Coatbridge, which had won the 1992 Curriculum Award: 'I would wish to pay my own personal tribute to yourself, your staff and, of course, your pupils for the magnificent work which must have went into the school's submission in order to achieve the award.'

SLOGAN on the side of a van belonging to an Asian-owned building company in Bradford: 'You've Used the Cowboys, Now Try the Indians.'

STRATHCLYDE police informed the media that '8,000 tons of EC mince' had been stolen from a Salvation Army warehouse in Cambuslang before it could be distributed to local OAPs. While the collective journalistic mind was attempting to cope with the concept of how anyone could purloin such a large amount of mince, the polis went on to say it was in fact 8,000 tins of mince which had been nicked.

FOLK singer Hamish Imlach told in his autobiographical tome, *Cod Liver Oil and the Orange Juice*, that he had an allergy to leather – every time he wakes up in bed with his shoes on he has a terrible headache. We asked readers if they suffered similar afflictions. Eric V. Hudson of Bearsden recalled his days as a Round Tabler and a colleague who, as he donned his dinner jacket before departing for the soirée, was asked by his darling three-year-old daughter: 'Daddy, why do you wear that jacket? You know it always makes you sick.'

READERS' WRITES

One of the features of Herald *Diary columns over the years has been their ability to involve the reader. Some say that this is merely a way of having the readers do all the hard work. The truth is that the* Herald *readership includes some extraordinarily clever people and it is very much in the public interest that their wit be published.*

THE first competition I ever ran was suggested by colleague Roddy Forsyth. He noticed that the book *Six Days of the Condor* had been made into a film called *Three Days of the Condor*. We invited readers to come up with their suggestions for other half-frame films. These included:

*Snow White and the Three and a Half
  Dwarfs
The One and a Half Musketeers
Five (Hard Luck, Bo Derek)
Stereophenia
One and a Half Coins in the Fountain
The Three-and-a-Half-Year Itch
The Magnificent Three and a Half
The Slightly Soiled Half Dozen
Fellini's Four and a Quarter
Catch 11
Farenheit 250½*

The winning entry was *The Wizard of 14 Grammes.*

The Diary was later inspired by Mayfest stand-up comedian Howard Busgang, who had in turn been inspired by Kurt Vonnegut's *Slaughterhouse Five*, to run a competition called Backward Films. In his act Mr Busgang related the plots of films which had been inadvertently run back-to-front:

- *The Godfather* is a happy story about some really bad gangsters who gave up a life of crime to lead a simple peasant life in Sicily, while *Friday the Thirteenth* is a tale about a nice person who goes round pulling knives out of people and making them better.

- *The Titanic* is a film about a giant submarine which surfaces, picks up lots of people who appear foolishly to have gone swimming or sailing in rowing boats in the middle of the Atlantic, and takes them back to Liverpool.

- *Psycho* is about this mental patient who overcomes his problems, rescues a girl trapped in a car in a murky pond, and cleans her up in the shower before she returns home.

- *Roots* is a backward TV serial much loved by members of the Ku Klux Klan. It tells how prosperous and integrated black people in American society are thrust back into slavery and, even better from the Klan point of view, are put into ships and taken back to Africa.

- In *My Fair Lady* a wealthy London lady has an upper-class accent she wants to get rid of so that she can communicate with the poor folk of Covent Garden.

- *The Sound of Music* is an unusual tale about a woman who gives a bunch of children aversion therapy to music by teaching them to forget various dreadful songs. She then makes curtains out of their clothes before going back to a nunnery.

- *It's a Wonderful Life* is the story of a crooked businessman who cheats the people of a small town before committing suicide with the help of an angel.

- *The Agony and the Ecstasy* is about a Pope on his death-bed who apparently has an aversion to his painted ceiling. He hires a chap called Michelangelo to strip the paint off. He then recovers his health.

- *Gone with the Wind* is the story of a wilful young woman who averts the American Civil War, puts out a major fire at Atlanta, extends slavery to all the states of America, and leaves her husband for a wimp called Ashley.

- *Gregory's Girl*, in the backward version, is about a lanky youth who likes to lie in the park in Cumbernauld with attractive young women. But he gives up girls to

concentrate on playing football for the school team.

- *The Dirty Dozen* is a sad story of Allied soldiers who fight their way out of a French chateau occupied by German troops. They escape back to England where they are untrained, put in prison and then charged with sundry crimes such as murder and rape.

- *A Bridge Too Far* is another war story but with a happy ending. An army of plucky soldiers are surrounded and vastly outnumbered by the Germans. They retreat, doing repair work on any bridges they pass, and escape back to England by jumping 10,000 feet back into their aeroplanes.

- *The Graduate*: A young man throws off the shackles of marriage to have a fling with an older woman, and experiments with rubber fetishism in his swimming pool, before going to college.

- *Casablanca*: The chief of police tells his men to allow the usual suspects to go home. Rick goes to the airport to meet Ilsa. They sit around in a café agonising as time goes by. They part but meet many years later and have a dirty weekend in Paris before splitting up forever.

- *Fatal Attraction*: A beautiful but impetuous woman is harassing a married couple by messing up their bathroom, kidnapping their child, and making constant phone calls. The husband solves the problem by meeting her, and taking her to bed, after which they part amicably.

- *Bridge Over the River Kwai*: Alec Guinness builds a bridge by the simple device of pulling up the plunger on a detonator device. His men then laboriously dismantle it before going back to a PoW camp where they sit around with nothing to do.

- *The Ten Commandments*: The Jews, fed up with Moses' strict laws, send him back up the mountain with the Commandments. His people stop having an orgy and decide to head back to Egypt where the Pharaoh is waiting for them. They are given council houses and celebrate by wiping the lamb's blood off the lintels. They get MSC jobs building pyramids and live for many a happy year by the Nile.

- *A Town Like Alice*: An Australian couple go to Malaya with a Japanese travel firm. They fall out over the inclusion of chicken on the menu. She goes to live in England. He goes back to Alice Springs to be a shepherd.

- *The Wooden Horse*: A hand-picked team of Allied soldiers tunnel into a German PoW camp, where they entertain the troops with gymnastic displays under the nose of the Hun.

- *Frankenstein*: An ugly chap goes to a doctor for plastic surgery. Instead, the doc dismembers him and buries the pieces in various local graveyards.

- *The Cannonball Run*: A bunch of crazy car drivers race backwards across the USA and it ends in a dead heat.

- *Guess Who's Coming to Dinner*: A couple are having a pleasant dinner with their daughter's black boyfriend. But he proves to be such a smart-ass they throw him out.

- *Whisky Galore*: The entire population of a Hebridean island decides to go teetotal. They search every nook and cranny of the island, collect every drop of the hidden hooch, and ferry it out to a beached freighter. The ship is refloated and sails off into the fog.

- *Geordie*: A strapping Highlander is Olympic champion hammer-catcher in Australia. He returns to Scotland to work as a farm labourer. He spends less and less time at the hammer-catching and eventually ends up emaciated.

- *The 39 Steps*: Robert Donat is watching a mind-reading act in a London theatre. He takes off for Scotland where he steals a car, makes a political speech and is shot. He leaps on to the Forth Rail Bridge, gets himself handcuffed to Madeleine Carroll, and goes back to London. There he dresses up as a milkman while someone is murdered in his flat.

- *Dracula*: A gang of Transylvanian villagers led by a doctor extract a big skelf from a local gent's chest. The grateful gent undertakes night-

ly visits to the bedrooms of anaemic ladies, restoring them to health by means of blood transfusions.

• *Greyfriars Bobby*: A wee dog is sitting by a plot in a graveyard in Edinburgh. The grave opens and a man (whom the wee dog obviously knows) emerges from the coffin. The man and dog go away and live happily ever after.

• *The Third Man*: An American in Vienna rescues a fellow countryman from a sewer while on the way back from a funeral. The rescued man disappears. The rescuer gets fed up being harassed by British military police and goes home.

• *Ice Cold in Alex*: John Mills and Anthony Quayle meet in a bar in Egypt. They have a few chilled lagers too many, hijack an ambu-

lance, drive into the desert and get lost.

THE idea of backward films led on to a wider examination of life as seen through a rear-view mirror. We had readers writing in with some very interesting Backward Concepts . . .

The year in question is 1988, and Celtic have celebrated their centenary year by winning the Scottish Cup and Premier League double. Then things begin to go backwardly bad:

First they climb back up the steps to hand the cup and individual medals back to Mrs Thatcher. There then follow a number of football matches where the Celtic forward line keep running away from the opponents' goalmouth and each game ends in a disappointing 0—0 draw.

Even more perturbing is the tendency of the Old Firm to take the field with only nine or ten players, with the missing players coming back on at different times during the game as the referee puts his red card back in his pocket.

The league season ends with all 12 teams in a tie for top and bottom places with no points and no goals scored. The Celtic board are obviously upset at this way of celebrating their 99th birthday and sack manager Billy McNeill in favour of Davie Hay.

MRS THATCHER'S career provided an interesting Backward Concept.

First she cancels the poll tax (this was pre-Major, please remember) in favour of a property tax. She nationalises British Telecom, British Gas et al. This is paid for by higher taxes on the rich.

After eight years of undoing Conservative legislation, she resigns as Prime Minister and goes into opposition. She makes a comeback as Education Minister under Ted Heath. After reintroducing school milk for children of all ages, she demits ministerial office for the back benches.

She leaves Parliament to be a housewife. Her husband Denis leaves to rejoin his first wife. She goes to university where she has degrees in law and chemistry taken away from

her as she begins to know less and less about the subjects.

There is a happy ending as she goes back to Grantham, Lincolnshire, to be the daughter of the owner of a corner grocery shop.

THE Glasgow Garden Festival of 1988 found itself a victim of Backward Concepts.

Millions of visitors gradually drift away from the Garden Festival site. One day in April the Prince of Wales performs a closing ceremony. The trees, buildings, exhibition pavilions and even the very grass are ripped out. The Scottish Development Agency takes its £35,000,000 back. The site lies derelict for many years. Then a flourishing docks and ship-building industry develops.

SCOTTISH industry, too, is very much a backward story.

The Linwood car factory reopens and trains its labour force to dismantle vehicles. The River Clyde becomes the centre of the world's shipbreaking industry. The scrapping of some of the world's largest ships become occasions for royal visits as the vessels are dragged ashore.

The revitalisation of these industries is accompanied by a population movement back to cosier, if more crowded, accommodation in inner city areas. Housing estates in Castlemilk, Easterhouse, Drumchapel and Pollok are demolished and the land returned to farming use.

Meanwhile in Lanarkshire, Fife and other rural areas, large numbers of immigrant workers are employed to bury coal in the ground before being sent back to Ireland and the Highlands.

A SPOKESMAN for Lothian Fire Brigade started it all when he said that a blaze had been started by 'some bampot'. The Diary reported that the Press Association news agency had to put out an explanatory paragraph to the English media saying that bampot was a Scottish word for idiot. Diary readers, as they often do, joined in the debate uninvited . . .

A bampot was, in fact, a section of thick bamboo filled with explosives, said one.

No, a bampot was the bowl or receptacle in a dry toilet and a bamstick (another common Scots word) is the stick used to remove the aforementioned bampot for the purposes of emptying.

No, bampot comes from balm, an aromatic substance used to mask the smell from this pot.

No, actually, bampot was named after the town of Bam in Iran.

No, definitively, bampot comes from the brewing trade where the froth on fermenting beer is called the barm. Thus a bampot is one whose head is in ferment or full of wee bubbles.

A scholarly reader had the last word when he claimed to have uncovered a Scots verb, to bamp, which means to harp on constantly about the same topic.

WE suggested that the Scottish Prison Service's recently launched newspaper, the *Informer*, might have been better named the *News of the Screws*. Readers' suggestions included:

Time Magazine
The Daily Stir
The Indepenitentiary
Inside Crack
Daily Mailbag
Peephole's Friend
The Two-Way Daily Mirror

THE *Evening Standard*, London's local newspaper, irked the Scots with a readers' offer for T-shirts bearing the words: 'There is No Life North of Watford.' Diary readers were quick to retaliate with such slogans as:

Scotland Borders on the Uncultured
Stuff London Up Your Arsenal
Grow Your Own Dope – Plant an Englishman
You're Very Welcome to London
London is Full of Tubes
Live South of the Tweed? Yer Aff Yer Heid!
When the Germanic Tribes Invaded Britain the Acute Angles Moved North While the Obtuse Angles went South
Living in London is Capital Punishment

THE rivalry between Prestwick and Glasgow airports led to a suggestion that the Ayrshire one be renamed Robert Burns International, in an attempt to retain the American tourist market. Naturally, the Diary

readers got into the act by proposing a name change for Glasgow airport. Suggestions included:

Jean Armour International
Peter McCann International
Dalriada International Airport
Ally MacLeod Memorial International Airport
Greek Thomson Holidays Airport
Keelie's Landing
Jimmy International
Cheerio, Cheerio International
Stanley Baxter International (he does such good take-offs)
Doo Lally International
Rab C. Nesbitt International
Charles De Goal International (after Charlie Nicholas)
George Younger Memorial International
Jock Tamson International
The Just Outside Glasgow Actually in Paisley Airport
Wheech International
Itsyersel International (Edinburgh airport to be renamed 'You'll Have Had Your Tea International')
We Aero People International
Hudgie International
Erranerri Errport

THERE were suggestions that Prestwick's new name should be Sydney Devine Ayrodrone or Princess Anne International (because it is fog-free).

TO mark the opening in Glasgow of a smart hotel and bistro called Rab Ha's, after the famous Glesca Glutton, the Diary asked readers to come up with a CV which would make Rab more of a Yuppie.

Rab's real name, we were told, was John Robert McTammany Hall. He emigrated from Glasgow to New York, where he rapidly rose through the political ranks. He left New York in disgrace after consuming the entire purvey for the mayor's Thanksgiving Dinner. He joined the Confederate Army catering corps and was billeted at Tara, near Atlanta, where his cooking inspired *Gone with the Wind*. After the Civil War he took up a job as chicken inspector for Colonel Saunders. During this period he cured himself of gluttony by inventing an aversion therapy called cold turkey.

Rab Ha' was actually a well-known but financially embarrassed roofing contractor in Glasgow last century. Creditors who called at his various places of work were invariably told by his apprentice: 'Rab Ha's on the slates' – giving rise to a famous piece of Glasgow slang.

Rab was actually the smallest of three brothers; the other two being Kelvin and Albert.

Rab Ha' was extremely fond of boiled food such as potatoes, fish and beef. He it was who came up with the slogan 'Glasgow Biles Better'.

Rab Ha' was actually a famous all-in wrestler. He competed under various pseudonyms including that of Garth (later to become a newspaper cartoon strip) and invented the Garth Arm Lock, a name subsequently given to an area of Glasgow. He was equally famous for his large appetite and was also known as the Maulin' Diner and had a burn named after him. His culinary skills were the talk of the city. He was the first chef to use Irn Bru in cooking – as a marinade for an entire ox. This Irn Bru Roast Ox (or IBROX for short) became so popular that a part of Glasgow was named after it.

AND finally, the slogan invented by Saatchi & Saatchi as part of their £2,000,000 campaign to promote Glasgow's Year of Culture in 1990 did not go down too well with the populace; 'There's a Lot Glasgowing On in 1990' didn't quite take off.

The Diary put forward its own suggestion: 'See Glasgow? See Culture?', and asked readers to come up with their own ideas. These included:

Glasgow's Piles Better through Its Arts
Glesca – City of Culture an' That
See Glasgow and Die
1690—1990: We've Walked a Long Way
1990: Culture for Everyone – You Can Even Draw the Dole

Glesca 1990 – Happy Birthday, King Billy
Glesca 1990: Four Old Firm Games with Musical Interludes
Glasgow: City of Lally and Dali
Who's Coming Out in 1990?
    Alfresco Glesco
Gie it Laldy, Vivaldi
Glasgow's Got Everything, But Be a Pert o' Glesca's Ert
The Cry Wis Where's Yir Culture Errzafishulculchur
Culture's the Berries
What's Glesca Up To in 1990? Its Oxters in Culture, That's Whit
Glasgow's Hoachin' Wi' Culture
Glasgow' Full of It
Up Yours, Embra
Keelies Aye No. 1
Tiny Toi Dig the Bolshoi
Haud the Bus, Sibelius
Beethoven, Yer Tea's Oot
Glasgow 1990: Culture's the Biz, So It Is
If You Know Rennie Mackintosh from Rowntree McIntosh, Glasgow's for You

ONE last entry was: Culture's the Jinkies, and came as part of a poem which went:

What we think is
Culture's the Jinkies
We chow up culture
Like a bloody vulture.
We erra peepul.

RELIGION

Over the years, the Diary has tried to maintain an even-handed approach to religion. We aspired to upset each sect equally . . .

THE wit and wisdom of Archbishop Thomas Winning: walking into an exhibition on St John Ogilvie at the Third Eye Centre, Glasgow, the archbishop was confronted by Pastor Jack Glass and a team of protesters, complete with an effigy of the Scottish martyr hanging from a gibbet. 'Nice day for it, Jack . . .' was the Winning remark.

LUIS Palau, the Argentinian evangelist, ran a five-week series of meetings in Glasgow in summer 1981. Like many well-dressed men of the world, the man of God with the presidential entourage and the film-star good looks made a pilgrimage to Ralph Slater's tailoring emporium.

Other customers were impressed by the way Mr Palau tested his four new suits for fit. As he tried on each jacket, he stretched his arms to the heavens and said: 'Yes, this will do fine.'

THIS story could equally well have fitted into our section on Rabbie Burns . . .

The pope and Rabbie died at the same time and, due to an administration mix-up, the poet went to Heaven while the pope went to Hell. After a few days, the mistake was noticed and a swap arranged. They met halfway and the pope said to the poet: 'I am about to fulfil my lifetime ambition, to meet the Virgin Mary.'

'I'm afraid you're too late,' said Rabbie, heading off to hotter climes.

THERE was a nun, we are assured, from the Sisters of Notre Dame whose ambition was to have her own car. After many years of saving, she managed to buy a Vauxhall Nova – and quickly became known as the Hatchback of Notre Dame.

A MINISTER and a priest were sitting together on the Glasgow-London shuttle flight. The stewardess asked if they would like a drink. The minister ordered whisky.

The priest, a vigorous abstainer, said: 'I would rather commit adultery!'

'I didn't know there was a choice,' the minister said to the stewardess.

THE suspension of Lord Mackay of Clashfern, the Lord Chancellor, by the Free Presbyterian Church because he had attended two Catholic funerals, gave rise to some jokes at the expense of the FPs.

The FPs used to be known as The Seceders. One wit, thought to be from the Free Church, said: 'The FPs are no longer to be known as The Seceders. They're to be called The Suspenders.'

A second FP joke subsequently surfaced, a reference to their immaculate ministerial garb. What do you call a Free Presbyterian minister with one button of his black Crombie coat undone? A poser.

Against all the odds a third FP joke appeared. It is the tale of an English tourist in Lewis who went for a walk one Sunday afternoon. He met a member of the local FP congregation on his way home from the service. 'I wonder if you could tell me where this road leads to?' he asked the local.

'If you're walking out for pleasure, it leads to Hell,' was the reply.

A follow-up joke had the English tourist protest that the Lord Jesus went walking on the Sabbath.

'That sort of behaviour might be all very well in Jerusalem,' the FP said, 'but not in Stornoway.'

Then there was the FP elder who died on a Sunday and went straight to Heaven where he berated St Peter with the words: 'And what are you doing working on the Sabbath?'

Finally, a definition of Free Presbyterianism: 'The uneasy feeling that some people, somewhere, are enjoying themselves.'

THIS tale concerns the many secessions that have plagued the Church of Scotland. The minister of a Highland

parish is wakened at 2 a.m. by a ferocious banging at the door. He opens the door to find one of his parishioners. 'What's the problem?' he asks.

'Ah'm awfy worried, meenister,' says the parishioner.

'And why are you worried?' the minister asks.

'Ah'm awfy worried about the terrible schisms in the Kirk.'

'The terrible schisms in the Kirk?' asks the minister, beginning to spot that the member of his flock has had a drink or two. 'This is not the time to be worried about the terrible schisms in the Kirk. Come and see me tomorrow morning and we'll discuss the matter. But mind and come sober.'

'Ah cannae dae that, meenister. When ah'm sober ah couldnae care less aboot the terrible schisms in the Kirk.'

TRADITION, the Jewish version of Trivial Pursuit, contains the question:

'Why do Jewish people always answer a question with another question?' Answer: 'Why not?'

Other, unofficial Jewish Trivial Pursuit questions included:

Where did the Jewish kamikaze pilot land his plane? In his brother-in-law's scrapyard.

What is Jewish optimism? A Jew who makes a purchase from another Jew and hopes to sell it on to a Scotsman at a profit.

THE Catholic Church also had its own version of Trivial Pursuit, called Limbo, produced as a fund-raiser by a Canadian RC charity. It was described as 'an opportunity for everyday sinners to test their knowledge of Church doctrine, trivia, ceremony and liturgy'. The more po-faced RCs might disapprove of the rule which determines the order of play for a game of Limbo. The Tim who has been most recently to confession gets first go.

A RECURRENT theme in the Diary is bigotry and we were grateful to Pastor Jack Glass for some historical background on the subject. The wee pastor's organ, the *Scottish Protestant View*, contained an article, 'Proud to be a bigot', which explained: 'In the days of the stake when Protestants were burned alive by Roman Catholic priests, the reformer was made to wear a yellow garment of shame with devils and flames painted on it . . . The reformer would say: "By God's grace we will not give in to false religion. By God's grace we will stand for Jesus and contend for the faith." Papists started to call them Bi-

Godites. Over time it became bigot. This is not a badge of shame for us.'

A RIGHT uplifting wee tract was pressed into the Diary's hands. It is published by the National Bible Society of Scotland who have entitled it *Hope!*. It begins: 'For many people life has no purpose or meaning. The years come and go, bleak without hope. There seems to be no light at the end of the tunnel. One Old Testament writer sums it up like this: It is useless, useless, said the philosopher. Life is useless, all useless. You spend your life working, labouring, and what do you have to show for it? Generations come and generations go, but the world stays just the same. The sun still rises, and it still goes down, going wearily back to where it must start all over again. What has happened before will happen again. What has been done before will be done again. There is nothing new in the whole world.'

(For best effect, it should be read in your best approximation to the cheerful tones of Rikki Fulton's Reverend I.M. Jolly.) At the end of the pamphlet are the words: 'Text from the Good News Bible.'

THE churches in the Western Isles held a Day of Humiliation and Prayer to intercede with the Lord on the vexed subject of the local council's losing £23 million in the BCCI bank collapse. The local kirks – Wee, Free, and plain Church of Scotland – were busy praying and humiliating themselves. The Western Isles Council, more usefully, chose that day to hold a committee of inquiry to establish who was at fault for the missing millions. Meanwhile, over in Edinburgh, in an office not totally unadjacent to the financial heart of Scotland, how did money brokers R.P. Martin spend the Day of Humiliation and Prayer? R.P. Martin, the very people who acted for the Western Isles Council in the BCCI matter, were holding a Christmas party.

WE hear that the Rev. Dr Ian Paisley has taken umbrage at one of the Christmas presents received by his wife. He threw out a basket of dried flowers with the words: 'There'll be no pot-pourri in this house.'

THE newsletter of Strathblane Parish Church reported that parishioners have been suffering from break-ins to cars parked at the church. There was an appeal for £400 to install extra lighting to deter the thieves. Appropriately enough, the theme for that Sunday's worship was 'Lighten Our Darkness'.

SECTARIANISM is on the decline but still reverberates in West of Scotland society. How else could you explain the thinking of the pupil at a school in the Pollok area of Glasgow who knocked at the staff-room door and blurted out the news: 'Please, miss. There's a Catholic dog in the playground'?

O TEMPORA! O mores! O Motherwell! What we are talking about here is the state-of-the-art Catholic first communion ceremony as reported to us recently from Lanarkshire's cathedral city. It appears that the ceremony has become a touch Hollywood. One of the Motherwell poppets, in a white gown that could have been made for *Dynasty*, was making her way back from the altar when she touched a button on her wrist. This activated a microchip which made her tiara twinkle. Another wee communicant lassie apparently arrived at the church in a horse-drawn coach with four page boys. The opinion among some of the older brigade out Motherwell way is that communion chic has gone too far.

PROOF, if any were needed, that the folk of Larkhall are not the Orange fanatics they're made out to be could be found in the recent district council elections. Two of the town's four councillors on Hamilton district are Tims. There is one Protestant and the fourth is a Muslim. Some of the old attitudes persist, however. When Mustaq Ahmed (he's the Muslim, by the way) was first elected he proudly claimed he was the first Asian councillor to represent an all-white ward. 'It's no' white, it's orange,' he was told. In a recent election there were rumours of some dirty fighting. 'You mean they tried to use the racist card?' he was asked. 'No. They were putting it around that my wife is a Catholic.'

SIGNS

I was going to call this chapter 'Semiotics', but decided that was too pretentious and dangerous since I don't know what it means. Anyway, here is a collection of signs, small advertisements and other public notices which were brought to the attention of the Diary.

SIGN spotted on the wall of the hut which serves as an air terminal at Sanday, Orkney: 'Orkney Islands Council Emergency Procedures – airfield manager, with assistants, cover engines with foam. Drag occupants out and clear of the aircraft, using hatchets if necessary, and apply medical attention.' Oh, and have a nice trip.

SPOTTED on the North Circular road in London, a road sign saying 'Golders Green 2 miles' and, added in neat script below, 'To you, 1½ miles'.

AN advertisement in the personal columns of the magazine *Country Landowner* indicated a down-to-earth kind of readership: 'Attractive, affectionate single lady, 35, having survived last winter in cold draughty inconvenient old home, seeks any unattached farmer with super new farmhouse. Send photo of farmhouse.'

FROM the small ads section of the *Cork Examiner*: 'For sale, gravestone. Would suit family called McCafferty.'

SMALL ad in *Oban Times*: 'Life-jacket, British naval standard size, near new. £16.50 – worth £25 (more if you're drowning).'

SEEN in Bridgeton, Glasgow, around the time of the Loyalist campaign against the Anglo-Irish agreement: 'Ulster Says No!' To which has been added: 'But the man from Del Monte says Yes and he's an Orangeman too.'

Heading in the *Catholic Herald*: 'Catholic MPs swing both ways on hanging vote.'

SIGN in toilet cubicles of C.R. Smith, the double-glazing firm: 'What are you doing sitting here when you could be out selling windows?'

A ROYAL Highland Fusiliers sentry on duty in heavy rain at Edinburgh Castle was approached by an American tourist for the umpteenth time that day. The tourist pointed to the motto *Nemo me impune lacessit* carved into the castle entrance and asked: 'Soldier, can you tell me what that sign means?'

Sentry (wearily): 'That says "No four-tonners beyond this point", sir.'

HANRAHAN'S, a watering-hole adjacent to Glasgow Sheriff court, commissioned an artist to create a spoof coat-of-arms. This was duly done, complete with motto *Quinque Lonicra Periclyneum et Piscis Prandium* which translates as 'Five Woodbine and a Fish Supper'. *Sic transit gloria mundi . . .*

A CAVEAT on a leaflet about the Cambridge Diet listed 'possible minor side effects'. These included 'headaches, halitosis, mild dizziness, constipation, diarrhoea, nausea, irritability and dryness of the skin'. Or you could also stay 'cheerfully chubby'.

THE sign announcing to travellers that they have arrived in the Kinross village of Crook of Devon had a piece of graffito added announcing that it had been twinned with the Thief of Baghdad.

A BUILDER'S sign in Kilmarnock was the subject of a few letters to the Diary. It read: 'The Poor Sisters of Nazareth New Sun Lounge Extension.'

FROM the *Dunoon Observer*: 'Fire – The old pouffe which started the fire at 7 Douglas Cottages as reported last week, referred to an item of furniture and not the owner, Mr Donnie McArthur.'

ERRATUM slip in the *Oxford Minidictionary of Spelling*: 'The following error escaped our notice – for illitterate read illiterate.'

PROPERTY advert in *The Scotsman*: 'Set on the outskirts of this charming West Lothian village this exceptional detached bungalow is set in ¼ acre mature gardens screened by established carnivorous hedging.'

FROM the minutes of Perth and Kinross District Council: 'Concern was expressed at dog fouling on footpaths and play areas and it was agreed to increase the number of hanging floral baskets next year.'

NOTICE in the bar of Castlebay Hotel, Barra: 'Helen Whaite is our credit manager. If you want credit, go to Helen Whaite.'

AND finally, a piece of arcane graffito spotted in Glasgow's Maryhill Road: a list of youths' names followed by the statement: 'F*** the Polis and BBC1.'

SPORTS

Sports, apart from football, occasionally fought their way into the Diary's columns.

GORDON Brown, Broon frae Troon (or Brown from Trown as he became known since his vowels changed slightly after becoming a star on English TV) has so many tales and anecdotes, we hope he doesn't mind us pinching a few. Like the one about referee Allan Hosie officiating at a towsy match between West of Scotland and Langholm. Brian Gossman, of West, tried to nip down the blind side of the scrum to be met by one Langholm player who got him in a neck-breaking hold, while another opponent punched him in the face and indicated that if he tried the ploy again it would be met with even stiffer punishment.

Gossman said to referee Hosie: 'Did you hear that?' The ref indicated that he had. 'Well?' asked Gossman. Hosie replied: 'If I were you I wouldn't go down the blind side again.'

SOME years ago, after a club match away from home, Broon discovered that his car had been moved from where he had parked it, a practical joke in vogue at the time. He returned to the bar and announced, loudly and aggressively, that if the blighters (or a word similar) responsible did not return his car pronto, he would have to do the same as he had down at Hawick two weeks before.

Given Broon's substantial presence, not to mention menace, the car was promptly located. 'By the way,' asked the club secretary of Broon. 'What did you do at Hawick two weeks ago?'

'I had to get a lift home,' said Broon sweetly.

US chaps on the Diary do not approve of violence but we could not help but smile when we were appraised of this overheard conversation in an Edinburgh hotel lobby on the Sunday morning after Murrayfield between two Englishmen, one sporting a braw keeker. 'Nigel, what on earth happened to you?'

'I was in a pub in the city centre after the match. We were having a perfectly normal discussion about the game when suddenly this Scotsman leaned across and punched me for no apparent reason.'

A RUGBY World Cup 'I Mentioned The War But I Think I Got Away With It' award went to Duncan

Paterson, Scotland team manager. Praising the Japanese for their tenacity at Murrayfield, and in particular a tackle by the Japanese centre on Scott Hastings, he said: 'They certainly don't take any prisoners.'

AUSTRALIAN women rugby fans are noted for the directness of their approach and explicitness of their language. During a British Lions Australian tour a player (who shall remain nameless) was approached by a local maiden whose convent education and finishing school in Switzerland had obviously not worked.

'You're a big lad,' she said to the player. 'How big are you?'

'I'm about six foot six when I'm standing up straight,' he replied.

Gazing below his belt, the shameless sheila asked a supplementary question: 'And are you in proportion?'

'Oh, no,' the player replied. 'If I was in proportion I'd be nine foot eight.'

A LOCAL restaurant was negotiating to put some sponsorship into Irvine RFC. The snag was that the restaurateur wanted the name of his establishment to be incorporated into the name of the club. The Irvine committee had to decline on the grounds that they could not see the SRU being too pleased with such scorelines as: Watsonians 6, The Gulab Tandoori Irvine RFC 11.

ISLAY rugby club played hosts to a David Sole select XV. The Diary reported that as well as enjoying the game, Sole and co. also had a grand

time at the post-match ceilidh. Freddie Bell, president of the Islay club, was intrigued subsequently to receive a phone call from a lady on the staff of the *Sunday Sport*. She wanted the full story of the goings-on at the ceilidh. It was very enjoyable but nothing unusual for Islay, he replied. Come, come, insisted the lady reporter. What about these international players taking their clothes off at the ceilidh?

Freddie confessed to not having a clue what she was talking about. 'You know what I mean,' she persisted. 'This strip the willow . . .'

AT a time when the community of Monklands district was riven with discord it was heartening to see the Corinthian sport of rugby going some way to ameliorate Lanarkshire's version of the Serbo-Croat way of life. The Waysiders club of Airdrie and Drumpellier from Coatbridge agreed to merge. After a poor season which saw both clubs relegated from their respective divisions in the McEwan's National League, a decision was made to have one rugby club represent the Twin Burghs of the Plain.

The union was achieved not without rancour, especially from Waysiders who had to forsake their clubhouse and make their way to the other side of the Monklands faultline for a pint and a game of rugby. The most memorable contribution to the merger debate came from a player

FAST EDDIES PLACE

WARM BEER LOUSY FOOD

COCKTAILS

who expressed his reservations in a typically North Lanarkshire down-to-earth manner: 'They're a load o' shite. We're a load o' shite. And if we amalgamate we'll have an even bigger load o' shite.'

ONE of the Diary's more esoteric interests is unusual line-out codes used by rugby teams. An observer at Westerlands playing fields at Anniesland was able to compare the secret codes of Glasgow University and their opponents Strathclyde Police. The yoonie chaps stuck to mundane numbers such as 'Seven, Six, Three, Five!'. The polis, you may not be surprised to hear, preferred such instructions as 'Foxtrot, Alpha, Tango, Romeo'.

ENGLAND won the war of words as well at the World Cup Sevens rugby at Murrayfield. While our fans were indulging in some booing and jeering of the English, one of the fans from down south came away with a moment of genuine humour. As Japan scored their 26th point against Scotland in the final of the Bowl, the cup for the runners-up to the runners-up, the Englishman turned to sundry nearby Scots and said in an impeccable Bill McLaren: 'Aye, they'll be smiling down in Tokyo tonight . . .'

RUGBY fans can have an engaging way of negotiating with ticket touts. A conversation outside Murrayfield:
Tout: It's £4 for a £1.50 ticket.'
Fan: 'I'll give you £1.50 or I could break your arm and take it from you for nothing . . .'
Tout: 'It's a deal.'

MANY years of visiting Paris for international matches has given Scottish rugby fans a fair smattering of the French language. One of the leading exponents of this is Mr David Shaw, of Clarkston Rugby Club. The man is damn near bilingual. *'Au secours, mon Robert,'* he can be heard to say in a bar where the prices are rather steep. In a moment of exasperation, he might even be heard to utter: *'Donnez-moi une fracture.'*

Mr Shaw is also credited with making this joke during a weekend in Paris:
Frappez, frappez.
Qui est là?
Nous.
Nous qui?
Certainement!

FANS at an Irish Gaelic football match proved themselves to be no animal lovers. The game, the Offaly senior championship, was delayed when a cockerel sporting the Tullamore colours was thrown on to the pitch. The situation was further confused when a dog started to chase the cockerel around the field. The bird, minus many feathers, avoided the jaws of death by escaping behind an advertisement hoarding. The Irish Times reported the incident under the memorable heading: 'Dog bites cock at Offaly final.'

PRACTICAL jokes are a way of life in Portree on the Isle of Skye. As evidence, take this story about the Skye Camanachd shinty team. The players in this auspicious outfit, one of the top caman-wielding teams in the country, like to repair to the Tongadale Hotel in Portree of a Saturday night after the match.

After a hard day at the shinty and a few drinks afterwards, the strapping lads of Skye Camanachd have taken, of late, to raiding the fridge in the Tongadale Hotel kitchens which are all too handy for the bar.

Despite warnings from the chef, the shintyists failed to desist from this practice.

The chef, deciding that enough was more than sufficient, baked a pie. It had beautiful flaky pastry but an unusual filling. Pedigree Chum.

The pie was left in the larder. Sure enough, after closing time, one of the shinty players, who shall remain nameless (although he uses his hands more than other team members), went through to the kitchen, spied the pie, and scoffed the lot.

The midnight snackster was

spotted by hotel staff, who knew the provenance of the pie, but, with difficulty, said nothing.

By the time of the next shinty match, the word had gone round the home fans about what had happened. The first the player realised was when there were outbreaks of uncharacteristic barking from the crowd. This was accompanied by the sight of people lifting their legs against the goalposts.

At the hotel, the post-match beer was served in saucers.

It is said that eight out of ten Skye players prefer Pedigree Chum.

THIS story about marathon malpractice just happened to involve an Irishman.

The occasion was the Inverclyde Marathon. A competitor from Antrim in Northern Ireland, who had finished well up the field in a very respectable time, had his medal taken back after an investigation by the race stewards.

They disqualified him after he admitted starting the race half an hour early and then cutting numerous corners. His excuse, that he was in a rush to catch the ferry at Stranraer, did not impress the stewards.

THE Diary's attention was drawn to strange signs in two municipal swimming-pools. Glasgow's North Woodside Leisure Centre, the old

Woodside Baths as was, had been refurbished in ancient-Roman style. The authorities, perhaps concerned that orgies may occur in such a setting, have put up a sign which includes among its prohibitions the words: 'No petting.' To reinforce the point, the sign is illustrated by a cartoon in which a well-endowed lady swimmer is saying to her male companion: 'No, I don't want to see your breast stroke.' Meanwhile, over in doucest Giffnock, the Eastwood pool has a sign which boldly states: 'Please don't pee in our pool. We don't swim in your toilet.' More appropriate to the area, we thought, is the sign in the shower area headed 'Protection of privacy' which urges swimmers to keep their swimwear on in the showers to avoid embarrassing others.

OUR reference to the *défense de pisser dans le pool* sign at Eastwood baths brought a rejoinder from Austin Lafferty of Pollokshields (one of the Diary's regular correspondents, now sadly deceased). He recalled the occasion when a man was being ejected from a Glasgow swimming baths. Why for? He asked the attendant. 'For peeing in the pool,' he was told. 'But other people pee in the pool,' he protested. 'Aye, but no' aff the dale,' the attendant replied.

MR LAFFERTY also took us back to his boyhood in Perth in the 1930s. 'It was before the days of recycling of water in the baths. The baths were filled every Monday, Wednesday and Friday morning from the nearby lake. Monday, Wednesday and Friday were described as fresh-water days, the

admission charge being thruppence. Tuesday, Thursday and Saturday were known as dirty-water days, and the charge (dysentery *compris*) was only tuppence. But at the end of a dirty-water day the contents of the baths resembled something like lentil soup, but without its flavour. It wasn't helped by the practice we boys indulged in. In the shower we were wont to lather our whole selves with the aid of blocks of carbolic soap thoughtfully provided. Then, to the manifest horror of the attendant, do a "soapy dive", leaving a submarine trail like Halley's Comet. Eventually the attendant would call you over, and, on enquiry, you said you had fully enjoyed the pleasure of the pool for a quarter of an hour. He was seldom persuaded and insisted on inspection of your fingers which, after a couple of hours, were so furrowed and bleached (by the chorine and urine) that you had no defence.' Happy days. Insanitary days, but happy days.

DOCTOR John Macpherson, a Dundonian now in exile as a GP in deepest Troon, weighed in with some Dundonian swimming-baths lore. 'The old Central baths are sorely missed. The second-class pool was known to turn from blue to red at about 5 p.m. every day during the summer. The reason for this was not any decree from the ruling Labour Party but berry juice washing off the schoolkids who had been "at the berries" that day.'

Social historians may be interested to note the phrase 'second-class pool'. The first-class pool was more expensive and a service to those who were prepared to pay a premium to avoid contact with Clootie City's great unwashed.

SOMETIMES the Diary became deeply philosophical and asked serious meaning-of-life questions like: Is Ally McCoist really the Greatest Living Ranger? Is Jim McLean really God? How long could Terry Cassidy get away with it at Celtic Park?

We were saved from the much simpler debate, 'What is sport?', when the Sports Council issued their Research Document No. 21 on this very subject: 'It was necessary to define clearly the concept of sport . . . This includes all activities which might be popularly recognised as sport . . . but excludes greyhound racing in which animals are the only active participants.' (The Sports Council chaps have obviously never been to Shawfield on a race night.)

The report continues: 'Popular physical activities such as dancing, snooker, billiards, pool, and walking (two or more miles for leisure purposes) are also included in this definition, but the game of darts is not included.'

So, there you have it. A chap who walks two miles from his house in Maryhill to a disco in town, meets Senga for a spot of dancing, and walks her home, has been doing sport. (No, we don't know if aerobic winching counts as sport.) The chap who stayed in the pub playing darts cannot be counted a sportsman but the guy next to him playing pool in the smoky confines of the boozer has been doing sport.

WISDOM, Weans, From the Mouths of: It appears that in our schools even jolly old PE has been blighted with academic jargon. No longer can gym teachers allow the bairns to go out to the playing fields and knock a ball about in the name of sport. Now that the pupils can do an O-level (or whatever the hell it is they're called nowadays) in gym, they have to be learnt proper. Thus we hear of one lady gym teacher trying to inculcate some O-grade hockey into her girls. As she demonstrated a few bits of hockey magic, she asked the class: 'Now what skill is this?' To which one replied: 'North Kelvinside, miss.'

THE British Amateur Gymnastics Association lost out when Coca-Cola withdrew as sponsors of their major awards scheme. But the good news was that the void was filled by Pedigree Pet Foods Ltd. Pedigree chose to name the award scheme after its Kit-E-Kat brand. Neat, don't you

think, with the comparisons between agile felines and supple gymnasts? But we felt that Mr Tony Murdock, the association's awards director, took things too far. He stated in a circular on the new sponsorship: 'We sincerely hope that all our current gymnasts who use the awards will support the sponsor and, hopefully, try out Kit-E-Kat cat food in the coming months.'

FROM darkest Midlothian came a tale which illustrates what a trusting lot bowlers are. Loanhead Miners Welfare were drawn to play Rosslyn at the neutral venue of Rosewell bowling club. To save travelling, it was agreed over a telephone call between the respective skips to play the match at either Loanhead or Rosslyn. 'Where will me meet to toss the coin?' asked the Loanhead man.

'Let's do it over the phone. I'll trust you,' replied the Rosslyn man.

'Okay, call.'

'Heads.'

'Sorry, it's tails.'

We can't see it catching on in less trustworthy pairts than Midlothian.

WORLD boxing champion Walter McGowan, explaining how he came to be a hungry fighter, described his upbringing in Burnbank, a garden suburb of Hamilton: 'It was the jungle in Burnbank that we came from. You had to sleep with your socks on if you wanted them in the morning. Pit-bull terriers had to run about in pairs up there.'

THE Diary attracted a number of golf jokes of uncertain vintage, like the story of an enthusiastic but inexperienced American who hacked his way around the Old Course in 170 strokes. He confessed to his caddie: 'Gee, I'm so dispirited I could jump into that ol' Swilcan Burn and drown myself.'

'Dinnae bother,' the caddie replied. 'I don't think ye could keep your heid doon lang enough.'

A WILLING but wanting lady golfer on a Kilmarnock municipal course was experiencing great difficulty making contact with the ball. After her third fresh-air shot, she turned to the party of schoolboys who were waiting their turn and apologised for the delay. 'That's all right, missus,' one boy replied. 'We started our school holidays today.'

A MEMBER of an Ayrshire club was playing a round with his wife. He drove his ball into a wooden shelter at the sixth hole. He was about to take a penalty drop when his wife pointed out that two planks of wood were missing, providing a slim but tempting chance of pitching to the green which was visible through the aperture. He attempted the shot. Unfortunately, he missed the gap and the ball rebounded fiercely, hitting his dear wife on the forehead and killing her stone dead. Some six weeks later, having overcome the grief, he was playing the same course with a friend. His drive at the sixth ended up in the same wooden shelter. He declared that he would be taking a penalty drop shot. His partner pointed out that there were two planks missing and he could possibly chip through and onto the green. 'Oh, no,' he said. 'I tried that before and it was a disaster.'

'What happened?'

'I scored nine.'

A TRUE story about the golfer who was practising his short iron shots in the privacy of his own back garden. As he practised with his eight-iron, his wife's beloved Yorkshire terrier ran through his legs, making a perfect connection with his downward swing. The poor wee thing was sent flying through the air. We would like to tell you about the powers of recovery of the Yorkie but the truth is it was dead on arrival at the vet.

Also true and in equally bad taste: An aged member's last request was that his ashes be spread on the eighteenth green. The club captain, charged with carrying out the request, did a less than perfect job. He simply up-ended the urn, leaving Old Tam's remains in a rather large pile on the green, hoping that the breeze would disperse them. Walking back to the clubhouse, he looked back to see that a ball had landed on Old Tam's ashes. The player duly lifted his ball, licked it clean, placed it clear of the obstruction and carried on putting.

STRANGER than fiction are the rules which various golf clubs invent to torment lady visitors. This experience from a woman who accompanied a male friend to Old Ranfurly Golf Club in Bridge of Weir: 'The problem arose in the bar. Drink in hand, I surveyed the room and decided that the best place to sit was near the window where the players

could be seen. As I walked towards a vacant table, my companion was asked by the barmaid to call me back to the bar. There, I was informed in embarrassed tones that ladies were not allowed to step off the carpet. The wooden floor was apparently the men's games area. No dividing screens were evident. I enquired from the embarrassed barmaid whether this rule was to stop high heels damaging the hard floor. No, she replied, ladies are just not allowed to step off the carpet area.'

WE are pleased to report a small but significant backlash on the subject of dress codes in golf clubs. Loch-winnoch Golf Club is part of a darts league which includes various local hostelries. When the players from another team turned up at the club-house wearing (*quelle horreur!*) denims and trainers, they were snootily received by some members. In revenge, when the golf club chaps paid their return visit to the other team, a sign was prominently displayed with the words: 'No Pringles allowed.'

IT appears that Canadian golfers are more laid back than us about the business of clubhouse rules. A club in

Sicamous, British Columbia, has a sign which warns: 'No spikes on dance floor.'

GOLFERS have to fill in those fallow winter months somehow. Some of the chaps at Williamwood, the select club on the South Side of Glasgow, decided to have a night during which a bird would be hired to get her tits out for the lads, as the current slang vulgarly has it. The performance in which the lady would be engaged to doff her garments purely in the pursuit of the lively arts was to take place in lockfast premises to avoid offence to the innocent. A member of staff, spotting the arrival of a lady ('a right darling' according to an eye-witness) in a fur coat and black stockings guided her into a side room and said she could leave her gear in there while she performed next door. The said member of staff quickly discovered that this is a surefire way of upsetting a member's wife.

FROM the world of horse-racing we heard the Runyonesque tale of Tam, an OAP who goes to Hamilton races with only a tenner. He puts the lot on his choice for the first race which duly romps home at big odds. He puts his winnings on an outsider in the second race which also wins. By the time the last race comes, Tam has £40,000 in his pocket. Being a true punter, he puts the lot on the favourite, a horse called Lucky Tam. It is beaten in a photo-finish. He goes home to the wife who asks how he fared. 'No' bad,' he replies. 'I only lost a tenner.'

ANOTHER tale of a superstitious punter who went to bed one night and dreamed all night long about bread — crusty loaves, sliced, pan, plain. The next morning, consulting his *Herald* racing pages, he was delighted to find a nag called Mother's Pride which was a cert for the 3.15 race at Hamilton. He went straight to the bookie and placed £500 on the horse. Returning to collect his certain winnings, he was disgusted to hear from a delighted bookie that the race had, in fact, been won 'by a big outsider'.

USEFUL

*One of the Diary's favourite topics is Things You Never Knew You Wanted Until You
Saw It In A Catalogue.*

There are some unusual items on offer
from The Engine Shed mail-order
railway-model company. Especially
arcane is their list of the wee people
that can be purchased to populate the
trackside of your average model-
railway complex. The list includes
your standard groups like 'waiting
passengers', 'track maintenance gang'
and 'arriving passengers'. Then,
further down the list, do we not find
'wedding group, Protestant' and
'wedding group, Catholic'. What, we
asked the man on the mail-order line
at the Engine Shed, was the
difference? Quite simple, he said.

In the Protestant wedding group
the vicar is wearing black and in the
Catholic one the vicar is wearing
white. So far, so good, if not an
entirely accurate representation of the
differences between Proddies and
Tims. But our attention was then
drawn to other items on the list like
'artist, sculptor, nude', 'nude bathers',
and 'doctor, patient, revue girl'. We
were particularly intrigued by this last
category.

Explain, we asked the man at The
Engine Shed. Quite simple, really.
'This group consists of a doctor with
a female patient stripped to the waist,

a striptease artist, a naked lady with a
towel, another naked lady with her
arm covering her bosom, and a lady
in a leotard.' Yes, of course, just
another day in the doctor's surgery.
(Does the BMA disciplinary tribunal
know about this chap?)

We didn't like to ask but we
presume that the respective groups
advertised as 'shepherd with dog and
sheep' and 'boy scouts' are more
mundane and of a different stamp
from the doctor and the coterie of
floozies. We should add, in defence of
Britain's railway modellers, that the
above items are manufactured in
Germany. And they carry a warning
that they are 'recommended for
model builder and collectors as of 14
years of age'.

OTHER Essential Items:
The Swiss Lady Fertility Watch
which 'uses the natural laws of the
menstrual cycle to help parents plan
for a baby boy or girl. Tests carried
out in Germany, and supported by
the German Research Foundation,
show that Swiss Lady's timing has a
90 per cent success rate.'

This combination of Germanic
efficiency and Swiss accuracy will

'help you keep a check on the right time for conception'. So how does it work? 'There's no need for complex calculations or complicated charts – you simply follow the easy instructions supplied.' We asked just how easy were these instructions. Actually, the watch comes with four A4 pages of instructions. The lady on the telephone confessed that she could not give us a simple, brief version. The watch is 'beautifully styled so it can be worn as an ordinary watch'. The watch face is black and green with the rather unsubtle logo of an apple with a bit out of it. So watch out. If you see a lady wearing such a watch, it is probably best not to ask her if she has the time. Another piece of totally useless, but interesting, information about the Swiss Lady Fertility Watch is that it is waterproof to 100 feet.

FROM the Pets Pleasure mail-order catalogue we present 'the new-style dog's waxed jacket with turn-back corduroy collar, suitable for either country or smart town wear'. It doesn't say if the doggie's waxed jaiket includes a poacher's pocket.

Also irresistible is the selection of kebab-shaped munchy treats on a biscuit skewer. Suitable, we presume, for smartly dressed dogs seeking a takeaway after a night out on the town.

BEANO, a product advertised in *Alive*, the Canadian Journal of Health and Nutrition, claims to be a 'revolutionary way to prevent gas'. It is a magic potion hailed as 'a new scientific and social breakthrough that helps to prevent wind from beans, broccoli, cabbage, whole-grain cereals and many other legumes and vegetables'. In fact, 'Beano lets you and your family enjoy today's healthful food without most gas distress'.

Also from North America – 'Haemorr-ice, an insertable rod for cooling and shrinking haemorrhoids'.

ANTIKA Sherds: 'Solve the riddle of the sands. Dig up sherds from their simulated desert sand, match the pieces and restore them, just as an archaeologist would. The result is a beautiful collector's piece that you will treasure and your friends will admire. Antika sherds are authentic replicas from a bygone age, hand-made by native potters using skills passed down through the centuries. Each pot is then turned into sherds just as the originals were shattered in the mists of time.' The result is a cracked pot for any crackpot to put on their mantelpiece. An archaeological adventure. Or perhaps, at £24.95, a very expensive and silly 3D jigsaw.